.

War in an Age of Risk

War in an Age of Risk

CHRISTOPHER COKER

polity

First published in 2009 by Polity Press

Polity Press
65 Bridge Street
Cambridge CB2 1UR, UK

Polity Press
350 Main Street
Malden, MA 02148, USA

ISBN-13: 978-0-7456-4287-1
ISBN-13: 978-0-7456-4288-8(pb)

A catalogue record for this book is available from the British Library.

Typeset in 11.25 / 13 pt Dante
by Servis Filmsetting Ltd, Stockport, Cheshire
Printed and bound in Great Britain by MPG Books Ltd, Bodmin, Cornwall

The publisher has used its best endeavours to ensure that the URLs for external websites referred to in this book are correct and active at the time of going to press. However, the publisher has no responsibility for the websites and can make no guarantee that a site will remain live or that the content is or will remain appropriate.

Every effort has been made to trace all copyright holders, but if any have been inadvertently overlooked the publishers will be pleased to include any necessary credits in any subsequent reprint or edition.

For further information on Polity, visit our website: www.polity.co.uk

Contents

Every age has its own kind of war, its own limiting conditions and its own peculiar preoccupations. It follows that the events of every age must be judged in the light of its own peculiarities.

Clausewitz, *On War*

War: the possibility at last exists that war may be defeated on the linguistic plane. If war is an extreme metaphor we may defeat it by devising metaphors that are even more extreme.

J. G. Ballard, *A User's Guide to the Millennium*

Preface

'Mine is the first generation able to contemplate the possibility that we may live our entire lives without going to war or sending our children to war', claimed Tony Blair, speaking at the beginning of his premiership (*Economist*, 12 May 2007). He spoke with the confidence of a man who knew little history. Assertions that we have seen the end of war are pretty commonplace these days, yet most can be dismissed as the hollow echoes of a misplaced Kantian confidence in the future. Many when examined carefully seem to be interesting only as evidence of a recurring need to find something different to say.

Blair went on to fight five wars and was eventually forced out of office by the last, Iraq. He soon found that we do not live only in the present; during our lives the past is constantly relived or renegotiated. He failed to grasp the power of the past to contaminate the present. His problem was that he had a sense of destiny – but not history with all its cyclical repetitions. In the course of his ten years in power, history provoked ethnic cleansing in the Balkans, spurred ancient tribal enmities in Afghanistan and tapped into stubbornly persistent religious hatreds between Sunni and Shia in Iraq.

The wars he went on to fight, moreover, were an authentic expression of our age. Every age, Clausewitz tells us, must be judged in the light of its own peculiarities, its distinguishing features, its preoccupations, even nightmares. In the case of the West it is not difficult to detect a Hegelian Zeitgeist, the notion that there is a common spirit of the times discernible in everything we do. *Geist*, loosely translated, means 'spirit' though it can refer to the mind as well as the intellectual and cultural landscape of our existence. The nineteenth century believed every age had a 'spirit'. The idea was poetic and for that reason appealing. And it appeals still for it permits us to make broad generalizations about the sweep of history and thus invest it with 'meaning'. Some of these generalizations are even true; the challenge is to distinguish what the philosopher Alfred North Whitehead called 'general climates of opinion' that may persist for a long time, from the 'shorter waves of thought which play on the surface of things' (Lewis 1993: 229).

In this study I shall invite the reader to look at the general climate through the eyes of sociologists, anthropologists, economists and others who address the subject of risk – the definitive theme of the age. On a Google search in September 2007 I found 347 million hits. To peep though the prism of risk is to shatter the monolith of life into myriad patterns but the fractured rhythms of this study are intended to cohere into a thesis. The eclectic range of authors upon whom I shall draw are there for a reason: to illustrate my principal thesis that war has become risk management in all but name, and that the risk age itself represents not 'a shorter wave of thought' but an entire era.

From Ulrich Beck I have taken the idea of risk as the predominant reality of our times, now recast specifically in terms of war as risk management. From another sociologist, Frank Furedi, I have borrowed the concept that we live in a culture of fear that long pre-dated the War on Terror. From Zygmunt Bauman I take the insight that our world has been liquefied and rendered more fragile with the demise of the 'long-term'. In each case I have tried to ground the way the West thinks about war in what Clausewitz calls its cultural 'grammar'.

Clausewitz tells us that every age fights wars in its own ways, which is why every era of war has its own defining characteristics. This is what he means by the word 'grammar' but it is not a word that comes easily to mind when looking at ourselves. When you speak your own language grammar is usually the last thing you learn; when you begin to study a foreign language it is usually the first. For the role of grammar is to make conscious the ways in which language unites meaning and function. Grammar is difficult for those who already know a language because meaning and function are fused and seem indivisible. This is why we often know so little about ourselves and why I have chosen to use the work of sociologists in this study in an attempt to throw light on the reasons why we practise war as we now do.

A preface's function is by definition to be prefatory, and space permits me to make only one further point by way of clarification. Although the word 'grammar' is very important, so is another that Clausewitz didn't use – 'language'. Its use is in keeping with a general mood in intellectual history. We speak these days of the 'languages' that different societies speak and the 'vocabularies' which structure every era's understanding of the world and how it works. 'The limits of my language are the limits of my world,' Wittgenstein insisted, somewhat gnomically. We can even speak of the 'mentalities' of different ages, provided we recognize that the meaning is not psychological. In his book *Demystifying Mentalities* G. E. Lloyd challenges all theories that suggest different cultures have distinct styles of reasoning, such as Vivian Levy-Bruhl's belief in a 'primitive mentality', or James Frazer's notion of magic, religious and scientific mentalities as the three historical stages through which higher civilizations have to ascend to realize their full potential. In discussing the significant differences between cultures and even between historical eras Lloyd is much more interested in discovering what questions they were trying to answer and identifying the different problems they were trying to solve. Lloyd finds that historical ages differ in styles of enquiry. The questions we ask define our age (Lloyd 1990). Every age then has its own 'language', its own mentality – it is these that give war a distinctive 'grammar'.

Every society, of course, asks, 'How safe is safe enough?' As human beings we are programmed to avoid risks, particularly those that constitute a 'clear and present danger'. But we are also programmed to take them. Biology explains the first, culture the second. What makes our age unique is that risk aversion is now so entrenched in the collective consciousness that we tend to write off almost all risk-taking as abnormal, or pathological (Douglas 1992: 41). What makes our age different again is that there is no necessary correspondence between our risk perceptions and the 'real' or 'objective' risks out there. Because of the questions we raise, the practice of war has become even more challenging for those governments or societies that still wish to remain in the war business.

'Our challenge in this new century is a difficult one,' remarked the former US Defense Secretary, Donald Rumsfeld, '(it is) to defend our nation against the unknown, the uncertain, the unseen and the unexpected.' This language has become the hallmark of the risk age. 'To accomplish (the task),' he went on, 'we must put aside comfortable ways of thinking and planning . . . [we must] take risks and try new things' (Devji 2007:157). War is evolving to meet this challenge; risk-taking is being recalibrated as precisely as we can. The grammar of war is different today from the one with which we were most familiar during the Cold War – why and in what ways is the subject of this book.

I am not the first pioneer in this field. Sociologists with a few exceptions are not much interested in war, and the security community, though interested in military sociology, is not much interested in venturing into deeper waters. But three of my former students have written three excellent books on war which embody the scholarship of writers such as Anthony Giddens and Ulrich Beck: Yee Kwang Heng, *War as Risk Management* (2006), Mikkel

Rasmussen, *The Risk Society at War* (2007) and Michael Williams, *NATO, Risk and Security Management from Kosovo to Kandahar* (2008). This book owes much to their work, but it does not seek to replicate what they have written. Instead it offers a different perspective – it is about the risk age itself as a response to the increasing complexity of life.

In the first chapter I shall sketch three case studies of the risk society at war; in the second I will attempt to foreground the risk age in the era that came before it when war seemed to be a condition of modern life. One age gives way to another slowly; historians are always spotting trends that anticipate the times to come. I shall trace the risk age back to the twentieth century's acute anxieties about the risks of going to war which began to transform the century in unexpected ways long before academics began writing about the risk society. The unexpected in history is always waiting out there. As the novelist Philip Roth once claimed, the main reason we study history is to discover how the unexpected becomes the inevitable.

In chapter 3 I will sketch the principal features of the risk age which have encouraged us to reconceptualize security in completely new ways, and to see war as an exercise in risk management. In chapter 4 I shall explain that when we go to war, or use military force for distinctive political ends, we are acutely conscious that everything has side-effects; we are aware that the consequences of our own actions can rebound on us; we are saddled with the knowledge that through our own actions we may pose the greatest threat to ourselves. Ours is an age of consequence management, and this is especially true when it comes to war.

In the fifth chapter I will sketch the new geopolitical imagination which takes risk as its defining principle in addressing three major challenges: terrorism, the rise of China and the negative aspects of globalization. The risk-management strategies are different in each case. Ours is not an ambitious age – quite the contrary. We are no longer in the business of nation-building; we have scaled down our strategic ambition. Our military interventions are largely tactically driven as I shall seek to explain with reference to the language we now employ when engaging in such intractable problems as Afghanistan: we tend to see countries less as states than 'complex adaptive systems', and the problems we try to address are 'wicked', not 'tame'.

In the final chapter I shall suggest that the risk age itself is only the latest stage of modernity and that history will move on sooner or later. At the heart of the paradox that constitutes the risk age is the fact that other societies are willing to take very great risks indeed. It is their predisposition for risk-taking that may force us to confront and overcome our own predisposition to be risk-averse.

Some critics of the risk society are predisposed to seeing 'the pervasive acceptance of risk governance' as oppressive (Aradau et al. 2008:151). I tend to find it hollow. There is a marvellous passage in James Blinn's novel *The Aardvark is Ready for War* which came to mind when I was completing this book. 'What am I afraid of', asks one of the characters in the novel which does for the Gulf War (1990–1) what Joseph Heller's *Catch 22* did for World War II:

> I am afraid of everything. You think war scares me? It does but so does nuclear winter, and fall out from Chernobyl, and Legionnaire's disease and killer bees . . . and crude nuclear devices and strip mining, and the vanishing rain forest and AIDS . . . and rising interest rates and falling interest rates and people with accents and Third World population growth . . . and botulism and E. Coli and unnamed Amazonian viruses and the little petro-skin floating on my coffee. I am afraid of my ignorance and things I can't see. But the main thing that frightens me is fear. Fear of fear, that is what I am suffering from. (Blinn 1997:127)

Blinn's hero is a product of the risk age. In quasi-Hegelian terms I would argue that the chief external threat which the risk society is fighting is its own inherent essence.

1

The Risk Society at War

The most difficult moment for an author observing an era and trying to identify what makes it distinctive comes at the very beginning, for the infinite variety of life moves in a continuous surge and everything for its explanation has to be referred to things that happened before. So how can one begin? How, so to speak, can one nose one's vehicle into the uninterrupted course of traffic? One device is to choose a convenient base and from it to look at the way, in the case of this study, military force has been used since 1990.

In order to do this I am going to move geographically around the 'arc of extremism' as the 2001 *Quadrennial Defense Review* called the region that stretches from the Middle East to northeast Asia (*QDR* 2001). It is a region, argues retired general Anthony Zinni, that is a breeding ground for instability, insurgencies and warlords, 'a Petri dish for extremism and for terrorist networks' (Osinga 2007:52). Zinni was a regional commander in the 1990s and he should know what he is talking about, because the War on Terror was foreshadowed much earlier in the first Gulf War (1990–1). It was the inconclusive nature of that conflict which was held responsible by some of President George W. Bush's inner circle of advisers for what happened in New York on 9/11. And it was the World Trade Center attack which precipitated the invasion of Iraq in 2003 which followed the war against Taliban in Afghanistan which is still continuing.

Packing a long perspective in a short time frame, I am going to look at each event in turn. What each illustrates is the existence of a different consciousness, a realization that war has changed in a way that gives the age its own distinctive style.

Case Study 1: The Gulf War and its Discontents

In 2003 the conservative columnist and writer P. J. O'Rourke visited the island of Iwo Jima in the company of a group of high-flying US Marine Corps cadets. The essay he penned after the visit is entitled 'Iwo Jima and the end of modern war'. On that island – which the historian William Manchester in his memoir of the Pacific War described as 'an ugly, smelly glob of cold lava squatting in a surly ocean', the Americans lost 6,000 men in thirty-six days of fighting, of which 2,400 perished on the first day alone. Of 353 Congressional Medals of Honor awarded during World War II twenty-seven were given for heroism on Iwo Jima – thirteen posthumously. After the flag was raised on Mount Suribachi the Secretary of the Navy, James Forestall, who happened to be present, proclaimed 'this means a Marine Corps for the next 500 years' (O'Rourke 2005:189). The iconic picture of the flag flying was later rendered in bronze at the Marine Corps War Memorial in Washington DC.

To O'Rourke and the young marines who accompanied him on his battlefield jaunt the battle though heroic might as well have occurred 500 years earlier. Because what was demanded of the Americans at Iwo Jima is no longer demanded of them today. They do not face military hordes by the thousand in all-out attacks. Today 96,000 uniformed troops are not thrown into a small space on the map. Combat has become a less crowded affair. And the US military is more dependent on machines and communication systems and less on men. Iwo Jima reminded O'Rourke of the astonishing slaughter of war in the modern age. He nominated the battle as important 'for its ugliness, its uselessness and its remoteness from all things of concern to the post-modern era' (O'Rourke 2004:187). As the US prepared to invade Iraq that summer Iwo Jima seemed a world away from what contemporary war has become, or is in the process of becoming.

The same was even more true of the first Gulf War which, in retrospect, can be seen as the first conflict of the risk age. For the invasion of Kuwait which provoked it had actually been foreseen – the US military had even gamed for it the year before. The risk age puts a premium on anticipating events; scenario planning has become the norm, although it was first perfected in the closing years of the Cold War. The present age fears the unpredictable. A scenario is a tool for ordering one's perceptions about alternative future environments in which today's decisions might play out. Scenarios involve a set of stories based on carefully constructed plots – put more simply they are a way of rehearsing the future (Strathern 2007:243) The problem with the method is not failing to predict events (the US did predict the invasion of Kuwait, just as it later predicted the 9/11 attacks); the problem is a human one – it is the failure to act on them. The brutal logic of risk is that it is cheaper to pay to deal with the aftermath of a disaster (if it is localized) than it is to prepare for the same event in different theatres; there is a huge difference between anticipating an event and being prepared for it. The US could have deterred Saddam from invading Kuwait but deterrence would have been expensive – in the event it was caught out when Saddam struck.

The Gulf War (1990–1) which followed was not cheap, though it was the first war for which the US issued an invoice: Saudi Arabia, Japan and Germany all paid for the campaign. And when it came it took the world by storm. The air war lasted six weeks; the land campaign only a hundred hours. It was described at the time as the first *hyperwar* in history because of its unprecedented precision bombing and its use of strategic surprise which rendered it so strikingly different from everything we know about modern battles such as Iwo Jima. The 'star' of the show, the F117A (the Stealth Attack bomber), was used for the first time to attack heavily defended targets such as command and control posts, air defence radar systems and military production facilities. They flew 1,300 sorties and delivered about 2,000 bombs. Of these over two-thirds fell within ten feet of the intended aim point. Considering the destructive force of a 2,000-pound bomb it is likely that 80 per cent of the bombs destroyed their assigned targets. This level of precision had never been witnessed before: it has made war more lethal but also less destructive. Destruction from the air is now highly specific, but wholesale within its own specificity. The plane of the hour, the F117A, was also marvellously risk-averse for the pilots flying them; during Desert Storm not one of them was lost to enemy fire (Nye/Smith 1992:252–3).

But despite all the hype the result of Desert Storm was strikingly inconclusive, even though it met the terms of the UN mandate under which it was launched. Saddam himself remained in power for the next twelve years. At a press conference two days after announcing the ceasefire President George H. W. Bush regretted that he could not share the same sense of euphoria as the American people. As long as Saddam was still there he could not provide them with the closure that his own generation had been given after Japan's surrender (Bush himself had had a distinguished career as a pilot in the Pacific theatre where he had flown 58 combat missions and received the Distinguished Air Service Medal). 'You mentioned World War 2,' the President told a journalist. 'There was a definite end to that conflict. And now we have Saddam Hussein still there – the man who wreaked the havoc upon his neighbours' (Buley 2007:79).

His survival committed the Coalition to a long siege which it knew at any time could be broken. Victory in war tends to last only as long as the coalition that produces it remains intact. Take the collapse of the Allied coalition against Russia that had imposed terms on the country in 1856.

With France out of the equation following its defeat in the Franco-Prussian War (1870–1), Russia was able to tear up the terms of the Treaty of Paris and restore the *status quo ante*. Similarly, the coalition which defeated Saddam Hussein soon dissolved, leaving only Britain and the US after 1995 to face him down by the overt threat of military action and the occasional use of force.

Hostilities were to continue for the next twelve years as UN arms inspectors laboured away at ending Saddam's nuclear programme until their expulsion in 1998. This in turn provoked Operation Desert Fox (1998), a three-day cruise missile blitz on Baghdad that destroyed what was left of the programme although this was not recognized until years later. Even the war on land continued in an attenuated form in the north, in the Kurdish areas, where a civil war was later to claim 3,000 lives.

Air power was the West's preferred option in the phase that followed the liberation of Kuwait. After the end of hostilities the Coalition continued to patrol two no fly zones in Iraq, one above the 36th parallel in the north, the other below the 33rd in the south. Both were established to protect the Kurds and the Marsh Arabs after their uprisings failed to unseat the regime. No fly zones were mandated by the Security Council on 5 April which deemed the Iraqi repression of these minorities to be a 'threat to international security'. In the course of time the air missions (some 200,000 sorties in all) became less an instrument for protecting those at risk on the ground and more a means of constraining the Iraqi leader's freedom of action by keeping the regime under constant surveillance. The mission was aptly named Operation Northern Watch. When George W. Bush sanctioned the first air sortie of his presidency in February 2001 he described the mission as 'routine' (*Washington Post*, 27 February 2001).

At another press conference in 1991, a few days after the formal end of hostilities, Bush announced almost casually that the sanctions imposed in the run-up to Desert Storm would continue until the regime had been removed from power. Yet the sanctions regime imposed by the UN was progressively watered down on humanitarian grounds (oil for food/medicine) and subverted by massive corruption within the UN itself. They still did enormous damage to ordinary Iraqis, decimating the country's middle class and reducing it to the status of a semi-criminalized economy. Over the next few years Basra was transformed from a wealthy city into a slum. By the time of the invasion in 2003 Iraq was poorer, its people more desperate and isolated, and the regime apparently more entrenched than ever. Isolation from the West was a virus which slowly killed the nation long before the Coalition forces inadvertently, of course, almost finished it off.

The mood of frustration was captured by some of the key Hollywood films that came off the production line in the 1990s. Take the scene in Wolfgang Petersen's *Air Force One* (1997) when the plane carrying President James Marshall, as played by Harrison Ford, is seized by Kazak terrorists while he is being briefed on a suspected Iraqi mobilization. In another film, *Independence Day*, which had hit the movie theatres the previous year, Bill Pullman's even younger Commander in Chief, Thomas Whitmore, is defined again and again by his service as a fighter pilot in the Gulf War. The repeated references to Iraq in the movie culminate in the nod of approval exchanged by Iraqi and Israeli pilots as they prepare to leave a desert airbase for the final assault against the invading aliens. America's commitment to 'whippin ET's butt' has even neutralized the aggression of one of the world's most dangerous states. 'At least America has a kick-ass President' was one of the original taglines for the movie. Although it was later rejected by the studio, it captured a widespread feeling of frustration that Desert Storm was a war that had not been declared, not fought to a conclusion and not truly won. The job had been left uncompleted (Handy 1997).

In outlining the principal reasons for this, which made the Gulf War the first conflict of the risk age, I am going to take my lead (at some risk to myself) from a book by the sociologist Jean Baudrillard, one of the leading figures in post-modernism and the theorist of the hyperreal. *La Guerre du Golfe n'a pas eu lieu* (*The Gulf War Did Not Take Place*; an obvious parody of Giraudoux's play *La Guerre de Troie n'aura pas lieu*) is composed of three essays: 'The Gulf War will not take place' (which originally appeared in *Libération* and was translated for and reprinted in the *Guardian*), 'The Gulf War is not really taking place' (originally published in *Libération*) and 'The Gulf War did not take place' (written for book publication only).

The problem with his work is that it is often annoyingly obscure. Baudrillard liked to provoke his readers, as French intellectuals have been doing since the mid-nineteenth century. Many of them like to 'dazzle' (the French word, *briller* has no real English equivalent). He was something of a self-professed 'poseur' like his compatriots Lacan, Foucault and Julia Kristeva, and like them he could be stubbornly obscure. But although obscure he was also a scintillating critic of our times, especially on the constructed nature of reality. He may have taken great pride in the subversive nature of his critique but we should take his wish to subvert seriously. Subversive writers are often the best commentators on our times. The Gulf War seems to have appealed to his sense of the subversive in that it appeared to 'subvert' most of the norms of war which the Western world had taken for granted. What astonished him is what should astonish every sociologist of our age and its obsessive preoccupation with risk aversion: risk aversion is a cultural construct demanding explanation. For the avoidance of risks involves serious risks too.

His aphoristic style and essay technique almost inevitably annoyed many of his fellow sociologists. He never engaged in field research and provided little data to support his propositions. The three essays he wrote on Desert Storm comprise a series of telling vignettes held together by a rather rambling commentary on hyperreality, lightened with an occasional touch of grotesque humour. They have been dismissed by some as a set of variations without a theme, and by others as a series of vanities awaiting a bonfire. But Baudrillard was a serious social thinker. Indeed, his wider philosophy and reputation would be largely unintelligible without the ongoing predicaments that make our age so intensely self-reflexive. As he wrote in the run-up to the fighting, 'what is at stake . . . is war itself; its status, its meaning, its future' (Baudrillard 1995:32).

All reflection is derived from the difference between appearance and reality. This is entirely a human discovery. Other species are stuck in an evolutionary rut, in a world of appearances. They have to make the best they can of how things seem, and seldom if ever worry about whether how things seem is actually how things are. We invented culture, writes Daniel Dennett, in order to leverage ourselves into new territory (Dennett 2003:165). Over time we have been forced to reflect more frequently as the gap between appearance and reality has widened, as we have come to recognize that we can never grasp all at once the increasing complexity of the world. In the risk age we are forced to reflect even more on our circumstances because the cost of getting it wrong has risen so greatly.

To be a risk society, however, is not just to ask oneself more questions, or to be even more troubled by doubt. A risk society has to accept ambivalence as a condition of its own existence. Insecurity, not security, is now the norm, but at levels that we may find more acceptable. The future cannot be secured but it can be made 'safer'. War can still produce more favourable outcomes (if we are lucky) but it is always a double-edged sword. For those who endanger the well-being of the international community and those charged with its protection may well be identical (even if in the case of the latter by default – the failure to anticipate the unintended consequences of their own actions). It was said that Colin Powell, the Chairman of the Joint Chiefs of Staff at the time of Desert Storm, displayed on his desk a quotation from Thucydides: 'Of all forms of power restraint is the best.' Actually, Thucydides never said it, but the quip has much greater resonance in our age than his. For it is no longer possible to externalize risks; we now internalize them as never before. This is what makes our societies so self-critical.

Reflection and reflexivity are quite different, despite what the adjective 'reflexive' might suggest, for the latter involves an element of *self-confrontation*. It is not only a question of fearing the consequences of war; it is fearing the consequences of our own actions. We have become acutely aware that we may pose the greatest danger to ourselves.

And although we have certainly reflected on wars in the past, on their consequences and even the cost of success (pyrrhic victories have been quite common), when going to war today we are engaged in self-confrontation as never before. 'With risks, avoidance imperatives dominate' (Beck 1992:9). Once something becomes a 'problem in itself' the issue of self-limitation comes to the fore. We entertain concepts of damage limitation, consequence management, safety, monitoring and responsibility even before the first shot has been fired. We debate responsibility for the risks we run when targeting other societies and the risks we ask others to run even after the shooting has stopped. Within alliances we are intensely preoccupied with who takes the risks and who shares them by association. And, of course, we are all acutely risk-averse.

In order to make war possible for itself, argued Baudrillard, the US had to cast the war as comparatively risk-free. The public was encouraged to see it as 'a war without the symptoms of war, a form of war which means never needing to face up to war' (Baudrillard 1995:43). In order to minimize the public's anxieties the Bush administration had to reassure it that the war would be largely risk-free. In this respect Desert Storm was not so much a 'hyperwar' as it was 'hyperreal'. For the outcome was never in doubt: the US never had to confront the prospect of defeat. Nothing was really 'real': the Iraqi air force flew to Iran where it was promptly impounded; the Iraqi army did not even bother seriously to contest Kuwait City. At no time was the Coalition's superiority made more manifest than in the closing hours of the ground war, when the Iraqi army was pummelled from the air as it tried to escape from disaster along the scarred ribbon of the Basra highway.

One of the war's 'selling points' was that it posed a much reduced risk of 'collateral damage'. Writing at the time in the *Guardian*, the author J. G. Ballard even hazarded that the absence of combatants, let alone the dead and the wounded, on the nation's television screens every night suppressed any reflexes of pity or outrage, and even created the barely conscious impression that the entire war was 'a vast demolition derby' in which almost no one was being hurt and which might even have been fun for all concerned – but especially for the Americans (Ballard 1997:11).

For Ballard and so many other spectators, in this, the first war to be televised in real time, what mattered most was not that the US overwhelmed the enemy but that the outcome was 'pre-programmed'. The war was scripted in advance and the Revolution in Military Affairs (RMA) was part of the script. So were phrases like 'full-dimensional protection', 'full spectrum dominance' and 'precision engagement'. These were the ideological inflections of the 1990s discourse on war. Inadvertently they disclosed the military's ambition for what the RMA promised – in the words of one US general, the chance 'to abolish Clausewitz'. It was a bold claim because Clausewitz is the man whose work has produced many of the axioms the military has taken for granted, including his insistence that in any war chance and friction can never be eliminated, and with them the risk that every conflict entails. John Warden was later to claim that 'dominant battle space awareness' had given way to 'predictive battle space awareness'. One government official went even further. In planning for the future, he remarked, the US military could discard the traditional inductive approach (i.e. learning from history and experience) in favour of a deductive method: it could now posit what the future would look like without reference to the past (Buley 2007:87).

The words we use reveal a lot, and the terms associated with the RMA – 'transformation', 'precision', 'digitization' said it all. All downplayed the existential value of battle-hardened combat; all played up a degree of control in an era in which the US military boasted that it enjoyed 'full spectrum dominance'. The Pentagon tried to tap into what a character in Don DeLillo's novel *Cosmopolis* calls 'the zero-sumness of the world, the digital imperative, one which promises 'an order at some deeper level' in the general chaos and mayhem of life through the rare power of the computer to compute the future. 'Computer power eliminates doubt. All doubt rises from past experience. But the past is disappearing. We used to know the past but not the future. This is changing too' (Updike 2007:487). Only in recent years has the US found that the RMA is merely the latest in a long wish-list of techno-scientific panaceas that have been sold as benefits without costs – they also include the 'peaceful atom', the space programme and modern eugenics (the ghost in the machine that haunts genetic engineering).

Desert Storm wasn't without its casualties, however. No war is, even if the final casualty toll is still debated. Baudrillard himself even acknowledged this after the fighting had stopped. A 'clean war ends up in an oil slick', he wrote in reference to the gratuitous burning of Kuwait's oil wells by the Iraqis as they pulled out of the country (Baudrillard 1995:43). It was an outrageous act which polluted the region and provided one of the iconic images of the conflict. In the days that followed, the world's television channels broadcast the picture of a helpless oil-caked cormorant as if it were the war's registered trade mark, a symbol of our own impotence when confronted with a grimly unintelligible event (Adair 1992:155). The burning oil wells reinforced contemporary anxieties about war, vividly showing that these days consequences extend far beyond the social realm; they can also have a devastating impact on the environment.

And so to Baudrillard's final observation. The less committed we are to a definitive outcome (victory) because of the risks involved in attaining it (in this case the removal of Saddam Hussein) the more we have to 'spin' the result. 'Spinning' becomes even more important than winning. In an age of hyperreality war is packaged for cable television. It is the narrative that is all important. This was especially true of Desert Storm for it provided only an illusion of success; it ended in a *virtual* outcome. It was spun as a success, rather than what it really was, a draw, which left the Iraqi army where it had been before the war, poised to invade Kuwait again in the future, the moment the Americans departed to fight other battles on other battlefields.

Now of course much of the argument was overdrawn. The only objective of the war was to remove the Iraqis from Kuwait, but it soon became clear that success on the battlefield had not produced a conclusive *strategic* outcome and had therefore fallen far short of success. Our wars, Baudrillard concluded, 'have less to do with the confrontation of warriors than with the domestication of the refractory forces on the planet' (Baudrillard 1995:86). In this he came particularly near to the truth, for the war's prevailing logic was consequence-management. It was fought to manage the consequences of allowing Saddam Hussein to invade and occupy Kuwait and thus to monopolize the supply of Gulf oil; the consequences, once the decision to oust him from Kuwait had been taken, of weakening him too much (given that Iran was still the West's principal adversary in the region). The US had to manage the consequences of the war itself – its environmental damage (should the oil wells be set alight); its collateral damage (should civilian casualties reach an unacceptable level); the material damage to the infrastructure of Iraq as a functioning state. So busy, in fact, was the US managing the consequences that it failed to secure an outright victory. In the language of our times, it was denied 'closure'.

At one point, of course, George Bush promised that the war would usher in a New World Order. In a speech before the UN General Assembly he promised a partnership of nations based on consultation, co-operation and collective action, united by principle and the rule of law (Mills 2001:25). The fact that this New Order was still-born set the seal on the era in which we have been living ever since. Baudrillard's most infamous charge against the war was also on first reading his most banal: 'First, safe sex, now safe war. The Gulf War would not even register 2 or 3 on the Richter Scale. It's unreal, war without the symptom of war' (Baudrillard 1995:26). But the 'safe sex' analogy was not entirely unjustified, however outrageous the metaphor. We make war, as we make love these days, with condoms. Safe sex is unreproductive sex, and the war's inconclusive end brought into question whether force could ever again be used to reorder the world.

If only for its symbolism, the absence of a declaration of war gave the game away. 'We ought to have been on our guard because of the disappearance of the declaration of war. There can be no real war without a declaration – it is the moment of passing from a word to the deed' (Baudrillard 1995:26). Historically, of course, declarations of war have become rare. In 1941 President Roosevelt told the British ambassador that 'declarations of war (were) going out of fashion' (Kershaw 2007:329). The US never declared war on North Vietnam and the British never declared war on Argentina in the Falklands War of 1982, and in Korea (a conflict in which the Americans lost 33,000 men) the US insisted it was involved not in a war but in a police action. The declaration of war, of course, used to be a timeless ritual which implied that every war had a beginning and an end: that every conflict usually ended in a peace treaty or at the very least an armistice. But these days wars do not always end even when the fighting stops. They have become an instrument of risk management, not order. To quote Ulrich Beck: 'risk problems are characterised by having no unambiguous solutions; rather they are distinguished by a fundamental ambivalence which can usually be grasped by calculations of probability, but not removed that way. Their fundamental ambivalence is what distinguishes risk problems and problems of order which by definition are oriented towards clarity and decidability (Beck 1997:8–9).

This was borne out at one point in the weeks before the fighting began when a former US ambassador to Iraq who knew the country well asked a USAF general whether he would like some political advice. He was told, 'Oh no, Mr Ambassador, the war has no political overtones' (Cockburn 2000:82). This would have horrified anyone brought up to take seriously Clausewitz's maxim that war is the continuation of politics by other means. But that is the point – it is the politics, not war, that has changed. What the general grasped (no doubt unconsciously) was that this was going to be a very different kind of conflict from any previously witnessed. It really only did involve targeting before – and after. Unlike other conflicts it would not end with Saddam's formal surrender.

It is ironic, of course, that in endeavouring to redress his father's legacy George W. Bush should have found himself in a bloody re-enactment of his father's fate. For the second Gulf War may indeed have removed Saddam from power but at a terrible cost. The US soon found post-Saddamite Iraq a nest of unresolved schisms, uncorrected ethnic imbalances and unrequited injuries. It soon discovered that it is naive to imagine that risk can be eliminated from war. War may put everyone in greater danger than ever. Risk management in other words is a risky business. And it is certainly no longer casualty-free. Instead of an antiseptic war in the desert the US soon found itself mired in operations in the concrete valleys that form the cityscapes of Baghdad, Tikrit, Najaf and Kirkuk. City fighting has become something of a norm in the risk age, witness the fighting in Basra, Beirut, Belfast, Grozny, Jenin, Mogadishu and Sarajevo. Urban warfare is not only timeless, it involves significant collateral damage. It is the closest the West has come to pre-industrial forms of warfare (Hills 2007:116). And the cities of the future in which Western forces are likely to be deployed will have even larger populations of underemployed, or unemployable, young males, precisely the group most likely to follow the lead of charismatic leaders. Despite the promise of the RMA, Western forces do not enjoy full spectrum dominance, or even information superiority (which is essential for precision-guided missions).

Looking back, then, Desert Storm may be considered the first conflict of a new age. Its after-shocks persisted for a long time. For those who lived through it and watched it unfold on the news stations every night, it is even legitimate to talk of events not 'before the Gulf War' but simply, and more bluntly, 'before the war', now that the risk age finally has a first-hand war to call its own.

Case Study 2: 9/11 and the Rise of the Safety State

As Zygmunt Bauman has observed, 'The insecure life is lived in the company of insecure people' (Bauman 1999:23). The September 11 attacks on New York which propelled the rest of us into the risk age can be traced back to the Gulf War and what followed. Many young Muslim radicals who joined al-Qaeda in the mid-1990s claim that they felt humiliated by what happened in the last days of the conflict, particularly the 'turkey-shoot' on the Basra road. Saddam's continued defiance of the West persuaded the US to build up its local presence in Saudi Arabia so as to more effectively contain Saddam, or in Blair's words 'confine him to his cage'. It was this presence which inspired bin Laden and his followers to take up arms against the Americans in 1998 when they launched their first military attack on American embassies in East Africa.

The attack on the World Trade Center when it came changed everything. Within hours the site became known as 'Ground Zero', a term previously used to designate the epicentre of the explosion of the Hiroshima bomb and the point from which its effects had radiated. The effects of 9/11 quickly radiated across the world. Like the Hiroshima bombing, the attack was seen by many as an apocalyptic event, a revelatory and prophetic experience that ruptured our sense of the continuity of time, forming a point of reference around which we have subsequently reinscribed our historical and political narratives. In his address at the Labour Party Conference a few weeks later, Britain's Prime Minister expressed succinctly this moment of uncertainty and fluidity: 'The kaleidoscope has been shaken. The pieces are in flux. Soon they will settle again. Before they do, let us re-order this world around us' (Blair 2001). The subsequent invasion of Iraq was part of the reordering.

Was 9/11, however, really a turning point? Turning points and historical watersheds are usually only observed by historians employing 20:20 hindsight. Take the moon landing in 1969, which was widely greeted at the time as the 'next chapter in evolution'. 'The Apollo landing', opined Arthur C. Clark, the doyen of space travel, 'may be the only achievement of ours remembered in a thousand years' (Cornfield 2007:27) – except that there hasn't been another lunar landing since 1972. Our generation has turned inwards. Space travel has not fired our imagination.

Instead of invoking historical 'turning points', we might choose a weaker variant, a concept made popular by the philosopher Richard Rorty. If only historians are really in a position to identify turning points, contemporary observers may at least be able to identify 'turns'. Rorty himself identified a 'linguistic turn' in 1967. Since then, others have claimed to identify 'a biographical turn', 'an aesthetic turn', 'a pragmatic turn', 'an ethical turn' and, of course, a 'global turn'. What all these claims assert is that a significant shift in cultural and intellectual *attitudes* has taken place which are real but hard to pin down in their direction and timing. Not all, for example, follow clear historical pathways (Cornfield 2007:106). So if I am allowed to employ this device I would contend that we have witnessed a 'security turn' since 9/11 which has led to a significant change in the way we conceptualize security. We have become increasingly anxious, and at the same time less strategically ambitious. Bush is the first American President to have taken the American people to war without promising them the prospect of a New World Order. It is called the 'new American Realism'. In July 2007

Condoleezza Rice defined the term to mean a foreign policy which deals with the world as it is, not as we might like it to be. 'We strive to make the world ultimately *safer*. Not perfect, just better' (*Washington Post*, 26 July 2007). And Americans in particular consider the world since 9/11 to be far less safe than it was before. In that sense al-Qaeda has transformed the way we look at the world. We have been left in a permanent state of watchfulness (Mythen 2004:138). 'When you change the way you look at things, the things you look at change', writes Wayne Dyer (Ford 2007:20). The US hasn't seen the world in the same light since and the world hasn't seen the US (which is why the great love affair with all things American may finally be over).

The War on Terror which George Bush declared shortly after 9/11 has produced what social scientists call a new paradigm, and like all paradigms it is self-validating because it supplies the criteria that warrant its own legitimization. To begin with, it taps into a deep concern about the vulnerability of the modern world. Completed in 1973, the World Trade Center was an instant icon of Western wealth. Yet the terrorist attack confirmed the fragility of the international economy. It almost wiped out the world reinsurance market. It also immobilized the Bank of New York, one of the two banks that provide clearance services for Wall Street's fixed-income transactions and institutions vital for US Treasury securities (Homer-Dixon 2006:120). And it led to a dramatic collapse in investor confidence in a market already weakened by the bursting of the dot.com bubble and the Enron scandal. Financial markets thrive on predictability; 9/11 plunged them into complete uncertainty. As Alan Greenspan reveals in his autobiography, *The Age of Turbulence*, as Chairman of the Federal Reserve he spent the next few months trying to stop the US economy (and by implication the world) from going into recession (Greenspan 2007:9–10).

The 9/11 attack was a close call in other respects too. Over time our urban networks have become ever more complex. If terrorists target the right hubs or nodes in an energy system, for example, they can have a devastating impact. The trick is to sabotage a critical but non-redundant part of the system. Al-Qaeda's attack took the lives of 3,000 New Yorkers but the eventual death toll could have been far higher if the terrorists had met with even greater luck. New York relies on its subway crews and 753 water pumps to keep the city from flooding. Beneath the van Sichlen Avenue station in Brooklyn for example, 650 gallons of natural groundwater gush from the bedrock each minute. The pumps rely on electricity. If the power fails, disaster is not far off. In the hours immediately after the attack an emergency pump train bearing a jumbo portable diesel generator had to pump out water twenty-seven times the volume of the Shea Stadium. Had the Hudson River as was briefly feared burst through the train tunnels connecting the city's subways to New Jersey then New York's transport infrastructure might have been overwhelmed (Weisman 2007:25). Long before hurricane Katrina and the flooding of New Orleans the city of Manhattan could have been waterlogged.

Twenty-first-century cities are far more vulnerable than their citizens suppose in other ways too. The attack hit home because it hit a raw nerve – its main impact was not on the economic or transport network but a neural one. The terrorists slowed down the internet and disrupted mobile phone lines as people across the world tried to contact their friends. The world was plugged into the television images of the carnage for days afterwards. The attack heightened a generalized sense of anxiety about our own vulnerability in an interconnected world which feeds off bad news, frequent warnings of environmental catastrophe as well as the many risks we confront on a daily basis in everyday life (Homer-Dixon 2006:121). In a word, the attack hit home where it mattered most – the imagination.

Every society, everywhere, has made a choice, a selection of the institutions that constitute its cultural life. One culture may ignore monetary values; another may hold them to be fundamental in every field of endeavour. One society may prioritize technology; another may marginalize it. Life consists of so many experiments in living, so many explorations of human possibility. We are told the globalized age is producing a single civilization, that it is a great leveller of difference. Whether we come to conclude that civilizational differences are real and still matter, or that globalization itself amplifies cultural diversity, is not the point. Even in the twenty-first century cultural differences are profound. The risk society itself is a product of one civilization – our own at a particular stage in its historical development. And what makes the West still distinctive is the peculiar texture of its urban life, from which derive not only concepts of citizenship, the social contract and civility, but even, etymologically, the word civilization itself.

The great Western cities have been the place where the West has looked first to see the shape of its own future, to divine the contours of history in the act of being made. Back in the 1930s the architect Le Corbusier saw the skyscrapers of New York as the 'white cathedrals' of the modern age. New York was, for him, a fantastical, almost mystical city, and what made it special was its plasticity. It was acutely unreal, and therefore even more real than reality for it was whatever you wanted it to be, or whatever you dreamed. The young Albert Camus, on a visit immediately after World War II, was less impressed. The city's skyscrapers reminded him of 'white sepulchres', not cathedrals, but even he would not have imagined that sixty years later that is exactly what the twin towers would become (Camus 1978:52).

Within a few years of 9/11 Europe's cities also came under attack: London, Madrid and Glasgow. Is it so entirely irrational that the Western world should yield so readily to fears of the breakdown of urban life? For Western cities are vulnerable in a way unique to themselves – they are the only 'world cities' that offer their citizens an ethnically diverse urban experience. 'Do you really think this is your city any longer?' asks the mayor of New York in Tom Wolfe's *Bonfire of the Vanities* (1988), 'It's the Third World down there.' With its sixteen different ethnic groups and its nine distinctive ethnic cores Los Angeles, not New York, can lay claim to be the capital of the Third World. But what would happen if the city's citizens were no longer to trust each other? In the film *State of Siege*, New York's Muslims are interned during a particularly brutal spate of bombings. That is the problem of the age – the War on Terror may exacerbate ethnic tensions, giving ghetto life a political charge that it lacks in Wolfe's novel where the tension is racial. Hollywood has a knack of exploiting our primal fears.

Hollywood offers us a chance to surf the Zeitgeist, a chance to locate ourselves in what Frank Furedi calls the new 'culture of fear' (Furedi 2006). Fear, of course, is a central feature of individual and collective experience alike. It is a response to our instinct for survival. We will always fear death, illness and loss of income. Such fears are more or less unchanging from culture to culture and from age to age. It is when fear is cultural, when it is framed by a range of beliefs and practices that surround it, that it becomes of interest to historians. It is when fear reflects the preoccupations present in the community or culture at large, it is when fear is socially patterned that it acquires significance for sociologists.

Today most of us are no longer haunted by the fear of war between the Great Powers as our forefathers were for much of the twentieth century. And the fears that concern much of the rest of the world do not keep us awake either, such as the prospect of famine. What makes us most anxious is what we *imagine*. What is remarkable is that our everyday anxieties do not correspond to our immediate experience of life. We are apprehensive about risks that we do not encounter on a day-to-day basis. Apprehension is anxiety about what *might* happen and it thrives in a climate in which we all feel ourselves to be constantly at risk. Our anxieties are less focused than our fears; they are also much less specific, less immediate and thus much less easily overcome. Anxious people are much harder to reassure than those who are fearful.

What makes us more fearful still is the breakdown of civil society. The language of risk is not new — it has been part of the modern experience from the beginning but for much of the time it has been inescapably 'social'. Specific risks were conceived with reference to the family, the neighbourhood, the company or the nation. Today, risk assessment has become intensely individualized, related to the safety of the person, disaggregated in some cases from the society of which the citizen is still part. Survival has become much more of a private concern, precisely because what we fear most is other people. 'It's not so much human survival, but the survival of our faith in humanity which is at issue,' claims Furedi (Furedi 2006:xii). And what alarms him most is the impact or imprint on history of our declining faith in the human condition. It would seem that we are not only polluting the environment, we are also polluting one another. We talk of 'toxic relationships', 'toxic parents' and children trapped in 'toxic families'. Not for some time has there been so much concern about the malevolent passions that affect us as a species (Furedi 2006:xvi).

As a result there has been a marked reduction in 'public space'. As the privatization of security hollows out social life so it becomes more difficult to mobilize moral resources such as civic pride or citizens' responsibility. So too we are more inclined to retreat into private spaces that make us more secure. Take the gated community with its elaborate two-storey guard houses and roll-back wrought-iron gates, which has come to reflect one of the chief characteristics of the risk age. Walls may represent power, but they also represent isolation and fear. Gated communities, after all, are only a second-best solution to safety, but we have all come to accept second-best solutions as the best on offer (Ellin 1997:104). This entire defensive landscape is one that is waiting for a crime to be committed, a crime that will awaken us, perhaps, to a more passionate world. For the moment, however, the passions that were once devoted to a struggle to change the world are now invested in trying to ensure we are safe. The label 'safe' has given new meaning to a wide range of phenomena such as 'safe havens' in Bosnia in the 1990s. Personal safety is now big business. Homeland security is supposed to increase the safety of the citizen. 'Better safe than sorry' has become a fundamental principle of public life.

And then there is the 'surveillance society' in which citizens' movements are on camera 24 hours a day. The CCTV camera is merely another example of modernity's endless quest for control which makes our civic culture increasingly less tolerant or inclusive and increasingly less capable of trust (Garland 2001:195). For the camera is not there only to provide evidence of a crime after it has been committed and the perpetrator apprehended; it is there to deter crime, by providing real-time management of the rest of us. Our governments have not lost their interest in control; instead they have developed new techniques to reassure us that they are still in control, and consequently that they can be trusted to protect us even if they no longer trust us.

We might well ask, of course: didn't the balance of nuclear terror under which we all lived for so many years, also bring into question the everyday-ness that constitutes civil society? Didn't the Cold War take to a logical conclusion one of the nightmare visions in Orwell's *1984* in which the three totalitarian states which manage the world ask nothing of their citizens but obedience. In Orwell's dystopian vision, all three super states provide their citizens with everything from social welfare to state-sanctioned pornography. Only one puts its own citizens at risk by dropping bombs on them from time to time to remind them that they are still at war, but it does so secretly.

In an article in the *Atlantic* in 1947 Cord Meyer, a retired US Marine officer, had taken this logic further. Steadily increasing national power, complemented by steadily decreasing national security, he speculated, might force the US to maintain not only an immense arsenal of arms, but to disperse the urban population in underground shelters so that war could be continued even if its cities lay in ruins. It might choose to guard against atomic sabotage by creating the most efficient intelligence system in the world, as well as a large security police force armed with powers of search and arrest. Ironically, in preparing for the ultimate showdown, the US might come to resemble its enemy, the Soviet state (Iriye 1985:49–50).

In the event, the Cold War never intruded into people's lives in quite that way. The US did not become the surveillance society that it is today. The Cold War produced a shadowy security state with surveillance of political radicals, the vetting of some public service employees and the suspension in countries like the UK of jurisdiction over US bases. Yet none of these measures challenged free speech, the presumption of the innocence of the citizen until proved otherwise, the right of asylum and even free movement across the country. Identity cards were not introduced either in Britain or the US. And the suspension of *habeas corpus* in Britain would have been considered unacceptable. The global war on terror is already much more intrusive in this respect for it is hollowing out the concept of the 'everyday'. Instead, order – regularity, peace, routine, everydayness which makes civility possible – is now organized around the everydayness of violence (Mbembe 2003:11).

Today, governments make us feel frightened all the time, though the terror under which we all live is not imagined; it is very real. Nowadays we

find ourselves living in what Appadurai calls an age not of total but of quotidian war, an age in which violence is an everyday possibility. And terrorists too connive at this, of course, by making us constantly fearful (or
vigilant). Much more insidious than terrorism in its various manifestations
is the state of mind it produces: terror – the name for any effort to replace
peace with violence as a guaranteed anchor of everyday life. 'It uses emergency as its routine' (Appadurai 2006:32).

Take the colour coding of threat levels at American airports (a direct consequence of the events of 9/11). The top three – Red/'dangerous',
Orange/'high' and Yellow/'elevated' – are all ominous, but it is not clear
why the third level – Yellow – should be any less threatening than the
second, Orange. The effort to link terror coding to weather coding adds a
spurious scientific validity to the exercise. More disturbing still is the fact
that public officials seems to think that the coding has now become a permanent feature of social life. As a Washington DC police chief regretted,
'we will never be green again. Normal was redefined on 9/11. Normal is
yellow' (Stearns 2006:44). Not only are America's airports colour-coded;
should the traveller decide to ignore the Red status and travel the same day
he will find himself entering a 'surveillance machine' in which he will be
scanned like a bar code, silently organized and processed through the terminals, a process that really invites critical examination along with the
underlying assumptions and concepts framing it (Lyon 2007:124).

For those who can afford it, there is always the private security industry. Ten years ago only four US universities offered courses devoted to disaster management. Today 115 degree courses are available, and a further
100 are under consideration. We can find twenty-four-hour status alerts
against terrorism on the internet, as well as supplies of potassium iodine
for use in an emergency, should we fear running short during a nuclear
attack. Back in the 1960s American newspapers ran advertisements for
deluxe fall-out shelters for those who could afford them. The wealthy consumer was offered every comfort, including wall-to-wall carpeting and
expansive lounge chairs as well as the latest state-of-the-art TV. Sold as a
family room during peacetime and a fall-out shelter should war break out,
the consumer was offered protection against nuclear war provided he
could pay the price. Here, wrote Herbert Marcuse in his book *One-
Dimensional Man*, was a vivid example of the introduction of con-
sumerism into death which traditionally had been beyond the range of
consumer choice (Marcuse 1991:37). Marcuse's irony seems somewhat
out of place in an age when the consumer has been empowered as never
before.

The problem is that the citizen would seem to be at greater risk than ever. Such is the risk society and the culture of fear to which it gives rise. It encourages all of us to be apocalyptic about the future, nostalgic about a supposedly more secure past and misinformed about how insecure the present really is. The protagonist of DeLillo's novel *Mao 2* argues that terrorism does what the novel once did as the inner life of American culture wanes. It feeds off our brittle anxieties, our manufactured fears, our second-hand neuroses. 'Now the bomb makers and the gunmen have taken that territory; they make raids on human consciousness' (DeLillo 1992:41). Terrorism feeds back into the risk society by entering our everyday consciousness, try though we may to escape its hold.

Case Study 3: Afghanistan and Liquid Alliances

My third case study is Afghanistan which the US attacked a few months after 9/11 in an attempt to root out bin Laden and expel his hosts, the Taliban. Subsequently NATO deployed an International Security Force (ISAF) to contain the Taliban once it reappeared as a political actor. The war is still continuing. At the beginning of September 2006, in support of the new Afghan government, it launched Operation Medusa to establish central government control over the Taliban-held districts in the south.

Operation Medusa was NATO's first land battle in its fifty-five-year history and it was a close-run thing. If the battle had gone the other way then the Taliban could – and probably would – have claimed victory and entered Kandahar, with all the implications that that would have had for the legitimacy of the NATO mission and the authority of the government in Kabul. If they had not been so foolish in their determination to defeat NATO in the way they had designed – a defensive battle – and had engaged in a 'mission analysis' as the situation on the ground changed, ISAF would have faced a crisis. It would have been outmanoeuvred. There were no reserves available. Every soldier was committed to the battle (Richards 2007:25).

NATO claims that it is a 'stability enabler' in Afghanistan but it is failing to provide the stability it promises. It has tried to enforce the rule of law in the south, the first serious attempt to do so since the Soviet occupation of the country, and has met with the same lack of success. The Taliban had been given five years to regroup and apply lessons learned from foreign fighters with experience of fighting in Iraq who brought roadside bombs and suicide bombers into the Afghan theatre. Since 2006 NATO has stopped talking of winning the war and removing the Taliban threat.

Instead, it is aiming to contain it. Its leaders have found that the country is made up of a vast and intricate web of human groups, feuds, ties and revenges.

NATO continues to insist that the enemy had no popular appeal. Indeed, only 5 per cent of Pashtuns supported the Taliban at any one time. More importantly, claimed Richards, although nearly 80 per cent of Pashtuns could be considered 'floating' voters, they all expressed a strong desire for the international community and the government in Kabul to succeed (Richards 2007:26). But that is the point. NATO has not yet recognized that the 'floating voter' is one of the definitive features of our liquid times.

Liquids, writes Zygmunt Bauman, do not keep their shape for long; they make salient the fractured, brittle nature of today's social bonds. And there are compelling reasons, he maintains, to consider fluidity or liquidity as an appropriate metaphor for the times. For what distinguishes liquid power from any other is the absence of commitment or the long term. What makes it sensible to call the current kind of modernity 'liquid', in opposition to other, heavier forms in the modern world, is the continuous, impenetrable fluidity of things (Bauman 2000:2).

In the modern age everything was heavy. We were obsessed with bulk and size, with tight, impenetrable boundaries. All this has changed. The massive workforces of the old industries have been downsized, and companies de-industrialized, in favour of the fluid service sector. With the rise of information systems 'software' capitalism has replaced 'hardware' capitalism. Transnational conglomerates increasingly outsource work to the developing world. Capital has become weightless with the concomitant liquidization of life. The overwhelming preoccupation of businessmen today is to acquire and downsize, to merge and move on. Business is always seeking room for manoeuvre.

Outsourcing is quite old – the transplantation of production to reduce costs. Off-shoring is more recent – the migration of white-collar work jobs from rich nations to poor ones with a well-educated workforce. Off-shoring affects jobs in back-end processing, call centres, accounting, software, product design and consultancy. With jobs migrating instead of workers, the global centre of gravity is moving from west to east. Capital is now weightless, or extraterritorial. We locate manufacturing bases 'offshore'. We invest in economies where labour is cheap, non-unionized and gendered (because in most countries women are still cheaper to employ). And we are always looking for an immediate, not a long-term return on our investments. Indeed, there is a popular saying on Wall Street: 'A long-term investment is merely a short-term speculation that has gone wrong.'

In short, there is something intrinsically 'light'-headed about post-modern capitalism; the free markets which now run rampant do not promote the wise management of assets or even promote long-term investment. The problem is that when markets are conceived wholly in terms of price and return and when asset wealth and the leverage that this provides become as concentrated as it was in the nineteenth century (which is what we are approaching) then markets tend to encourage irresponsible behaviour. Before 1973 the ratio of investment to speculative capital was 9:1. Since then these proportions have been reversed. So huge have the numbers, leverage and derivative instruments become that their value now far exceeds the total economic value of the planet (in 2003 the value of all derivative trading was $85 trillion while the size of the world economy was $49 trillion).

In our private lives, too, brief encounters have replaced lasting associations. By 2035 a third of all Britons are expected to be living alone (*Sunday Times*, 2 September 2007). Even now we fall in and out of love quickly, and just as quickly in and out of marriage. The nineteenth-century Victorian family ideal which expressed the solidity of family life reflected the civic model of a patriarchal state. Today, no single family pattern is statistically dominant. Divorce has become so common that today's families are frequently organized around relationships between ex-spouses and step-parents. In Britain there are over 400 divorce cases every week. By 2020 on current projections, married people in the UK will be in a minority, and long before then, within families, step-fathers will outnumber fathers for the first time. No wonder that children have become the last remaining primary unit that engages married partners. For if partners come and go, children remain. The child, writes Ulrich Beck, has become 'the final alternative to loneliness that can be built into the vanishing possibilities of love' (Beck 1992:118). Hence our morbid preoccupation with the risks faced by children, especially from paedophiles, and a national obsession in Britain in 2007 with the fate of a single vulnerable little girl, Madeleine McCann.

Our military alliances too have been downsized. Once they were rooted in fixed defences, anchored to flanks, fronts and theatres. Now they are interest-based, multi-purpose, global and increasingly short-term. Lack of commitment, however, is a mark of our liquid times. The 2006 *Quadrennial Defense Review* expresses a strong preference for transforming 'static alliances' into more liquid 'strategic partnerships' in which the partners will be evaluated on the military contributions they can bring to the campaign (*QDR* 2006). Unfortunately, 'discretionary alignments' or 'coalitions of the willing' tender to foster temporary partnerships, not lasting commitments.

They help members navigate their immediate insecurities while promising nothing that will make them feel more secure in the long term. And once insecurity feeds in there is a reluctance to commit further.

They also show an impatience to accomplish the mission and move on. This is exactly the situation that the NATO force commanders found in Afghanistan after the US left the country with the job uncompleted, and the Taliban and al-Qaeda still in the field. Indeed, the qualified success of Operation Medusa can be traced back to the speed of the original American campaign to topple the Taliban government in 2001. The Americans committed few ground forces. Instead, they relied on over-whelming air power – distant punishment as opposed to physical coercion. Air attacks produced high casualties and prompted many semi-independent commanders within the Taliban to switch sides. The US was able to reactivate the military networks of the United Front and the anti-Taliban Pushtun command. When the regime imploded these local allies were able swiftly to consolidate their position. The north and west of the country have remained relatively stable ever since under the institutionalized control of the warlords who dominated the political landscape in the 1990s. But the south has disintegrated into a system of small micro-commands whose leaders still use extortion, crime and drugs to pay their followers and sustain their own networks of power. The subsequent reluctance of ISAF to deploy sufficient forces in Helmand forced it to rely on the national Afghan army which was hopelessly unprepared to fill the vacuum – which Taliban could.

Why we might ask was the US in such a hurry to move on? An answer can be found in the remarkable response by General Franks to a question he was asked in an off-the-record session with officers studying at the Naval War College in Newport, Rhode Island in the spring of 2002, not long after the biggest battle of the Afghan war, Operation Anaconda. 'What is the nature of the war you are fighting in Afghanistan?' asked an officer. 'That's a great question for historians,' Franks replied, side-stepping the question (Ricks 2006:127). It would have been a fine answer for a sergeant to offer, but not a senior general. Generals attend staff colleges where the military are taught Clausewitz's maxim that a country should never get involved in any war unless it understands its nature.

Franks, however, was thinking about the next war in Iraq, which the administration had already resolved to fight. It is the nature of liquid life, adds Bauman, that our most acute, stubborn fears are of being caught napping, of failing to catch up with fast-moving events, of falling foul of over-long 'use-by' dates. Afghanistan, for the Americans, was already a 'use-by date' by the late summer of 2002. The next rendezvous was Iraq, and after that probably Iran.

This would not have mattered perhaps, had the US and its allies committed more forces to the campaign. In not doing so it threw into relief another feature of war in the risk age. A commander's first priority these days, writes Rupert Smith who had personal experience as a commander of UN forces in Bosnia, is not to lose his force, rather than use the force at any cost to achieve his aim. No commander, of course, has ever wanted to suffer more casualties than strictly necessary. But in the twentieth century it was possible to replace losses. The production lines allowed this: conscription, training depots and formations and reserves in the case of soldiers, and industrial assembly lines in the case of the weapons which they used. Most of these production lines have been shut down. Today Western forces are unable to replace losses and as a result have become excessively risk-averse. 'We fight not to lose the force for the same reason the guerrilla fights that way: it is expensive to acquire, move and prepare new men and equipment. And politicians at home, uncertain of the people's support for the venture, wish to keep the costs to men and material within what is politically sustainable in the circumstances' (R. Smith 2005:303). Unfortunately, in a counter-insurgency campaign numbers matter. They are needed to dominate the terrain and the environment. Even an extra battalion would have enabled Richards to stop the Taliban from fleeing in good order in September 2006.

Everything I have highlighted betrays the unwillingness to commit that is such a marked feature of the age. Richard Sennett talks of 'the corrosion of character' which has followed the end of the idea of the 'long term' in the new economy and the human consequences of 'flexibility', downsizing and the new management culture. ' "No long term" disorientates action over the long term, loosens bonds of trust and commitment and divorces will from behaviour' (Sennett 1998:31). The flexible behaviour that brings success in the marketplace is weakening the character of the successful. Another sociologist argues that modern institutional networks are marked by 'the strength of weak ties' by which he means that fleeting forms of association are more useful to people than long-term connections and that strong social ties like loyalty have ceased to be compelling (Sennett 1998:24).

The corrosion of character, of course, is far more serious on the battlefield than it is in the boardroom or on the factory floor. For the longer a military campaign continues, the more the members of an alliance are likely to suspect that they are being put unnecessarily at risk. Sharing risks is one thing; the trouble is that in an alliance some members are willing to take more risks than others, and some find themselves being put *at risk* by the risks that others are willing to take.

By default, NATO itself has become a coalition of the willing. Even when countries do commit forces they often hedge them in with 'national caveats' on their use. In Afghanistan this has seriously compromised the Alliance's operational credibility. Some countries will not even allow their soldiers to leave the ISAF HQ. Others will not allow them to engage in combat. The ISAF command has been unable to get soldiers out of their vehicles and onto the streets. Even when units do venture out of their barracks or Provincial Reconstruction Teams (PRTs) they are so over-protected that they both inspire fear in the locals while appearing to be fearful of them at the same time, a disastrous combination which undermines the credibility of the mission.

In short, Afghanistan is a good example of how risk leads to the *reshaping* of political life and the hollowing out of alliances. Risk determines the way the Alliance has changed in recent years – I would say 'evolved' were it not for the fact that the metaphor implies improvement, and whatever else we may conclude from the history of recent years, NATO is both less important and less powerful than it was twenty years ago.

Perhaps looking back, Afghanistan should never have been a NATO mission. There is a striking passage in one of Nietzsche's greater works, *Human, All Too Human*: 'The overthrow of beliefs is not immediately followed by the overthrow of institutions; rather the new beliefs live for a long time in the now desolate and eerie house of their predecessors which they themselves preserve because of the housing shortage' (quoted Schmidtchen 2006:165). Despite the 'housing shortage' after the demise of the 'old belief' in communism, NATO may not have been the best institution to take the West into the risk age. Risk management may even have detracted from its core interest: European security. The many ways in which institutional risk management can deflect organizations from their core business has been highlighted by others (Gaskell 2007:107).

But then risk has become the organizing principle for allied decision-making. Missions are set, tasks determined and national caveats put in place according to the risks involved. Risk is not only conceived as something which the Alliance must address, such as the next state to collapse, or the next one found to be sponsoring terrorism. It has also become a method for regulating its own activities.

And there's the rub. For increasingly, in our liquid times, what we want from alignments is immediate satisfaction, not long-term outcomes. We want the mission (which is always changing) to determine the coalition, not the coalition the mission. Our risk culture gives rise to an obsession with the present, not the future, a frantic wish to secure today rather than tomorrow. 'Liquid life is a succession of new beginnings – precisely for that reason it's the swift and painless endings . . . that tend to be its most challenging moments' (Bauman 2005:2). Unfortunately, endings are rarely swift in war and rarely painless. Wars are often inconclusive; they don't always end when hostilities cease or armistices are signed.

The problem is that of time more generally. In our liquid societies time has been liquefied too. Liquid alliances tend to weaken each member's commitment to its partners and increase the costs of being associated with them for too long. There is a general retreat from commitment. Without commitment, every member looks to restrict its losses in the field to the minimum. As Bauman tells us, what interests us is the immediate, the 'on the spot', and the immediate satisfaction of desires – all of which translates into a fading of interest over time (Bauman 2000:118). We are rooted not to the future but to a present which is potentially 'endless'. As the Yale philosopher Agnes Heller writes, we 'post moderns' are living in the 'absolute present tense' (Heller 1999:83). In the words of Jean Luc Nancy, we find everything historical but nothing 'historic'; we have lost our power to objectify the present in terms of a future we are anxious to reach (Nancy 1993:144). The present has become a theme and problem in itself – which is what makes the risk society in Beck's words so self-reflexive.

Elsewhere in the world the past holds people in its sway. In the western Balkans and Afghanistan, the West finds itself trapped not only by its own history but the histories of all those whose lives it has chosen to shape. It brings its own past with it, and so it should come as no surprise that as current issues become interwoven, impacting on one another, both pasts should exert their pull. The Alliance may want to move on; history prevents it.

What happens when the risk society encounters history can be found in a fictional realization towards the end of Kurt Vonnegut's novel *Cat's Cradle*. There we hear the sound of the sea freezing into ice. This is not the freezing of the ocean as a new Ice Age dawns. It is the outcome of dropping a block of *Ice-9* into the waters and transforming the ocean from a fluid into solid. 'There was a sound like that of a gentle closing of a portal as big as the sky. The great door of heaven being closed softly. It was the great *"ah-whoom"*' (Vonnegut 1965:163).

Such transformations between solid and liquid are called 'phase transactions'. Philip Ball writes of such transactions in society; so do many others.

Malcolm Gladwell calls them 'tipping points' in trends, norms and fashions. Even Thomas Kuhn's 'paradigm shifts' (of which more anon) have been called phase transactions. The term is not merely a convenient allegory for an abrupt shift in modes of behaviour and thinking; phase transactions really do occur (Ball 2004:102). And that is Vonnegut's point. This is the nature of freezing. It is abrupt. Either a substance is liquid (and mobile), i.e. it is above its melting point, or it is solid, rigid and below it. There is nothing in between. Water does not become sluggish before it turns to ice. There is an *ah-whoom* factor too in politics and it tends to occur when the international community tries to manage the risks which local politics produce, and finds itself stuck.

Conclusion

All three case studies I hope illustrate that in today's risk age we are concerned with the 'risk management of everything' (Gaskell 2007:92). The central political issues in all our societies are becoming the reduction or legitimation of the risks we are asked to run. Risk has become the *lingua franca* of modern life. It has become the language of business, politics and public policy, and so we should not be surprised that it should also have become the language of war.

All three case studies are also examples of what is called 'risk colonization' (Gaskell 2007:93), a term borrowed from the Organizational Studies literature where it is used to describe those external pressures for change which penetrate into the 'genetic codes' of organizations and transform their core outlook and practices. The logic of risk colonization since 9/11 has fundamentally changed traditional concepts of security. It has led to the concept of a 'long' or 'never-ending war', an *astrategic*, tactically driven risk management policy which locks the West into an endless process of risk management. A risk society is necessarily a safety society, one that is permanently on the defensive.

Risk also drives the evolution of the institutions designed to address it. Chicago School theorists have long argued that powerful organizational practices shape regulation in their own interests (Gaskell 2007:95). Lobby groups have a direct interest in expanding risk regulations. In so far as risk management depends on knowledge of the risks that are 'out there', knowledge in turn can generate even more risks which must be addressed, managed, regulated and controlled. In the case of war this has given rise to the doctrine of pre-emption which is rooted in turn in the Precautionary Principle, another product of the risk age that became part of environmental law in 1992. Pre-emption has been a feature of modern wars from the Japanese attack on Pearl Harbor in 1941 to Israel's strike against its Arab neighbours in 1967. But never before has pre-emption been the resort of the strong.

Increasingly, the language and method of risk analysis is also applied not only to the way we conceive war but also the way in which we conduct it. Some have referred to this paradox as 'the duality of risk' (Gaskell 2007:93). Contending that risks are better managed by diversified agencies, the state now distributes risks with others: with other states in the case of torture (it is called 'extraordinary rendition'); with private security companies or 'Coalitions of the Billing'; and even with its own citizens (Homeland Security is a glorified Neighbourhood Watch scheme). And if the risk age shapes the way we see the world, it has also begun to reshape the military themselves in terms of their own ethos and training as I shall try to explain in my penultimate chapter.

My three case studies I hope illustrate the extent to which war has been repackaged or remarketed in an age of risk. There is a framework for stitching together these insights into a single theory or model that is capable of making sense of them – a kind of unified theory of everything. It is a model that was popularized in the 1990s by a number of authors, three of the most important being the British sociologist Anthony Giddens and two German writers, Nicklas Luhmann and Ulrich Beck. This book is an attempt to understand war as it has evolved, and is evolving. It is an attempt by a political scientist, not a sociologist, to read our age in the same way that a critic reads a text.

But the risk age did not suddenly come upon us: it has a history like everything else and first we need to study it. The only real voyage (of discovery) argued Marcel Proust was not in seeking new landscapes but in looking back at the old with new eyes. We need to see the past in a new light in order to see the origins of the risk age.

2

Complexity and War

> However forcefully a man develops and seems to leap from one contra-
> diction to the next, close observation will reveal the *dovetailing* where the
> new building grows out of the old. This is the task of the biographer; he
> must think about the life in question – the principle that nature never
> jumps.
> (Nietzsche, *Human All Too Human*, The Wanderer and his Shadow'
> Section 198)

'I greet you at the beginning of a great career which you must have had a
long foregrounding somewhere for such a start' – Emerson writing to Walt
Whitman in 1855 (Bloom 1999:737). The foreground Emerson saw in
Whitman's career was not, as he makes clear by his unique use of the word,
a background. The latter term is used by historians to explain the context
in which we should locate events, whether political, social, economic or cultural. Emerson means a temporal foreground of another kind within which
events are made sense of. 'Foregrounding', the verb, means to make permanent or draw attention to particular features of a phenomenon. In the
case of the risk age and in the specific case of war I shall contend that we
can foreground it in an acute appreciation of the growing complexity of the
world and the increasing risks that inhered in going to war, at least (and
perhaps only) for the leading powers. The risk age did not emerge in a void.
It had a long gestation period. It was not something that was either previously unthought or even unthinkable. It is not, writes the French philosopher Alain Badiou, to put it more pithily, one of our century's 'un-inherited
thoughts' (Badiou 2007:3).

William James Glimpses the End of War

In 1910, the American philosopher William James was commissioned
to write a pamphlet by the American Association for International
Conciliation which we know today as his essay *The Moral Equivalent of War*.
James was a pacifist by conviction, but he was a pacifist of his time. His

reflections were the product of a time and context quite different from our own. Indeed the title of his paper gives him away. He acknowledged that he liked the martial qualities, such as intrepid behaviour, contempt of softness and obedience to command. 'The competitive passion', he added, 'is our fate.' As a species we are by nature competitive (Wilshire 1984:350). Clearly what James found most seductive about the competitive passion was that it introduced a few welcome moments into the boredom and monotony of life. War allowed some to live for a time at an unaccustomedly heightened level of intensity. The fact that we have still not found a moral equivalent for war explains its continuing appeal.

James is an important figure because he was a utilitarian thinker, and utilitarianism has great appeal in a post-metaphysical age – an age such as ours which has turned its back on great causes and utopian ideas. Even so, the Anglo-American discourse on war since the late nineteenth century has largely been instrumental, or utilitarian. We set out ends (such as making the world safe for democracy) and ask how we can best attain them. For us, war is merely a means to an end, and not end in itself, as it was for fascism and still is today for many terrorists. It is worth adding that James believed war to be part of the tragedy of life. This does not mean that it is a fixed part of the human condition. Indeed, he invited us to imagine a world without war. The point about dreams is that they require effort, and effort must be based on the difference between the world we find and the world we would prefer. It is this ability to see it as 'other than it is' which marks us out as a species. But we have an equal responsibility to face reality. Hopes such as peace should be *cashed* out, James insisted, in the human experience, not human hopes.

James, in other words, was a supreme pragmatist whose case against war was moral only in so far as being consequentialist. A practice is usually right (or true) if it is profitable to pursue it. An idea is also usually right if it is profitable to believe in it. 'The true is only the expedient in our way of thinking . . . our obligation to seek truth as part of the general obligation to do what pays' (Wilshire 1984:350). We should be careful of rejecting any idea, in short, if it continues to pay dividends on belief.

Some critics have been put off by James's language, but it was very much part of a distinctively American desire to be philosophically profound and street-wise at the same time. Oliver Wendell Holmes (a contemporary) also insisted 'the best test of truth is the power of thought to get itself accepted in the competition of the market' (Lieven and Hulsman 2006:3). What was so distinctive about American thinking was that its voice, even turn of phrase, were all authentically market-driven. Writers deliberately employed market terms, more as a medium than a message – to bring their ideas within the reach of the man in the street, then still a creature in no immediate danger of disappearing into the anonymity and uniformity of an iPod world.

And on his own reading of the times James came to the conclusion that modern war had become unprofitable, and especially dangerous because of the complexity of modern life. It asked the warring parties to run more risks. It was now 'so expensive that we feel trade to be a better avenue to plunder' (Wilshire 1984:350). The 'piratical wars' of the past may have turned a profit, but the two Anglo-Saxon economies now found profiteering in peacetime to be infinitely more remunerative than piracy. 'No legitimate interest (of any of the powers) would seem to justify the tremendous destruction which a war to encompass it would necessarily entail.' Extravagant ambitions, James insisted, would have to be replaced by 'reasonable claims'. The only two countries that still appeared to be 'bent on loot' were Germany and Japan (Wilshire 1984:351), and even they would find war did not pay if they were ever foolish enough to put it to the test.

Was James necessarily naive? One thing we do know: the period before 1914 was even more globalized than our own on some measurements: such as world trade as a percentage of world GNP; transnational capital flows as a proportion of total world capital; the rate of transnational migration worldwide *vis-à-vis* the rate of world population growth. And for the first time in history there was evidence of commodity price convergence worldwide – the emergence of a 'law of one price,' the economic *sine qua non* for talking about market integration (Krugman 1998:73).

Over time, in other words, the Industrial Revolution had created an 'acute peace interest,' a point reaffirmed by later writers including Karl Polanyi in his book *The Great Transformation* which was published at the height of World War II. The international character of many of the new businesses, especially railways, shipping and pharmaceuticals, and the development of the bond market which held a substantial proportion of most government public debt, had made the international economy more complex than ever, and raised the risks of war significantly. In the case of a general war in Europe, the bankers insisted, military operations couldn't be allowed to go on for more than six months; the gold reserves would soon run out (in 1914 gold-backed coinage was common) leaving governments with no alternative but to print money which would mean galloping inflation (Stone 2007:30).

The bankers were not wrong. Although the case was perhaps over-sold, judged against the long perspective of history most economies were to be devastated by war, the British in particular. The nineteenth century did witness pivotal changes in the entire nature of the economy which produced a watershed between the pre-industrial and industrial ages. And the key, as always, was complexity – the 'deepening' of investment, and the onset of technical changes in business which involved a significant change in 'production functions' (Matthias 1967:4). The international system involved a growing division of labour driven and powered by globalization (then in its early stages) which deepened and intensified interconnections and interdependencies. In other words, quantitative changes in long-standing commercial relations were beginning to produce a qualitative transformation of global life.

James's reputation has tended to suffer because we know how the story ended. Reputation too often becomes reality. To be known as disingenuous is to become subsumed by that identity in the end. James, however, was only expressing a common belief at the time, one which found its most forceful and enduring expression in Norman Angell's book *The Great Illusion*. War was essentially a business transaction which had long outlived its usefulness. 'International finance had become so interdependent and so interwoven with trade and industry . . . that political and military power can in reality do nothing.' 'These little recognised facts, mainly the outcome of purely modern conditions (the rapidity of communications creating a great *complexity* and delicacy of the credit system), have rendered the problems of international politics profoundly and essentially different from the ancient' (Howard 2007:48).

Angell's work had enormous influence. His book was translated into twenty-five languages and sold two million copies. It sold particularly well in Britain which was at the time the most globalized country in the world and one especially aware of the growing complexity of the global economy. It may well have fallen behind the US and Germany in manufacturing, but it remained the dominant power in the world of banking, insurance and shipping. Its invisible exports more than compensated for its declining manufacturing base. And invisible trade needed market stability.

What James observed was how late capitalism had produced a fundamental transformation in the nature of *state power*. The starting point of any country's development is the state and what Max Weber called its monopoly of legitimate force over a defined territory. But while the state begins with coercion ('war makes the state and the state makes war' as Charles Tilly famously reminds us), the modern industrial state soon finds that it must constrain its own exercise of power in the interests of long-term economic growth. A truly effective modern state is notable as much for the constraints it puts on itself as its ability to coerce others.

Where James and Angell erred was not only in the narrowness of their analysis, but its application to the contemporary European scene. In the first place they paid too much attention to economics and not enough to ideas. The twentieth century was intensely ideational. Nationalism, communism and fascism all derailed globalization in the 1930s. In the second place they ignored the extent to which the European Great Powers had so concentrated power in the course of the nineteenth century that it could probably only end in greater competition between them. Nietzsche knew why the world wars would come – he called it the twentieth century's 'compunction to grand politics'. And the grand ideas included the most seductive and compelling idea of all: a world without war.

The world wars that followed were grounded in a universal 'will to power' that consumed the Great Powers. The time line went back to the Enlightenment. For the great expeditions of the eighteenth century, most famously those of Bougainville and Cook to the Pacific, may have been scientific in inspiration but they provided the information which made possible subsequent imperial expansion. Knowledge of the Outer World led rapidly and inexorably to an attempt to gain power over it. In the nineteenth century this expansionism was contained within rules: a loose alliance of values, religion and interests enabled the great imperial powers to expand in their respective spheres without coming into conflict with each other. Their industrial power was projected outwards rather than squandered on the inter-state rivalry that had taken up so much of the previous three hundred years. By 1914 they had taken direct or indirect control of 84 per cent of the planet.

Africa saw the last major land grab within the rules, but the rules only just held. In Africa imperialism turned into a race after 1870: a 'scramble' for the British, a 'steeple chase' for the French, a *Torshluspanik* for the late-comers, the Germans – a race to get through to the other side before History slammed the door shut. The importance of this craze is brought out vividly in John Borman's film *Hope and Glory* (1987) which depicts the wartime childhood of the young Billy Rohan, a boy who is determined to carry on being British in spite of the Blitz, with barrage balloons overhead and a gas mask beneath his school desk. Pointing out the pink bits on the world map his teacher asks the class, 'What fraction of the Earth's surface is British?' Billy doesn't know but Jennifer the school swot does. 'Two-fifths,' she replies. Mrs Evans declaims, 'Two-fifths *ours* – men are fighting and dying to save all the pink bits for you.' The bits were only painted pink because of an extraordinary national investment.

World War I saw a land grab for what was left of the world – in the Adriatic, Eastern Europe and the Middle East. World War II also involved another land grab, this time by Nazi Germany and imperial Japan. By the time it ended, however, it had unmade the old global empires and given birth to the international order we have today in which states have found that they must limit their own power both at home and abroad in order to realize their market potential. Economic rationality demands the growth of institutions such as the World Trade Organization and the World Bank and they in turn demand that their members recognize that self-interest should be the basis of political decision-making, not the realization of political passions. Such institutions, in turn, tend to promote much greater transparency in their operations and trust between the members. James would consider himself vindicated were he alive today.

Let me return to his second argument for this too was perceptive, if premature. Not only was war becoming unprofitable, he insisted, it also was becoming distinctly *embarrassing*. Ministries of War were renamed Ministries of Defence. 'Pure loot and political mastery' were no longer 'morally viable aims', certainly not, he added, for the two countries he knew best, the US and Britain. It was a point that was made by many others (Wilshire 1984:351). What James did not appreciate was the extent to which the Great Powers tried to secure their own future by imposing order on a disorderly world. 'Modern war', explained Quincy Wright, 'tends to be about words more than about things, about potentialities, hopes and aspirations more than about facts, grievances and conditions' (C. H. Gray 1997:97). And what was distinctive about the Americans was that they dreamed for other people, not only themselves. What they promised was a complete break with the past; history would no longer ask what societies were fighting against, but what they were fighting *for*. America's only purpose in war, claimed Woodrow Wilson when the Congress declared war on Germany in April 1917, was 'to vindicate the principles of peace and freedom'. The US, he insisted, had no selfish end, sought no indemnities and would demand no compensation for the sacrifices it would make (Hagen 2007:106). What it did insist on was a New World Order in which war would be banned.

There is a sociological explanation to hand to explain this. Kant had predicted that when the middle classes displaced the aristocracy from power, war as an aristocratic pastime would come to an end. But the middle classes had their own dreams based in part on a Kantian conceit that republics (i.e. democracies) do not go to war against each other. If there was still a place for knights in the modern age it was as instruments of social improvement. 'We had better proclaim ourselves the knights errant of liberty and organise at once a crusade against all despotic governments,' President John Taylor had proclaimed in 1852. There was still a place for the use of the sword but only to advance what he called 'the doctrines of republicanism'. The only legitimate reason for war was the improvement of the human lot. War could educate for freedom. There have been many different variations on this theme. Wilson's ringing phrase, 'Making the world safe for democracy', remains its most famous expression.

The young Karl Marx was afforded a striking intimation of this vision when working as the London correspondent for the *New York Daily Tribune*. In 1856 he covered a parliamentary debate on a conflict, the Arrow War (1856–60) between the ailing Chinese empire on the one hand, and the modern world on the other (in the shape of Britain and France). Although the chief *casus belli* was free trade, the conflict was seized upon by radical Benthamites as a unique opportunity to frogmarch the Chinese into the future. It was the Conservative opposition which censured the Liberal government for thinking that war could, or even should, be fought in the interests of humanity. And Marx was quick to point out the irony: 'The Earl of Derby, the chief of the hereditary aristocracy of England, pleading against . . . Bentham, pleading for humanity against the professional humanitarian; . . . appealing to the *vox populi, vox dei* against the greatest-benefit-of-the-greatest-number man; the descendant of the conquerors preaching peace where a member of the Peace Society preached red-hot steel . . .' (Hurd 1967:56).

It is ironic, of course, that the transcendence of the national interest as the legitimating factor for war turned out to be the project of the despised boring bourgeois elites, not the proletarian masses. But then as Pierre Rosanvallon argues, once we stop thinking of liberalism as a doctrine and assess it as a mode of thinking or a field of vision then everything connects up. Economic liberalism (the open market), democratization (open minds) and nation-building (open government) appear so intertwined that they are inseparable (Trouillot 2003:54). The novelist Robert Musil had a nice phrase for it when he called moral freedom 'a philosophical appendix of free trade' (Musil 1979:361).

James can be faulted for failing to recognize that this put the use of force on a uniquely different footing. He failed to note how morality had become a source of power, as well as the main ground for taking risks – to be moral was to abolish war in the future; it was the promise that inter-state relations might one day soon be put on an entirely new, risk-free level. To turn the old Clausewitizian principle around, writes Ulrich Beck, 'military violence . . . is a continuation of the morality of human rights by other means' (Beck 2005:233). Long before human rights became a stock phrase, or even a concept, the West had begun to formulate moral demands for the behaviour of others. War became something it had never been before – a way of getting others not only to see reason but to accept another culture's point of view. It became a way of persuading recalcitrant societies to behave more 'reasonably'.

Perhaps the plight of others didn't really inspire Western countries to consider military action until after 1914, but what one historian calls 'the thrill of horror' which ran through British public opinion from time to time can be detected in the response to the Armenian outrages in the early 1890s. Gladstone is supposed to have muttered 'those poor Armenians' on his deathbed – probably a first for a British ex-Prime Minister. But the 'preachers of red-hot steel' were at it again in Kosovo 150 years later for another humanitarian principle: the punishment of ethnic cleansing.

What has changed in recent years is that, for all the talk of human rights and global governance and global civil society, the West is much more circumspect in its use of force: war is about interests, not values. Military force is now applied largely to one end, and one end only – managing the wild zones, the *zones grises*, the fragile states and failing societies from which the main risks it faces now emanate. War has been scaled down, as too has our strategic ambition; the West is no longer in the business of building a New World Order but managing the Global Disorder instead. Even in the US the neo-conservatives, the last knights who are willing to venture out to remake the world in their own image, have come to recognize that it is a hopeless task to wage war on inhumanity. The task is to mitigate it. The task, as Condoleezza Rice says, is to make the world, not perfect but a little safer.

Let me return to James's essay one last time. His third argument was that the world had become so complex and war such a risk that the Great Powers now had to arm themselves not in order to go to war, but to deter others from going to war against them. They armed themselves solely to promote peace: 'It may even reasonably be said that the intensely sharp competitive preparation for war by the nation is the real war, permanent, unceasing, and that the battles are only a sort of public verification for the mastery gained during the peace interval' (Wilshire 1984:350). The same insight was grasped by a diverse set of writers from Nietzsche to Engels who understood that the arms race both underwrote deterrence and undermined it at the same time. What these writers saw was a world that was arming itself in order to avoid war, not to provoke it.

All this would have puzzled the great proponent of Perpetual Peace, Immanuel Kant. The greatest evil, Kant suggested in the *Speculative Beginning of Human History* (1786), was that which civilized peoples derived not from 'actual present or past wars [but] from the never-ending and constantly increasing *arming* for future wars' (Smith 2007:82). But James was not a Kantian philosopher, and had little time for metaphysical principles, or Categorical Imperatives. Instead, he was a realist and believed that the realist approach to relations between nations was the only morally serious approach to policy. The best we can hope for is what Hobbes calls 'commodious living', and in the case of war at least a commitment to some civilized restraint in its use.

The need for restraint was already becoming urgent. All cultures institutionalize the practice of war. Considering the advantage of being better at it than one's neighbours, it makes sense to cultivate practices such as rewarding good warriors, to highlight concepts of 'us' and 'them' and to develop the means of maximizing societal participation in conflict. Nation states, as it happened, were more successful at all three than any other: they professionalized armies and educated their soldiers; they demonized their enemies in generic terms such as class and race; and they proved particularly adept at mobilizing entire societies to fight. But arguably they were too successful to be successful. The wars of the twentieth century almost destroyed the nation state itself. James was proved right: in the end the nation had to curb the passions that nationalism evoked.

Unfortunately, of course, disaster happened: war broke out, and our reading of James's essay is inevitably coloured by this knowledge. His confidence in the future was not only misplaced. His experience is a warning to the rest of us that we cannot be confident in anything. The etymology of confidence includes trust (confide), hope (confidence) and faith (*fides*). None of these inhere in the future. Instead, the words tend to remind us unnervingly of our losses – one of which is the faith in progress which James's generation took for granted. For the world wars which followed were marked by a level of barbarism that the nineteenth century confidently thought it had put behind it. As an author James would have been especially saddened to have been told that the century would open with the destruction of the great library at Louvain as the Germans advanced towards Paris. 'It was an act that rendered the condition of the century terminal. Nothing ever since has surprised me,' remarks the narrator of Thomas Keneally's novel, *A Victim of the Aurora*, the tale of a murder during an Edwardian polar expedition. In the book the crime is not only terrible in itself but also in its implications. The same might be said of the destruction of one of Europe's oldest libraries. And that was just the beginning. If only for its symbolism the twentieth century can be said to have ended with the burning of the library in Sarajevo in 1992 (a piece of barbarism which destroyed medieval manuscripts as yet unedited or reproduced, and incunabula not yet reprinted).

So what went wrong? What James failed to discuss in his essay was the complexity of the great diplomatic system 'managed' by the Great Powers in the hope of deterring each other from going to war. Unfortunately, the system broke down in 1914. It is always tempting, of course, to explain events like World War I as an accident waiting to happen. Franz Ferdinand's assassin, after all, might have obeyed the order to abort his mission sent to him by the military conspirators in Belgrade. Franz Ferdinand himself might have cancelled his trip as his wife begged him to do, or he might have followed the advice of his advisers and left Sarajevo immediately after the ceremony at the city hall. If the Archduke's driver hadn't taken the wrong road and his young assassin who had failed earlier in the day in his mission had not just happened to be in the right spot at the wrong time the assassination would not have taken place. But then we must also ask whether there are real coincidences in history or whether it is just history's way of saying that we haven't been paying enough attention to the risks we run, given the complexity of the systems we are required to manage.

History, in fact, is punctuated by upheavals like 1914. Recent mathematical ideas, writes the physicist Mark Buchanan, point to the possibility that a single scaffolding of logic lies behind tumultuous events like the stock market crash which precipitated the Great Depression. We are usually aware of the risks of systems failure such as an economic crash or a major war but we are not always aware that many of our most important networks are poised perpetually on the very edge of instability (Buchanan 2002:11–12). This is because they are so complex. And systems are complex because they are made up of many interconnected parts.

Take the international system in 1914 which was composed of Great Powers and small, banks and corporations, and ideas that floated freely, recognizing no frontiers. But that is not the end of it. If it were, a complex system would merely be complicated (like a machine with interconnecting parts). Complex systems have other characteristics. What distinguishes them from non-complex systems is that they produce a diverse range of behaviours (Homer-Dixon 2006:21–2). A car engine may be made up of diverse parts, but it either works or it doesn't. If it does, it will take you to your destination. If the engine breaks down, you are not going anywhere fast. By contrast, a complex system, like a stock market produces behaviour that cannot be attributed to any particular part. Whether we find ourselves trading in a bull market which is going up, or in a bear market which is going down, both are the result of buying and selling on the part of many different investors.

Unfortunately, the actors did not understand what was necessary to keep the European balance of power in an equilibrium state. All systems operate in a self-organized critical state. Wars are the result of tensions that observe a power law, for the smallest (or biggest) event can tip them over into conflict. The problem with the European system was that it had developed complex patterns of connections which made a breakdown more likely, not less. Harmful feedback loops such as the arms races between the powers (often called 'vicious circles') were one contributory factor. The naval arms race between Germany and Britain was one of the most pernicious for it further reinforced a general sense of insecurity. But equally damaging (though not often discussed) was the fact that some actors such as Germany spent too little on defence, not too much. Indeed, one of the explanations for Germany's willingness to go to war in 1914, writes the Harvard historian Nail Ferguson, was its fear that the military gap between itself and its enemies was beginning to close.

In 1913 Germany was spending only 3.5 per cent of its GNP on defence, less than either France or Russia. Resistance within the parliament to increased taxation was matched by the impossibility of borrowing further money without widening the bond yield gap between itself and its western rivals. Ferguson concludes there were a number of ways in which Germany could have increased spending and thus kept up with its rivals, and thus underwritten the system of deterrence. Increased borrowing would still have left the German debt smaller as a fraction of GNP than the French or Russian, and its debt service ratio smaller than Britain's as a fraction of non-lethal expenditure. Increased taxation would have brought tax levels into line with Britain's as a share of GNP and still left taxation lower as a percentage of public spending. The fact is – Ferguson reminds us – by the third year of the war total public spending had risen to more than 70 per cent of GNP. The state had sharply increased its share of revenue and expenditure and parliament was supporting the war effort by huge levels of short-term lending to the government. 'The fact that the Reich had been able to sustain the cost of waging total war on three fronts for three years suggests that it could easily have borne the much lower cost of averting war without difficulty' (Ferguson 1998:142).

The problem was that although the Europeans understood the component parts of the system, such as the naval arms race, the alliance systems, even the financial markets, they did not fully understand the system as a whole. It became impossible to anticipate all the possible combinations of the component failures, or the possible negative synergies of combined failure. This process prevented true equilibrium from being attained, with the result that a small and in principle containable crisis in the Balkans came to assume disproportionate and catastrophic proportions. The process is called 'self-organizing criticality' (SOR). What happened in 1914 was that the system went critical because it had already begun to develop an 'emergent property' – a general level of instability that eventually precipitated war.

Systems, moreover, tend to break down when 'nodes' in the network (i.e. the elements of the system) are tightly coupled (Homer-Dixon 2006:115–16). The European system in 1914 was so tightly connected that it allowed very little margin of error whenever a crisis arose. The system, in a word, had very little resilience. A resilient system, writes Homer-Dixon, can absorb large disturbances without changing its fundamental behaviour. The Europeans needed to prevent foreshocks from triggering synchronic failure. They needed to rein in their mobilization schedules; they needed time to think before they panicked; they needed a buffering capacity. For the resilience of a system is an 'emergent property' too (i.e. it is not the result of any one of the system's parts, but of the synergy between them).

And unfortunately, once war did break out the system encouraged its *deepening*. No one, for example, intended the war to go global, not even the British who stood to lose most, but the connections in the system ensured that it would go global fairly quickly. This dynamic first became critical in 1905 during the Morocco crisis when Germany sought to bolster the independence of the country against French colonial ambition. The crisis revealed that regional rivalries could no longer be handled in a self-contained fashion as they had before. They were now liable to be both 'Europeanized' and 'militarized' at the same time (Strachan 2003:37). But other *connective* factors were no less decisive in ensuring that war would spread and deepen at the same time. Of these none was more important than the links between the financial markets in New York and the City of London which enabled Britain to transform itself from a late-nineteenth-century economy into the world's first modern war machine. And this, in turn, enabled it to continue the fight after the French were exhausted.

Historians will continue to debate whether the Great War was inevitable or not; they will continue to engage in counter-factual arguments that have gained in popularity in recent years. On my own reading of events the system was bound to fail because as the complexities accumulated so the system became increasingly unstable. In the end, it collapsed because it was not resilient enough. What followed was a disastrous war in which battles proved indecisive, and attrition eventually took its toll.

The System Holds 1949–89

Many historians tend to see the era 1914–89 (the 'short twentieth century') as a continuum with the inter-war years, as an armistice between two campaigns we call World War I and World War II. The second conflict probably would have been avoided if Hitler had never come to power; 'Hitler's War' was the vision of one man, and it was willed by one individual. Its outbreak can be assigned to the moral failure of one man and/or a political movement rather than causal responsibility (the unforeseen and unintended breakdown of a system). But even Hitler could not have accomplished what he did on his own; the blitzkrieg tactics that the German army employed so effectively had been learnt in the Great War. In a sense the old imperial army in which he was so proud to serve had scripted World War II long before he himself came up with the project.

In 1945 there was no peace treaty, no Versailles Conference. The fighting stopped only in Europe. It continued elsewhere off stage in Indonesia and soon Korea, though this time much of the fighting involved, not the victorious powers but their proxies, the Koreans and the Vietnamese, the Salvadoreans and the Cubans. But peace held between the superpowers themselves, and it did so very largely because it was underwritten by nuclear weapons. Nuclear deterrence gave the system its shape and in the end its stability.

It was Carl Schmitt who famously claimed that the discrimination between friend and enemy is the basis of politics and constitutes the chief rationale of the state. It also constituted the chief rationale of the international order after 1945. For as Schmitt acknowledged, an enemy does not have to be considered demonstrably bad (which would rule out any hope of accommodation). It does not have to be demonized or rendered entirely unsympathetic. It does not even need to be a serious competitor; it may still be possible to do business with it, and defend oneself against it at the same time (Laidi 1998:86). This was certainly the case after the brief anti-Soviet moralism of the early 1950s. Even John Foster Dulles dropped talk of 'liberating' Eastern Europe and 'rolling back communism'. Even Ronald Reagan's Evil Empire speech was intended for domestic consumption, not an international audience. As Schmitt maintained, what is important is that we can live peacefully with the enemy but never be *at peace*. Any accommodation (such as détente, trade, etc.) can never rule out the possibility of war.

Fortunately, nuclear weapons made the prospect of war so uninviting that the two superpowers accepted deterrence as the prevailing principle of international security in an even more complex world. The nuclear age was ushered in with Hiroshima on 6 August 1945. Only a few months later a Yale University professor, Bernard Brodie, published a book entitled *The Absolute Weapon*. In it he and his fellow authors put forward the startling proposition that not only were nuclear weapons there to stay, but that they had changed decisively the rules of engagement. Henceforth, they wrote, the chief purpose of military establishments would no longer be to win wars, but to avert them. General MacArthur recognized this early on. Only days after the US dropped the two atom bombs in Japan, effectively ending the war at a stroke, he remarked to the journalist Theodore White, 'White, do you know what this means? Men like me are obsolete. There will be no more wars' (Ruggie 1996:350). Instead there was an armed peace, but it was peace of a kind. No further armed conflict was possible no matter how thoroughly each side might plan for such an eventuality. We are surely right to view as 'peace' a war in which the winning side made every effort not to fire a shot and the losing side could have no recourse to its weapons even when facing the final endgame.

But we must also acknowledge that the nuclear peace held despite the technology not because of it. 'Weapon ranges have a special magic: all that destructive technology concentrates on the production of nothing. The closest we can get to certain obsessional states of mind' J. G. Ballard in the annotated edition of his 1970 cult book, *The Atrocity Exhibition* (Ballard 1995:15). Weapon ranges defined the landscape of the Cold War such as the atom bomb testing site on Bikini Atoll. And like all obsessions it was dangerous for the world's health. Not only did the superpowers build larger and larger megatonnage weapons, they even tried to build the ultimate weapon, the third of what became known as the 'alphabet' bombs. We know about the first, the A-bomb, which incinerated two Japanese cities, and the H-bomb which blasted its way into public consciousness a few years later. But we tend to forget the C-bomb, a hydrogen bomb that could 'transmute' an element such as cobalt into a radioactive element about 320 times as powerful as radium. The C-bomb, though never built, soon found its way into the bestsellers of the time, such as Neville Shute's *On The Beach* (1957). It even found a mention in Bruce Chatwin's autobiographical book, *In*

Patagonia (1977) in which he tells us that as a schoolboy he had pictured a dense blue cloud bank, spitting tongues of flame at the edges. He had imagined himself alone on a green headland, scanning the horizon for the advance of the clouds. Patagonia seemed the one place on the map that he could survive while the rest of the world blew itself up (P. D. Smith 2007:395).

The cobalt bomb was largely forgotten after the Cuban missile crisis came and went, so too was the Doomsday Machine, a bomb which appeared in *Doctor Strangelove*, Stanley Kubrick's trenchant take on the Cold War. What Kubrick did for nuclear war so he was to do for space in his later epic, *2001*: he intensified it, making it more theatrical and giving it more depth at the same time. In the film the Doomsday device is designed to trigger a country's nuclear weapons if it finds itself under attack. Hermann Kahn, on whom Dr Strangelove was partly based, went to his death in 1983 firmly convinced that the central problem of arms control was to delay the day when the Doomsday Machine would be built. Only after the Berlin Wall had been breached and the ice of the Cold War had begun to thaw, did military analysts realize the Russians had actually built a version of the device. It is still in place. At its heart is a computer system code named 'Perimeter' which went fully operational in January 1985. Its job is to determine whether there has been a nuclear detonation on Russian territory and to check whether communications channels to the Kremlin have been severed. If the answer to both questions is 'yes', then the computer will conclude that the country is under attack and activate its nuclear arsenal. All that is then needed for the launch of the missiles is final human approval from a command post buried deep underground. It would be a brave officer who, having been cut off from his superiors in the Kremlin, would be prepared to ignore the advice of such a supposedly foolproof system. In other words, far from exiting the nuclear age, we find ourselves still trapped inside it. The West still faces the prospect that Russia's strategic nuclear warheads could be launched by a computer system designed and built in the late 1970s. For those of us, adds Ballard, who still think *Doctor Strangelove* the most telling commentary on the nuclear age, the system remains a vivid demonstration, arranged for our benefit by the machine, of our own dispensability as a species (Ballard 1997:76).

Indeed, in retrospect, we were fortunate to have survived the Cold War, not only because the C-bomb was never built but also because the technology that was put in place did not always serve the system as expected. Deterrence held, but control of nuclear weapons was not foolproof. Indeed, there were several disturbing failures in combat operation centres designed to detect the enemy. Constructed in 1961, the US Air Force's Ground Combat Operations Center at Cheyenne, Colorado, experienced alarming software failures. For eight tense minutes in 1979 it mistook a test scenario for an actual missile attack, a mistake that could have triggered a nuclear release. The following year a computer-chip failure mistakenly alerted the Strategic Air Command against attack. False alerts continued, especially following the installation of new computers. The complexity of the technology at the heart of nuclear deterrence made it particularly accident-prone.

The sociologist Charles Perrow calls failures in complex systems such as computer malfunctions 'normal accidents' and tells us that they are most likely to occur in tightly coupled systems in which various components interact quickly over rigid connections (Hughes 2004:90). Such a tightly coupled system was the European alliance system in 1914. In the nuclear age it took a technological form. An intercontinental ballistic missile, for example, with propulsion tightly coupled to its guidance systems, was particularly prone to 'normal accidents'. In the case of Three Mile Island, a cascading series of failures involving interacting physical components and hardware failures almost produced a nuclear meltdown. In the case of the weapons of the Cold War, we are probably still not fully aware of how lucky we were to win a reprieve.

Hollywood as usual succeeded in capturing the deep anxiety about the accidents out there waiting to happen. The film *Fail Safe* (1964), one of the most serious though dramatically lifeless renditions, depicts a computer malfunction, in this case a simple failure on board the lead bomber of a SAC patrol that orders the planes to drop their bombs on their pre-arranged target – Moscow. Once unleashed they cannot be recalled. Bringing the picture up to date, another film, *War Games* (1983), showed a teenage computer wizard hacking into the US National Defense computer. Believing that 'Thermonuclear War' is just another game, the teenager takes the world to the brink of disaster. The film was a wry comment on the dangers inherent in superpower war-gaming; we now know that a NATO war game later the same year almost triggered off a real conflict.

Today we live in a risk age which was foregrounded in the nuclear era in two respects. We once believed that technology was a form of 'functional simplification', one which gave human operators and programmers an illusion of control. Once we came to recognize that accidents were 'normal', and that there would always be a ghost even in the most sophisticated of machines, we had to rethink the place of technology in life in general. And once we accepted that tightly coupled diplomatic systems often fail we had to develop more *resilient* systems to prevent war between the major powers from breaking out. Half-way through the nuclear era we began to cultivate 'habits of co-operation', such as summit meetings between political leaders, arms control agreements and confidence building measures that reinforced the message that nuclear war had to be avoided at all costs. Today's international regimes that regulate the international system are also far more transparent than the old and, as a result, tend to evoke more trust between members. The multilateral institutions that have arisen since 1947 have altered the regional landscape of war and peace. They have established new normative standards, communication backchannels and institutional practices which have modified greatly the behaviour of states. This is a world of which James would have approved, but it is our world, of course, not his.

Looking back from our unique vantage point we can see that the hopes that James put forward in his essay were only an expression of a general idea that had begun to dominate liberal thinking by the end of the nineteenth century. James gave it a philosophical twist, others an economic and social one, but whatever form it took, the idea was expressive of the conviction that war had exhausted its possibilities and that history was taking mankind in a different direction. No sensible liberal thinker ever denied that there might not be setbacks along the way but none could have predicted a setback on the scale of World War I and none could have anticipated the horrors that were to be unleashed by World War II, let alone the Armageddon that would have been unleashed by a third.

The problem with James's vision was the problem of his philosophy. He asked his readers to ask themselves what good was likely to follow from their own beliefs and practices, that is what benefit would follow. He was an inveterate pragmatist who, true to his own school of thought, saw philosophy as an instrument of knowledge (for fostering common sense) not an answer to the enigmas of life or metaphysics. He sought, claimed Bertrand Russell, to build 'a superstructure of belief upon a foundation of scepticism', and, like all such attempts from Berkeley on, the attempt succumbed to the fallacies entertained by their proponents. Russell called all such attempts part of 'the subjective madness' that characterized the modern age (Russell 1971:773).

James's particular fallacy was his belief that human beings are guided entirely by self-interest, that they are always asking only one question: *cui bono*? Human beings in reality have impulses which are not always selfish. He himself acknowledged that the human mind is ineluctably poetic – that great ideas are precisely those that enable us to dream. It is curious that for all his talk of the growing complexity of life which was beginning to make war so unattractive that he never stopped to ask why states often want power; they want power to impose order, to secure a permanent peace, and in the twentieth century societies were willing to risk all to realize their dreams. They are much less willing to do so today, partly in the knowledge, of course, of what happened after 1914.

But our reluctance to hazard all in battle is also grounded in the knowledge that war is a particularly imperfect instrument for realizing any vision, just as revolution is invariably a wasteful way of reforming any society however stubbornly resistant it may be to change. Liberals like James would have been on much stronger ground had they identified that the problem was war itself and its growing complexity. They would have been better advised to have argued, not that war was proving too costly in economic terms, or too embarrassing to pursue with a good conscience, but that those countries that were still in the 'plunder' game such as Germany and Japan were unlikely to be intimidated by the cost or embarrassed by the practice as long as they believed that war could deliver a quick victory.

Complexity of War

Long before 1914, more enlightened generals knew what a long war would mean. Instead of a brief conflict, they would probably find themselves engaged in an endless contest that would require the total mobilization of populations and industries. What would occur is what Clausewitz predicted if combat were no longer guided by the 'will of a leading intelligence'. War would take on a will of its own, becoming in the process a complete, untrammelled, absolute manifestation of violence (Finkelkraut 2001:72).

By the early twentieth century war was becoming more dangerous because it was becoming more complex; and its increasing complexity mirrored the increasing complexity of life. We now talk of complexity theory all the time, but it is not to be thought of as a hypothesis about the history of the world so much as a description of a state of affairs that has been there from the beginning. The technology theorist Langdon Winner is right to suggest, however, that only since the 1970s have we begun to recognize complexity not only as a fact but as a problem. 'If there is a unique quality to the modern era it is that the conditions of existence have changed to such a degree that something explicitly recognised as 'complexity' now continually forces itself into our awareness' (Winner 1975:49). Complexity is certainly not unique to our own age, but it has become the main prism through which we interrogate our own practices. Complexity is at the heart of the risk age, and its growing self-reflexivity.

Indeed, one of the striking findings of modern historical research is the extent to which historians have identified a long-term trend towards complexity. It is built into everything, beginning with the Big Bang and the creation of the universe which became more complex as it began to expand. At the moment of its birth matter and energy could not be distinguished from each other, any more than could such fundamental physical forces as gravity and electro-magnetism and strong and weak nuclear forces. As it expanded and began to cool, so it became more complex. Matter and energy went their separate ways. Stars appeared, compressed and heated by the force of gravity. As larger stars died in supernovae they created heavier elements which provided the raw materials for complex chemical structures including living organisms such as ourselves.

In E. M. Doctorow's novel *City of God*, there is a brief description of the origins of the universe, from the moment, fifteen or so billion years ago, to which we date the Big Bang to that second in which 'a chance array of carbon and nitrogen atoms that fuse into molecular existence as a single cell', produced, 'the first entity in the universe with a will of its own' – ourselves (Doctorow 2000:6). As a novelist, Doctorow can be allowed a little poetic licence. Whether the creation of human life was an accident, or intelligently designed as many contend, is not the point. What is the point is that life is a prime example of irreducible complexity. A living cell contains some 100 million proteins of 20,000 different types. The genome of a simple bacterium has a genetic code some four million letters long.

The expansion of the universe did not imply that the appearance of our species was inevitable, but it does suggest that the appearance of increasingly complex systems was part of a larger, universal trend toward denser energy flows and greater chemical complexities. It takes little or no energy, for example, to sustain the simple structures of interstellar space. It takes a great deal of energy to sustain more complex systems. On our own planet complexity is seen in the appearance of life itself: the evolution of biological control over sunlight through photosynthesis, and the appearance of multicelled organisms which need, and can manage, much larger energy flows than single-celled organisms (Christian 2006:23).

Let us return to Doctorow's 'end point' – the creation of the first species 'with a will of its own'. What is distinctive about humanity is that we are infinitely more complex than the universe itself. By counting the number of neural configurations the human brain can accommodate, it has been estimated that it can produce about $10^{70,000,000,0000,000}$ possible 'thoughts'; for comparison, there are only about 10^{80} atoms in the entire universe. The brain is rather small. It contains only about 10^{27} atoms but the feeling of limitless thinking that we possess derives not only from this number alone, but from the vastness of the number of possible connections that can exist between groups of atoms. This is what we mean by complexity. Were our minds significantly simpler then we would be too simple to know it (Barrow 1996:19).

It is these neural connections that allow us to learn collectively. Equipped with language, we can share what we have learned as individuals. We can do so with such precision that more knowledge accumulates within the collective memory than is lost. As a result, our species has access to a vast repertoire of ideas, behaviour and techniques. *Collective learning* (i.e. the capacity to accumulate knowledge at the level of the community) is what makes us different from every other species on the planet.

In terms of historical development in the last 6,000 years collective learning has continued to evolve as human society has evolved ever more complex social structures: from the hunter-gatherer tribes, Neolithic farming villages, the first civilizations and today's 'cosmopolitan web'. And human webs, claim the McNeills, increase chance encounters. Kinship, common worship, economic exchange, political co-operation and especially military competition stem from the webs we have forged. In all such relationships people communicate information and use that information to change their behaviour (McNeill and McNeill 2003).

What gives knowledge an increasingly *corporate* character is that we have discovered that collectively we can make much more sense of the world than we can alone. Recently James Surowiecki has explored a deceptively simple idea, namely that large groups of people are smarter than an elite few, no matter how brilliant. They are better both at solving problems and fostering innovation. Ask a hundred people to run the marathon and average their times, and every time the average will be worse than the time of the fastest runner. But ask the same number to solve a problem, and the average will be at least as good as the answer of the smartest member. With most things, the average means mediocrity. With decision-making it usually means excellence. 'You could say, it's as if we've been programmed to be collectively smart' (Surowiecki 2005:11). The economic historian, Joel Mokyr, has attributed the Industrial Revolution to 'chains of inspiration' (Robert Wright 2001:190–1), the fact that one idea leads to another. Such chains can explain the whole history of technical advance which, after all, has been driven by the collective social brain. Our own history shows that the sharing of knowledge is increasing all the time because of another factor – technology, the dominant motor of complexity since industrialization began. History is the evolution towards complex structures, created and manned by information flows which today are managed electronically.

The importance of this for war may not be immediately self-evident but it is real. It was Charles Peirce, the founder of American Pragmatism, who first claimed that the 'meaning' of any single message (i.e. the meaning we derive from the information we process) is the behaviour it induces. The behaviour appropriate to the information the message carries about the state of the environment usually leads to behaviour appropriate to the information conveyed. In short, complexity is fostered by the processing of *information*. Consider the locomotive. Its engine is not only the cutting-edge processor of energy, it has a governor – a feedback loop – and thus processes data about its own state. Societies too tend to become more networked over time; multiple feedback encourages people to come together. If modern societies become complex at a faster rate that is because they are much more receptive than pre-modern societies to new information – they tend to embrace it, and do so collectively (Wright 2001:248). In a word, they learn faster. Cultural evolution can be said to be Lamarckian in the sense that acquired traits and skills can be passed on over generations at ever faster rates. History, of course, is full of fits and starts ('punctuated equilibriums' in the language of evolutionary biology), but the direction is clear enough to most historians. It is a direction away from simple sameness to diversity, towards complex sameness which we call, today, globalization (McNeill and McNeill 2003:320).

If history, however, is a story of rapid, accumulating change it is misleading to call this Progress. 'Progress' itself is something of a cultural construction, in its present form an Enlightenment concept which over the last two centuries has been translated into an ideology of life. It found particularly strong expression in Kant's 'hidden plan' and even Adam Smith's championship of the middle class as the vanguard of a superior economic and moral order. Its most sublime expression is Hegel's belief that history is the story of freedom becoming conscious of itself.

We can, if we wish, incorporate into history a concept of 'development' without smuggling in normative assumptions – if by development we mean nothing more than increasing complexity. Indeed, it is far more credible to claim not that history is progressive, but rather that it is *directional*. And what is directional is our capacity to learn, to adapt to our environments and to learn increasingly quickly. Our civilization has survived for that reason. What makes us learn quickly (to learn more, though not nec-

Table 1 Living Systems versus Auotmated Evolution

Nature's Evolution	Automated Evolution
A biological plant/creature	A process or software
Glacially slow evolution	Very fast evolution
Immense complexity	Low complexity to date: eventually complexity exceeding that of nature
No long-term goal in mind	Long-term goals that are set
Random trial and error	Steered by an intelligent-design team
Survival of the fittest	Selection based on design criteria
The selected version cannot be immediately replicated	The selected version is replicated and spread through the internet
Methods of evolution rarely change	Methods of evolution evolve rapidly
Each plant or creature that evolves is physically separate	Evolutionary software can be interlinked on the internet

essarily to know better) is the exchange of information which is now facilitated, as never before, through technological advance and global networks, especially the internet. In 1965, the engineer George Moore spelt out the principle that has become known as Moore's Law: the capacity (i.e. the speed) of micro-processors doubles every eighteen months. Recently this has been supplemented by Gilder's Law, which states that the transmission speed (or bandwidth) on the net doubles every year.

And the new technologies are important for a reason. If natural selection shows no evidence of intelligent design, automated evolution does. Automated evolution is targeted, purposeful and intelligent and it is promising to make life more complex still. In automated evolution technologies change as they learn. The algorithms do not remain the same. Complexity inheres not in the original design but 'evolutionary engineering' (Martin 2006:190–1). Natural selection can provide localized improvements (as genes continue to adapt); evolutionary engineering allows human intervention as a system reaches an evolutionary dead-end. Evolutionary engineering is not random because humans set goals, of which the most important is performance. If you invent software for foreign exchange trading, for example, you want the system to function optimally. Procedures refine themselves by going through endless mutate-select cycles, all with one end in mind: improving the return on your investment. When the system ceases to function optimally, the programmers change the algorithms. In the marketplace where the profit motive is the 'survival goal', it is vital that technology evolves, adapts, learns and improves itself. Daimler-Chrysler, for example, uses goal-driven evolution to refine the designs of diesel engines. The aerospace industry has used it to refine jet engines. And software can be refined indefinitely.

Automated evolution is going to change history faster than ever by making it more complex still.

Complexity, War and the Decisive Battle

Clausewitz never formally identified complexity as part of the nature of war except in claiming 'everything in war is simple, but the simple is *increasingly* difficult.' The word 'increasingly' is my own addition to his text. War has become increasingly complex and as a result increasingly indecisive. This didn't mean that war was fated to become redundant by some implacable law of history. Complexity did not spell this out – instead, it forced societies to be more creative. Far from spelling an endgame as James and others hoped, it inspired societies to play the game a little longer by coming up with different rules.

This development has also raised the opportunity costs of war. As war became more complex, so those who practised it had to anticipate the consequences for themselves, for the larger economy, for social and political stability at home, as well as in the international order. Even on the battlefield, when drawing up tactics, generals need more foresight than ever. Politicians have to ensure that allies do not become enemies, or vice versa. Indeed, the problem with complexity in warfare is the questions we have to ask at the beginning of every war: who are our allies; what are our true long-term interests; how accurate is our assessment of the enemy? These are all rational calculations, of course, but they become more complex as societies evolve and as the cost of getting the calculations wrong has risen. In the end, we have found that war is not as decisive as we might have expected.

Some years ago the historian Russell Weigley wrote a book, *The Age of Battles*, to challenge the popular belief that the history of war in Europe was the history of the decisive battle. As Weighey reminds us, modern history is replete with commanders such as Napoleon, Robert E. Lee and the German High Command in both world wars who went on to achieve one tactical success after another only at the cost of strategic ruin. His was a bold claim and a controversial one too because battle has always given war its theatrical appeal and no era was more theatrical in this respect than the Napoleonic. A fifth of all battles in Europe between 1490 and 1815 were fought in the twenty-five years of the Revolutionary and Napoleonic wars

(Bell 2007:7). Napoleon's own career ended with Waterloo, one of the last battles to pit uniformed armies marching against each other in parade-ground formations, drums rolling, bayonets flashing in the sun. Clausewitz himself took part in the Waterloo campaign, so it is not surprising that he should have been influenced by the prospect of risking all on a single throw of the dice.

In the Western imagination the decisive battle has an even longer pedigree. In the battles between Greek hoplite forces and Roman legionary formations, Machiavelli and other humanist writers of the Renaissance found an 'ideal type' of war. Even Hobbes, although correctly noting that 'war consisteth not in battle only, or the act of fighting' insisted that the interval between fighting was important only because it was a 'track of time wherein the will to contend in battle is sufficiently known'. In the course of the nineteenth century Western theorists gave particular prominence to battle as the objective in war towards which all effort should be directed.

But many military historians have begun to challenge the romance of the decisive battle as the supreme expression of the will to power. They have even begun to question the decisiveness of many of the battles of the modern era, even the most famous. One of the most admired of American military historians, Walter Millis, reflected in his most famous book, *Arms and Man*, that: 'Waterloo was the final and most decisive of these grim dramas. It was not often to be repeated [thereafter]. War was beginning to lose its one virtue – its power of decision' (Weighey 1993:xii). All students of military history must be struck, adds the historian Brian Bond in his book *The Pursuit of Victory* (1994), by the 'ambivalence, irony and transience of military victories' in the late modern era, however spectacular or decisive they might have appeared at the time. Wars have increasingly been won through attrition because they have been increasingly determined by economic and social factors, as much as by the performance of armies on a battlefield.

From 1850 onwards the powers which won their wars tended to be economically stronger than their adversaries: France against Austria in 1859; the North against the South in the American Civil War (1861–5); Prussia against France (1870–1); the West in both world wars, and finally the US and its allies in the Cold War that followed. The victories of the losing side though often tactically impressive, availed it little. Field Marshall von Manstein later talked of Germany's 'lost victories' in 1940–1 (Weltman 1995:65). None of the battlefield successes that Germany secured in 1940–1 (perhaps the most impressive in modern history) could be translated into a decisive strategic outcome.

In that respect, writes Jonathan Bailey, Operation Barbarossa was more a metaphysical than a military plan, the product of an article of political faith rather than dispassionate operational analysis. Convinced that the Soviet Union would collapse under repeated hammer blows, Hitler stripped the German invasion force of much of its firepower which would only be needed in an attritional campaign. Any assumption that firepower would prove decisive would have undermined the ideological tenets that under-wrote the whole enterprise. And indeed in the first six months the Wehrmacht did win some notable victories which still encourage us to see the early months of the offensive as a master stroke in manoeuvre warfare. But the cost was excessive: 830,000 casualties, more than Germany had incurred in the battles of Verdun and the Somme combined (Bailey 2007:56). Although ground was indeed gained, the war was not won. It was to continue for a further three years during which the fighting degenerated into an especially grim and barbarous series of encounters.

Unfortunately, in an attempt to defy this logic, war for some countries became a *metaphysical* ideal designed especially in fascist ideology to test the superior 'will to power' of the participants. And the chief distinguish-ing feature of the Third Reich was its willingness to risk all. Hitler saw himself as a gambler first and foremost, a man who took risks: 'there is no success without risk either politically or militarily' (Bessel 2004:86). He was not interested in politics as the art of the possible. The possible sought to eliminate risks; politics here was conceived as efficiency, function and purpose. The will to power was apolitical; it was measured by the risks a state was willing to take. 'It is ultimately a matter of indifference,' declared Hitler, 'what percentage of the German people make history. The only thing that matters is that it is we who are the last to make history in Germany' (Koselleck 1984:203). Hitler thought his will greater than the cir-cumstances in which he was forced to operate, which is why he took the risks he did; he gambled all and lost everything, and by his failure ensured that never again would the German people forget that politics is based on risk calculation.

But then the Nazis showed an antipathy to complexity of any kind. A society, wrote Hegel, is near the brink of dissolution when it displays a 'morbid intensification' of its own first principles. Germany had defined war as essential to its being – the Nazis merely intensified this into a fact of life. The Social Darwinist ideal of constant struggle in which the nation would be renewed on the field of battle tapped into another idea: nineteenth-century militarism. In essentializing war the Nazis ran true to form. Their whole phi-losophy subtracted variety from the human experience. They were the great simplifiers of the age. They tried to simplify war as they tried to simplify life by removing whole peoples from it, principally but not only the Jews. They tried to essentialize war and were overwhelmed in turn by its complexity. In the end, appearances notwithstanding, they were not very good at it.

Speeding to Defeat

If the increasing complexity of life was increasing the risk of going to war by rendering it less decisive, the solution for the weaker side seemed to be speed. War was becoming faster. Speed has always been central to the successful prosecution of war – getting an army onto the battlefield first and outmanoeuvring an enemy – but in the industrial era speed became something of an addiction, and a dangerous one at that.

The increasing addiction to speed provoked a great deal of comment in the course of the nineteenth century. To appreciate why, let me invoke a counter-factual, a 'scenario in reverse' (as counter-factual history is often called), one which involves a nineteenth-century world in which the computer has been invented and put into general use. Charles Babbage did not build a difference engine (the prototype of the first computer), and he never came close to realizing plans for its programmable successor, the analytical engine, but in 1830 he did come closer to inventing the computer than anyone else for the next hundred years.

In their novel, *The Difference Engine* (1988), William Gibson and Bruce Sterling offer an alternative history for the Victorian era which assumes Babbage's machines were actually constructed. Keats is found running a cinema, D'Israeli is a gossip columnist, and the hard ironmasters are in control. Babbage himself sits as a 'merit lord' in a reconstructed House of Peers. Data criss-crosses the kingdom by telegraph on punched cards and endless spools of ticker tape. In the Central Statistical Office (a grotesque invention worthy of Dickens's Circumlocution Office), serially connected analytical engines process dossiers on every man, woman and child in the kingdom. Smaller engines check customers' credit on the counters of small shops. But London is not a happy city. In another fictional realization of Babbage's analytical engine, Peter Ackroyd's *Dan Leno and the Limehouse Golem* (1994), an engine attendant remarks, 'I know that with notation we might take away all sorrow' (Spufford 1996:22). In the Sterling/Gibson version it doesn't; indeed, their imagined world is speeding towards systemic collapse (Spufford 1996:277).

Of course, the novel is not, in a strict sense, a proper counter-factual at all. For it is riddled with anachronisms. As Francis Spufford writes,

'Sterling and Gibson have invented a world of sluggish mainframe computers, analogous to the IBM machines of the 1960s, but have infused it with youths in frock coats that we could meet today on Wall Street. Theirs is a world of cinema-screen size kinetropes with its tens of thousands of mechanically rotated pixels. In their Britain Victorian computer graphics is available in the absence of cathode-ray tubes' (Spufford 1996:203). But it is precisely this anachronism which enables them to capture what was so disturbing about the Victorian world even at the time: speed told no one of their destination. 'It has come to me that some dire violence has been done to the true and natural course of historical development,' remarks a character in the novel, an aristocrat, a revolutionary communard who regrets that the aristocratic moment in history has passed and that the bourgeois era has dawned, for he finds himself estranged (as do so many others in the tale) from a purely Benthamite world of utilitarianism.

In that respect, as in so many others, the birth of the modern world marked a decisive break with the pre-industrial life that had come before it. History began to accelerate and has been accelerating ever since. Power began to be defined in terms of energy and the speed which it promoted. Until the Industrial Revolution scientists had been interested in discovering the rules and rhythms of nature. Afterwards they were concerned with transforming nature into order, the better to obtain power from her and make a profit. In time it became clear that heat is a form of energy which can be converted into other forms at a fixed rate of exchange. Energy was transformed into force: the translation of political energy (or ideas, such as revolution, nationalism and state power) into overwhelming force at a precise point of impact. Energy subsequently became the central concept of war.

No one understood better than Napoleon the concepts of mass, time and the distance that went into the creation of energy. Trained in the artillery sciences, Napoleon had a keen grasp of the principles of physics and the concepts of energy and force. Manuel DeLanda sees Napoleon's army as the manifestation of an abstract motor:

> Napoleon himself did not incorporate the motor as a technical object into his war . . . but the abstract motor did affect the mode of assemblage of the Napoleonic armies: 'motorised' armies were the first to make use of the reservoir of loyal human bodies, to insert these bodies into a flexible calculus (non-linear tactics), and to exploit the friend/foe difference: to take warfare from clockwork dynastic duels to massive confrontation between nations. (DeLanda 1991:141)

While clockwork mechanisms merely transmit motion along a pre-ordained path, heat engines generate their own energy and therefore motion. Even before the arrival of the railway age, Napoleon was able to push his soldiers harder than anyone had done before, marching them fifty miles in thirty-six hours. 'The Emperor has discovered a new way of waging war,' wrote a veteran of his campaigns many years later, 'he makes use of our legs instead of our bayonets' (Bell 2007:196). Robert Leonhard, one of the foremost US contemporary military theorists, takes as illustrative of Napoleon's 'culture of velocity' his march to Ulm in 1805. In sixty days he covered 400 miles. Some corps moved at the rate of eighteen miles a day in the last stretch of the march between the Rhine and the Danube (Leonhard 1999:132). Napoleon may not have been able to move his armies by rail (imagine what he might have accomplished if the railway age had dawned earlier), but there was a mechanistic principle at work in his own thinking about war.

But speed in itself did not challenge its basic principles. To appreciate this think of war as a business. In a market investors have to guess what a majority of people with money will consider tomorrow to be a prime source of revenue. The point is to buy now and sell in time to make a profit. In the late modern age the logic of speed in war was not dissimilar (Trouillot 2003:51). Speed was intended to demoralize and undermine the enemy's self-belief, to win today what couldn't necessarily be won tomorrow because speed could not be sustained indefinitely. The trick was to get the enemy to focus on the 'short term', not the long because in the long term everything could change. In the financial world short-term performance is often everything. Long-term investments, projects and possibilities take time to show results. R&D payoffs, slow yet sustainable growth and calculated yet potentially rewarding risks all take time to yield dividends which is why financial markets often encourage a preoccupation with the short term.

The problem with speed is that all energy dissipates – speed is entropic as Napoleon himself discovered in 1812 when he reached Moscow. Speed is unavailing when an army reaches what strategists call 'the culminating point of operations', the point at which it has advanced so far and so quickly that it cannot sustain itself in the field. All armies – especially the most ambitious – discover that energy diminishes the further it discharges itself. As one British strategist wrote, 'The offensive carries *a priori* in itself a fatal germ; it weakens itself by its own success' (Virilio 1986:122). It is foolish to preach that speed itself is a virtue, as if it is a teaching that brooks no argument. It is foolish because it primes soldiers to take tactics more seriously than strategy. The primary virtue in war is not speed, it is intelligence.

The Age of Abundance

These limits were clearly recognized by some of the generals who took their countries to war in 1914. Whatever they told their publics (and sometimes themselves) that it would all be over by Christmas, many suspected the worst. It was likely to last for years and in the end produce no overall winner. Even the architect of Germany's war plan in 1914, von Schlieffen, had warned the Emperor that a future war 'will be a national war which will not be settled by a decisive battle but by a long, wearisome struggle with a country that will not be overcome until its whole national force is broken, and a war which will utterly exhaust our own people, even if we are victorious' (Strachan 2003:43–4).

This logic had first become apparent in the first major conflict of the modern era, the American Civil War (1861–5). As the conflict dragged on the Union widened the focus of its operations. General Sherman's devastation of Georgia and South Carolina was a portal into the future. He has been described as 'the first of the modern totalitarian generals' for he waged war on a people, not only on armed men (Hagan 2007:82). This time the people were not 'collateral damage', they were the intended target. His aim was the destruction of factories and agricultural crops, and in the case of Atlanta, an entire city. Weighey aptly characterizes the strategy as 'the American way of war'. Industrialized warfare introduced a new factor into war; the country (or coalition of countries) that won would do so by out-producing its enemies. Wars in the pre-industrial era had been determined by finite inputs. World wars by contrast involved abundance, not scarcity: abundant manpower, weapons and even a space of operations which in the end turned the whole world into a theatre of conflict.

The classic study of war, like neo-classical economics, was grounded on the notion of scarce resources. There was a limit to the number of men who could be put in the field. War couldn't be fought on the cheap. All wars cost the taxpayer. The art of strategy was to engage in a series of successful trade-offs: trading space for time, long-term objectives for short (or those more easily attainable). When going to war governments assumed they had to deal with limited, not abundant, inputs. But the twentieth century was an era of abundance. Nations could fight on for years without experiencing economic collapse. World War II finally lifted the US out of the state to which it had been reduced by the Great Depression. The pathetic 'Okies' described by John Steinbeck in his novel of protest *The Grapes of Wrath* began to enjoy a middle-class income. The GI Bill (1944) gave an entire generation an education it would never have had. In the case of the Soviet Union, the mobilization of state industry stimulated nothing less than 'a second Industrial Revolution' (in John Erickson's words) (Keegan 1997:170). In short, the marginal costs of war – like the marginal costs of manufacturing and distribution (two of the main scarcity functions of classical economics) – were not as great as expected.

More than a decade ago, George Gilder, the apostle of abundance, offered his readers a good way to think about all this:

> For most of human history, most people have believed that economics is essentially a zero-sum game – that scarcity will ultimately prevail over abundance. Pastor Malthus was the famous exponent of the view that populations increase geometrically while agricultural output increases arithmetically. In the Malthusian view, food scarcity eventually chokes off growth. Karl Marx saw all economics ultimately reducing to a class struggle over scarce 'means of production'.
>
> The economists' focus on scarcity stems from the fact that shortages are measurable and end in zero. They constrain an economic model to produce a clearly calculable result, an identifiable choke point in the industrial circuitry. Abundance is incalculable and has no obvious cap. When they are ubiquitous, like air or water, they are invisible 'externalities'. Yet abundance is the driving force in all economic growth and change.

So how to reconcile this with neo-classical economics? Gilder recommended that we should embrace waste.

> In every industrial revolution, some key factor of production is drastically reduced in cost. Relative to the previous cost to achieve that function, the new factor is virtually free. Physical force in the industrial revolution became virtually free compared to its expense when it derived from animal muscle power and human muscle power. Suddenly you could do things you could not afford to do before. You could make a factory 24 hours a day, churning out products in a way that was just incomprehensible before the industrial era. It really did mean that physical force became virtually free in a sense. The whole economy had to reorganise itself to exploit this physical force. You had to 'waste' the power of the steam engine and its derivatives in order to prevail, whether in war or peace. (Anderson 2007:145–6)

Abundance gave the allies a critical advantage in both world wars. They could afford to lose the early battles until they worked out how to bring their main material strength to bear.

Most impressive of all, perhaps, were the extraordinary manpower resources of the Soviet Union. In the greatest battle in history, between

October 1941 and April 1942, seven million men were thrown into the fighting before Moscow; the Russians alone lost two million. The Soviet high command expected to lose two to three men for every German soldier. Stalin's wasteful strategy was only made possible by the knowledge that manpower was an inexhaustible resource. In 1941 the average survival rate of new recruits in some units was only four or five days. They were expected to go into battle with instructions to strip equipment from fallen comrades for they had no weapons of their own (Connelly 2006:29).

Even so we must recognize that, like speed, abundance does not, in itself, challenge the principles of war any more than it actually challenges the laws of economics. For as Gilder reminds us, abundant resources are just one factor in a system otherwise constrained by scarcity, and they do not challenge economic orthodoxy simply because they serve to lower prices and increase productivity. Likewise in war, abundance did not deliver victory to the allies. The Central and Axis Powers lost because they expected that a series of spectacular tactical victories would be enough to win them the strategic initiative. They lost because they ignored the complexity of war, including its increasing zero-sumness.

Complexity and Non-zero-sumness

Had this concept been available to William James there is no reason to suspect that he would not have invoked it. Drawing on the notion of *zero sum* and *non zero sum* games in which there are no winners, and those in which there are no losers, Robert Wright explains how history over the past 5,000 years has woven people into a larger and more complex web of networks. Historically, whatever aids complexity tends to be non zero sum; whatever threatens it tends to be zero sum. We tend to think of war as zero sum, of course, because soldiers get killed. Usually, there is a victor and a loser. But even in war, there tends to be a non zero sum dynamic.

As societies became more complex war generated non zero outcomes. 'To put this dynamic of cultural evolution in the Darwinian language of natural selection', Wright writes, 'what is selected for is larger and larger expanses of *non-zero sumness*, but one of the main selectors is the *zero-sum* dimension of war' (Wright 2001:64). It pushed some people into an organic solidarity. It posed an external threat that required even closer co-operation. In explaining this, Wright actually quotes James's essay *The Moral Equivalent of War*: 'If we think how many things beside the frontiers of states the wars of history have decided, we must feel respectful awe in spite of all the horrors. Our actual civilisation, good and bad alike, has had past wars for its determining condition' (Wright 2001:54). Even a pacifist like James had to acknowledge that not all conflicts are zero sum. They often bring together communities the better to co-operate on a common end. Neo-Darwinians define war as 'coalitional intra-specific aggression'. Primitive societies, according to the neo-Darwinian hypothesis, show that what makes us human is our Machiavellian intelligence which we share with the great apes, especially chimpanzees. We can imagine what others are thinking. We can enter into alliances. We can deceive others. Only that sort of social cognition makes possible genuine coalitional behaviour. In other words, our breakthrough into humanity required a further advance in Machiavellian intelligence as humans found themselves engaged in a 'cognitive arms race'.

Co-operation, in turn, led to the development of increasingly hierarchical social structures. Walter Bagehot, the early editor of *The Economist* explained it this way: 'The tamest are the strongest' (Wright 2001:57). Alliance-building beyond the village was the next move. In time, villages were consolidated into cities. The cities in turn may have succumbed to the depredations of the nomads at various times of history, but the nomads were emasculated by their conquests. Over time their private passions, such as ferocity, avarice and ambition, were transformed into public virtues. Ferocity became patriotism, avarice capitalism and ambition politics.

In short, the more one understands the anthropological origins of war, the more we can say that war has not always been zero sum. Despite his vision of a world at peace, even Kant wrote about the usefulness of 'unsocial sociability'. We all have programmed into us a desire for honour, power and status. Without these asocial qualities (which are far from admirable in themselves) we would never have developed. The drive for status has widened our circle of acquaintance over time, and we increasingly wish to be respected, not feared. Kant's 'cosmopolitan purpose' offers us an inner dynamic that, not without many detours and major setbacks, has made the world a more secure place. Indeed, what he eventually perceived in this 'hidden plan' was the eventual end of war. War, confidently asserted the sociologist Herbert Spencer, 'had given all it had to give' (Wright 2001:238). It had exhausted its co-operative possibilities. The next stage of complexity requires the world to be at peace with itself.

Unfortunately, this logic did not hold for the twentieth century, which should remind us that there is no linear direction to history. Instead, there are numerous setbacks and elisions. The zero-sumness of war (as many understand it today) is not, alas, necessary for humanity. It is certainly not predetermined. There is no evidence of a master plan or even a 'hidden hand' at work in history. Global warming or a major economic meltdown could arrest, or even reverse, globalization as it did in the 1930s. All I am prepared to claim, recognizing the contingent in history, is that the increasing zero-sumness of war represents a trend. War is becoming not only dangerous, it is also becoming incredibly difficult to wage with success. Speed offers no solution, and attritional strategies no longer have such appeal. There is even some reason to suspect that we may not see another major inter-state war providing, of course, that the movement towards greater complexity is not derailed by war itself.

At the non-state level the picture is less reassuring. Globalization may be bringing the world together but it is also forcing it apart at the same time. The internet is adding more and more communities of interest which cross dangerous fault lines: the boundaries of religion, nationality, ethnicity and even culture. It is aiding protest movements such as al-Qaeda. It is fostering virtual communities of hate and religious extremism. Unfortunately, some of the new actors that the risk age has thrown up, including terrorists and transnational criminal syndicates, are playing emphatically zero sum games. The risk age may not like war but it has chosen to remain in the war business by rebranding it as risk management.

Conclusion

As Nietzsche remarked, there is no 'leap' between historical eras; one usually gives way to another gradually. Historians are right to be wary of sudden breaks with the past; they are encouraged to detect the signals that might have been ignored at the time, the clues that only in retrospect look significant. This is why de Tocqueville when looking back at the greatest break of all in his country's history entitled his book *The Ancien Regime and the French Revolution*. Conjunctions such as this are necessary to make the past intelligible rather than the story of random events. History evolves slowly.

The risk age did not come into being overnight; it was foregrounded in the age that preceded it, especially in the growing recognition that the world was becoming so incredibly complex that everything had consequences, many of which could not be foreseen, which is why we now interrogate ourselves more intensely than ever. We have become irredeemably self-reflexive and as a result increasingly risk-averse.

Self-reflexivity is essentially a condition of modernity, as Max Weber tells us. The perpetual questioning of reality by reason is the mark of the modern age. In many ways Weber's anxieties about the moral implications of modernity have been reproduced in our own uncertainties about the reality that lies behind modernity itself. It is reflected in a profound pessimism grounded on the gap that is said to exist between our knowledge of the world and the world itself. Because we actually know so little about the mechanism of the world we live in, any attempt to transform it on the basis of knowing what is real and what is not can lead to disaster. This suspicion is now so deeply entrenched that it has even led to an unreasoning sense of fear. Weber, at least, was clear in his own mind about one thing. He anticipated that in its own distinctive way the twenty-first century might be as dangerous as his own. We are no longer prepared to take the world or reality on trust for that reason. Today we are much more sober about the future. Although we still accept that history may be progressive, we also recognize there is a price to be paid for whatever progress we make.

3

War in an Age of Risk

The more we rehearse disaster the safer we'll be for the real thing. Life seems to work that way, doesn't it? (Don DeLillo, *White Noise*, 1986, p. 205)

'Who is the nice lady,' asks a character in Don DeLillo's *Great Jones Street*. 'Security,' he said. 'Her name's Epiphany Powell. Maybe you've heard of her? She used to sing, she used to model, she used to act. Now she's doing security' (DeLillo 1978:181). And why not? Security is a growing industry. It is expanding all the time. So too, more alarmingly, is the concept itself. In his election campaign in 2001, the French Prime Minster, Lionel Jospin, proclaimed 'a battle against insecurity' (Bauman 2003:120). And that is the problem: many things now make us insecure. Some of us own financial securities that are at risk in a volatile market. Others have lost some of the 'security benefits' they took for granted. Many of us have even lost the security of our foundational beliefs such as progress and science. Insecurity is now a permanent feature of the world in which we live. The point is that in every age there is a turning point, a new way of seeing and understanding the coherence of the world. Ours is an age of risk, and insecurity is its definitive feature.

What's in a name? Plenty. Language matters because it constructs the categories by which we understand the world. Understanding the nature of our situation matters in international affairs because it structures our political and military response to events. Where once we were worried about defence / deterrence, we are now concerned with 'security' and the word is now so ubiquitous that it has become what one writer terms the 'grammar of violence' of the risk age (Tripp 2007:30).

A World of Risk

We used to speak a different grammar. Once we were more optimistic about the future. In the classical age security (derived from the Latin *securitas*) referred to tranquillity and freedom from care, or what Cicero termed the absence of anxiety upon which the fulfilled life depends. In his *Theory of Moral Sentiments*, Adam Smith mentioned only the security of the sovereign who possessed a standing army to protect him against popular discontent and thus being 'secure' himself was able to allow his subjects the liberty of political 'remonstrance'. Other Enlightenment thinkers dreamed on a more ambitious scale. Condorcet suggested that the economic security of individuals was an essential condition for political society. Fear – and the fear of fear – were for him the enemies of the political vision. In the course of the twentieth century governments went much further in offering their citizens 'freedom from fear' and 'freedom from want', both of which were the cornerstone of Roosevelt's vision of a New World Order that would be forged on the anvil of war.

What makes us especially insecure is that a New World Order is no longer a realistic goal, given the endless risks we find ourselves confronting on a day-to-day basis. War seems to have escaped the narrow parameters that it was given in the course of the twentieth century – deterrence and defence. Its principal theme is now security in its various, often mutually exclusive forms. And what we are securing ourselves against is a kaleidoscope of risks, defined or ill-defined, real or imaginary, external or internalized, all of which make us more anxious than ever. The *Washington Post* columnist Robert Samuelson captured the essence of this change in a piece entitled 'Rediscovering Risk'. The events of the post-9/11 world, including terrorism and the looming war in Iraq, were all 'metaphors for the defining characteristic of a new era . . . it is risk' (*Washington Post*, 23 October 2002).

We find ourselves living in risk societies, a term popularized by, among others, the German sociologist Ulrich Beck. Since I shall be invoking his work quite often in the course of the next two chapters, let me add that the word he used in his 1992 path-breaking book is elastic in its German idiom. As his English translator notes, *Sicherheit* may mean 'security', 'safety' or 'certainty' (Adam 2003:27). And 'risk' in English conveys a

Table 2 The Transition to the Risk Age

War as defence	War as security
Threats	Risks
States	Non-state actors/rogue states
Regimes	Collapse of regimes (non-proliferation treaty)
Ideologies (state)	Ideologies (non-state)
Fear	Anxiety/individual safety
Defence (regional)	Security
New World Order	Global disorder

similar penumbra of invented meanings. Economists are obsessed with risk capital; our societies are obsessed with children at risk; sociologists analyse 'high-risk behaviour'. The title of Beck's book, *The Risk Society* is as evocative today as was Herbert Marcuse's *One-Dimensional Man* when it was published in 1968. Although both titles are more quoted than the arguments, they have been deemed to articulate more vividly than most the existential crisis of a particular generation.

Beck's main thesis is that we have witnessed a radical change in social politics and cultural experience which defines a new stage of modernity. The risk society perspective is a heuristic device which allows us to observe and probe the peculiarities of our world, and to ask why it is pervaded by an extraordinary degree of anxiety about the future.

We are anxious in part because the idea of 'risk' has none of its earlier positive connotations. 'The world belongs to risk. The world will soon be a matching of risks, a scramble for the most daring', insisted the French writer Georges Bernanos. William James went further: 'It is only by risking our persons for one hour to another that we live at all.' It was the risks which inhered in war that gave the enterprise its moral character (Manguel 2005:23). Courage allowed the soldier to give of his own life for something greater: unit, regiment, country or cause which made life worthwhile. What James feared most was not a world without war but a world without the challenge of risk-taking, which is why he was so anxious to find a moral equivalent to war.

There was such a thing, in short, as a good risk, provided we had the courage to take it. Courage, insisted Hannah Arendt, is demanded of practically everything we do. It is the bedrock of political life. Courage is one of the cardinal political virtues. For the political realm comes before us and it will survive our passing and it does not hold life itself to be the primary concern. Courage liberates us to fight for what makes life worthwhile: our beliefs, our freedom or simply other people (Arendt 1977:132–5).

Today, most risk-taking is discouraged. Indeed, the very language we use reflects our unprecedented preoccupation with its negative aspects. Take the stock term 'at risk'. A search of British newspapers indicates it was used 2,037 times in 1994. Six years later its usage had increased almost nine-fold (Furedi 2006:xviii). Frank Furedi seizes upon this point to argue that to be 'at risk' today is to be 'powerless to shape the environment'; even worse, to be at risk is to have a very diminished sense of responsibility for one's own actions. It is this lack of direct agency which reinforces the anxiety we now feel. This is especially true of international security to the extent that our social experience generates the suspicion that we are at risk most of the time from terrorists and transnational organized criminal syndicates, as well as new global pandemics such as HIV-AIDS. Since 2008, the British government has published an annual national risk register setting out the likelihood and potential impact of a range of different risks that may directly affect the UK. Like everyone else in the West, the British find themselves living in a world in which anxiety has become part of the 'everyday'.

An Age of Anxiety

If Sainte-Beuve is right that every age has its own special malady then anxiety may well be branded the malady of our own. If disquiet is probably a normal enough symptom of human existence, it is when fear becomes conscious of itself that it is in danger of becoming a profound neurosis that feeds upon anxiety itself, a state the Germans call *Angst vor der Angst*. Anxiety here is very much a social construction; how we look at the world and life in general determines our level of anxiety. Some of us are by nature more anxious than others. An optimistic sensibility, doctors tell us, leads to a longer life.

A telling example of our anxiety levels is what happened in August 2002 when a pair of snipers killed ten people in the Washington DC area. The two perpetrators were capricious in their choice of targets and they did not profile their victims ethnically or socially; they chose them at random which made their attacks even more disconcerting for the public at large. More alarming still, however, was the overreaction they provoked from government and citizen alike which reveals more about the character of our times than we may like to acknowledge. Some citizens bought bullet-proof vests in which to do their shopping or mow their lawns. Many school districts placed their classes under Code Blue, forbidding a million children from going out for lunch or taking part in outdoor activities. At some schools October college aptitude tests were cancelled. School field trips were postponed. About fifty Starbucks stores removed their outside seating. Many people stopped going to health clubs. A DC soccer league involving more than 5,000 players called off its games.

What is particularly telling is that all these measures had no discernible statistical justification (Sunstein 2005:90–1). For the number of citizens in the Washington area who were at risk numbered over five million. Even had the snipers killed one person every three days, the statistical risk would only have been one in a million, a much smaller number than those associated with everyday activities such as driving a hundred miles or smoking two cigarettes or taking ten trips by air, or for that matter drinking thirty diet sodas with saccharine. Even some of the precautions taken by some local residents such as driving the extra distance to Virginia to purchase gasoline added to the risks of everyday life.

Many factors accounted for their unnecessary fearfulness. One was a predisposition to fear gun-related crimes which had been heightened by the post-9/11 fear of terrorism. It was compounded, in turn, by the predisposition of a risk society to fear the unknown, or the unfamiliar. Risk is fundamentally a belief or attitude, a way of thinking about the world. To the extent that our social experience generates the suspicion that we are at risk most of the time we tend to feel even more anxious.

This is the peculiar insight of quantum physics. The problem is that the physics is so inaccessible to the average person that its insights have been applied only spasmodically to the social sciences – except for one of its foundation stones, Heisenberg's Uncertainty Principle. This principle states that all observations are unreliable because we cannot observe nature in itself but only nature exposed to our method of enquiry. The observer influences the events or phenomena observed; the participating mind changes the reality in which it participates. The nature of reality affects the mind just as the mind affects reality; the senses distort it, but they also make it up.

Of course much of the risk society argument poses the same problems as quantum physics – it is difficult to validate empirically the claims of both through experimentation. We do not know whether string theory is right in positing a universe that consists of eleven dimensions where all matter is generated by the vibrations of microscopically tiny loops of energy. Yet string theory is widely held to be true. It is not entirely unwarranted to argue, as some scientists do, that physicists have no business wasting their time on a theory that postulates a new feature of nature some 100 million billion times smaller than anything we can directly probe through our senses, enhanced or otherwise (Greene 2000:212). The debate is informed only in part by physics. It also involves distinct philosophies about how physics should be done. The 'traditionalists' want theoretical work to be closely tied to experimental observation. Others think we are ready to tackle questions that are beyond our present technological ability to test empirically. The same could be said of many of the claims that risk sociologists make. In the end, it is a matter of faith that the risk literature has identified important trends unique to a particular age.

For my own part I am convinced that it provides a unifying framework for thinking about the different style of war in the risk age. Take a highly revealing remark some months after the invasion of Iraq, long after it had become clear that weapons of mass destruction would not be found. Unmoved, the American Defense Secretary Donald Rumsfeld insisted, 'the Coalition did not act in Iraq because we had discovered dramatic new evidence of Iraq's pursuit of weapons of mass murder. We acted because we saw the existing evidence *in a new light* through the prism of our experience on September 11' (Buley 2007:100). Even in science, as Heisenberg wrote in *The Physicist's Conception of Nature*, 'the object of research is no longer nature itself, but Man's investigation of nature. Here, again, Man confronts himself alone' (Lukacs 2005:68). The implications of this have long been known in science. We are just beginning to recognize when discussing security that there is a much closer connection between mind and matter than is often thought to be the case. There is no such thing as an *objectively* secure world. Whether we feel secure or not is a matter of perception.

Complexity and Subjective Insecurity

The risk age has given rise to its own unique consciousness. The postmodern age has been defined as 'a more modest modernity' (Lipton 1999:11), a time when modernity is coming to terms with its own limits. It has been forced to recognize the global consequences of its own initiatives and projects. Concern about risk is no longer a peripheral matter: it is built into the environment, into our culture and especially the everyday routines that guide our lives. In this sense, we can indeed be said to be living in a 'risk age' because we have become aware somewhat late in the day of the complexity that inheres in life.

The industrial era, by contrast, had a very uncomplicated view of life, especially humanity's relationship with nature. Relentless modernization stripped the planet and ruined much of the environment, especially biodiversity. The world population also increased exponentially, 'funded' not by natural income but by the running down of natural capital (notably fossil fuels and a stable climate). It was not that we set out to extirpate other species – we didn't. The matter was more complicated than a killer instinct that never relents until another species has disappeared. We succumbed instead to acquisitive instincts that we didn't always recognize, instincts that couldn't tell us when to stop until something we never intended to harm had been fatally deprived of something it needed. Today, we have a quite different relationship with nature. We recognize that nature is unimaginably complex, as too are our own immune systems The fact that we talk of 'eco-systems' is indicative of a change of sensibility, for systems are complex in different and diverse ways.

It has become clear to us late in the day that the environment had been damaged, perhaps irreparably, by our own actions. Of all the *unintended* challenges to global security, perhaps the most important is environmental degradation. It is one of our urban myths that as great swathes of the Amazon were burned in 1987 the smoke could be seen from space, along with another work of man, the Great Wall of China. Neither happens to be true but the perspective of space has been vital in producing a major change of consciousness. Changes *in* consciousness are quite frequent whenever we become aware of new challenges to which we have to respond. From time to time we become more sensitive to the plight of others, not only ourselves. A change *of* consciousness, however, is more profound, for it represents not only a response to the world; it is frequently accompanied by a wish to change the world for the better.

The risk age represents just such a change of consciousness. We now recognize that we consume more history than we produce. The modern era tended to treat human nature as it did the rest of the natural world, as a standing reserve. As C. S. Lewis grasped, the problem with the totalitarian systems of belief like communism was that they were wont to treat human beings as a standing reserve too. Stalin famously called communists the 'engineers of the human soul'. We were always trying to subdue Nature, Lewis wrote, because it was the name we gave to what we had to some extent already subdued. As long as the process stopped short of the final stage, humanity could well hold that the gains outweighed the losses. But as soon as it took the final step of reducing itself to the level of nature the whole process threatened to end in disaster; the being who stood to gain and the being to be sacrificed threatened to become one and the same (Mitchell 2007:1).

Over 100 million people fell victim to utopian engineering programmes in the course of the last century. Many of these programmes in Nazi Germany, the Soviet Union, Mao's China and, most recently, Cambodia involved genocidal projects. Genocide was once defined by J. G. Ballard as 'the economics of mass production applied to self-disgust' (Ballard 1997:277). Totalitarian states were especially disgusted at human fallibility. It is not easy to reform a society, any more than it is to redeem a human being. In the wake of a dreadful century we have come to realize that complexity reigns supreme – human nature cannot be fixed, any more than the human soul can be re-engineered. Complexity inheres not in externalities (politics: forging a New Jerusalem or a socialist utopia); it inheres in internalities (how people think and feel and perceive the world and themselves). The Heisenberg Principle again. We are part of the nature we observe and seek to dominate. Our response to the world and our understanding of our place in it is inherently subjective.

We have found after the bloodiest century of the modern era that people tend to achieve most when they are set free to open up the narrow window through which they are accustomed to view the spectrum of human possibilities. But they must be allowed to do so themselves. More important still, even the freedom to acknowledge that actions have consequences is one of the liberating benefactions of an open society.

The problem our societies face is that the benefits of following a particular course of action may well outweigh the risks, but we have no common currency in which to compare the consequences of different actions. All risk concepts are based on the distinction between reality and possibility. The concept would not make sense if the future were predetermined, or independent of our own actions. Fears about the future are linked to anxieties about the outcomes that follow from our own actions. For many of the risks we confront are associated with the *unintended* consequences of our own actions.

This challenge can be validated through experiment. In his book *The Logic of Failure*, the German psychologist Dietrich Dorner reveals how harmful effects can be produced in complex situations without anyone necessarily intending them. In one experiment he asked the participants to address some of the risks faced by humanity in different regions of the world, such as poverty, poor medical provision and pollution. Each participant was able to apply a variety of programmes including childhood vaccination schemes, improved programmes for the care of cattle and increased drilling for water. The effects of these programmes were then projected into the future by computer modelling. Some were found to genuinely alleviate human distress. But others provoked disasters that the participants had not anticipated, a fault that was largely of their own making. The programmes ended in disaster because they had fixated on problems in isolation; they had not appreciated the complex systems-wide side-effects of introducing the programmes in question (Sunstein 2005:46).

In our complex world everything is interconnected. This was brought home in 2002 when Brazilian scientists reported that 9,300 square miles (24,000 sq km) of the Amazon rainforest had been lost the year before. It was an environmental disaster but one triggered by the decision to clear new land in order to raise beef and soy beans for the booming (mostly European) demand for risk-free GM-free food (Wright 2005:185–6). In other words, an attempt to limit risks to health in one sphere amplified risks in another, something that no one deliberately intended. In this case, environmental changes brought about by human interference in one field of human endeavour were not coordinated with actions in another, with near fatal results. The same was true of some of the initiatives launched by the participants in Dorner's experiment who did not appreciate the environmental cost of drilling more water holes or the problem of over-grazing when their policies increased the size of cattle herds significantly. The problem is that precautionary moves taken to deal with a problem can end up with a different series of risks which may prove to be even more serious than the original problems they were designed to redress.

Risks, in other words, have become a *structural* feature of advanced industrialization (Adam 2003:7). We can no more avoid them than we can stop technology in its tracks. And contemporary hazards, especially those associated with new technologies, differ from the risks of the past because they cannot be delimited either in time or space (what happens thousands of miles away in the Amazon can impact on all of us). Nor can they always be anticipated by applying the usual rules of cause and effect – many are unintended. Worse still, we cannot insure against the disasters that may result. Consequence management is the prevailing rationale of risk management but we know that the risks we run do not always arise from bad decisions or inadequate strategic thinking or even lack of imagination. They often arise from the fact that everything we do usually has side-effects.

As Emerson wrote, with every influx of light comes new danger: 'there is a crack in everything God has made. It would seem there is always . . . this vindictive circumstance stealing in unawares . . . this back stroke, this kick of the gun.' Side-effects bring into question the assumption of agency in classical sociology. They devalue capital, destroy trust and muddy agendas. 'The side-effect, not instrumental rationality . . . becomes the motor of social history,' writes Beck; as I shall argue in the next chapter it has also become the motor of war (Beck 1997:31).

The security community has its own term for this: 'blow-back'. Thus one writer traces the rise of Islamic terrorism back to American support for al-Qaeda in the Afghan War in the 1980s, which he characterizes as an American *jihad* against communism (Mamdani 2004). This proved to be a telling case, of 'reactionary blowback'. For not only this relationship but many others the US cultivated during the Cold War, particularly in the Islamic world, have come back to haunt it. 'To a significant degree, the disorders of the post-Cold War era are a consequence of the paradoxical character of the American victory in the Cold War' (Saul 2006:66).

Even many Pakistanis have come to rue their former support of the Taliban. In the past few years military operations against pro-Taliban groups in the country's tribal areas involving over 100,000 troops have been compromised by Islamabad's previous willingness to cede vast swathes of territory to tribal militants. This has paved the way for the so-called 'Talibinization' of much of north and south Waziristan and emboldened the militants to stamp their authority over key urban centres in the Swat valley (Shaikh 2007:19). Blowback involves the reaping of what one sows, a suitably biblical metaphor for paying for a previous generation's bad judgement. Most of the violent groups we now face, such as the world's jihadists, even acquired their expertise in bomb-making either from the CIA or, in the case of the Taliban, from Pakistan's Internal Security Agency. And even in the case of Iraq, the Iraqi National Accord movement was setting off car bombs in Baghdad under CIA supervision long before the invasion of 2003. In this regard, we are all bear some responsibility for the current phase of terrorism.

The Risk Society at War

In Beck's book *World Risk Society*, published in 1992, he identified three types of global threat that were central to security in the risk age, and which stemmed from the complexity of our globalized world. The first were threats to the environment. Appreciation of these had been prompted by a change of consciousness first identified by the report *Our Common Future* which was commissioned by the United Nations in 1983. 'In the middle of the 20th century we saw our planet from space for the first time. Historians may eventually find that this vision had a greater impact on thought than did the Copernican revolution of the 16th century, which upset the human self-image by revealing the Earth is not the centre of the universe' (Bordo 1992:168). Satellite pictures brought home to the world its fragile position in the universe. They showed the planet in a new light in relation to ourselves. Symbolic of this change was *Time* magazine's editorial decision a few years later to turn away from its sports heroes and politicians and to name the planet 'Man of the Year'; it did so because environmental degradation had now placed it in mortal danger.

What is important about the environment is that it poses a different challenge from most other security issues for it has no political or moral standing independent of the interest that political actors invest in it. The environment itself is not a threat. It is not one of those mysterious 'others' against which we are planning to defend ourselves in the future. It is the environment which is threatened by human activity and, by extension, the activities of states. In turn, it is state activity that, through the medium of global warming or climate change, threatens local eco-systems as well as the planet. And this, too, has forced us to entertain the suspicion that the state might be the problem, not the solution.

Beck also identified a second group of risks that were directly related to poverty which is also held to be responsible for much of the environmental destruction of recent years. The critical difference is that whereas wealth-driven ecological threats stem from the externalization of production costs, in the case of poverty-driven ecological destruction it is the poor who are threatened by toxic waste (sometimes imported from other countries) and obsolete technologies (the chemical industry).

In recent years there have been claims that the current violence in Darfur, while involving tribal and ethnic factors, can also be seen as a land-use conflict exacerbated by climate change. It is a controversial judgement, at least to the extent that it tends to absolve the politicians of blame – why do so when you can blame the weather? Nevertheless, climate change is certainly going to influence why and where future conflicts break out. In linking poverty and the environment, the risk age challenges us once again to rethink our traditional notions of what should constitute the security agenda.

But Beck also identified a third threat, the existence of weapons of mass destruction (WMD), a term first coined in 1937 by the scientist J. D. Bernal. For most of the twentieth century the threat was posed by states, and Beck himself identified it at the time as a *residual* threat left over from the Cold War. But he also conceded that it was part of a larger trend: the privatization of violence as fundamentalist and terrorist groups sought to purchase the most destructive weapons they could.

Although the privatization of violence was not of great concern for much of the twentieth century, in retrospect it should have been. For it lodged itself in the imagination early on. Shortly before World War I, in his novel *The World Set Free*, H. G. Wells wrote of a hand-held nuclear device. He also reflected more generally on the increasingly destructive properties of technology, its unrestricted application for the purpose of war and its lethal consequences for world politics.

> Certainly, it seems now, that nothing could have been more obvious to the people of the earlier 20th century than the rapidity with which war was becoming impossible. And as certainly they did not see it. They did not see it until the atomic bombs burst in their fumbling hands. Yet the broad facts must have glared upon any intelligent mind. All through the 19th and 20th centuries the amount of energy men were able to command was continually increasing. Applied to warfare that meant that the power

to inflict a blow, the power to destroy, was continually increasing. There was no increasing whatever in the ability to escape. Every sort of passive defence, armour, fortifications, and so forth, was being out mastered by this tremendous increase on the destructive side. *Destruction was becoming so facile that any little body of malcontents could use it; it was revolutionising the problem of police and internal rule. Before the last war began it was a matter of common knowledge that a man could carry about in his handbag an amount of latent energy sufficient to wreck half a city* [my italics]. (P. D. Smith 2007:200)

No one described the end of the world like Wells. He was the master of the doomsday moment when people stare into the abyss and blink. In this particular case Wells got the idea of a hand-held nuclear bomb from reading Frederick Soddy's *The Interpretation of Radium* and merely combined it with his own unease about how 'the world still fooled around with the paraphernalia and pretensions of war' (Strathern 2007:90).

In another story, 'The Stolen Bacillus' (1895), Wells even described how a suicide terrorist infects himself with a deadly virus so that he can spread the disease in a city, a possibility which no longer reads like fiction now that the codes of diseases such as Spanish flu and smallpox are publicly available (P. D. Smith 2007:200). The genomes of other diseases, including hepatitis C, HIV and hemophilus influenza, are owned by private entities. Not even Wells could have envisaged a world in which common and not so common diseases would be patented by universities and private corporations.

In identifying all three types of risk Beck insisted on distinguishing them from the other dangers societies had had to face in the past. He insisted on reserving the right to identify the 'risk society' as one unique to one era, our own. For today risk has changed everything, especially the way we conceive security. What is interesting is the way in which this knowledge has worked into the collective mindset. We talk of the 'War on AIDS' and the 'War on Want' and the 'War against Crime'. The metaphors, in turn, invest the risks with even more apocalyptic overtones, and even greater global resonance.

The point is *not* that we live in a more insecure world than we did before 1989, or even that we are in greater danger. Neither claim is actually true. What is specific to many of our own anxieties is that they exist in the absence of any looming historical disaster – even global warming and climate change will not impact on most of us for another twenty years. The incidence of inter-state warfare is decreasing all the time. The existential threat of nuclear war has also been lifted – we were all at much greater risk of destruction during the Cuban missile crisis than we are today. In 1962 the USAF was planning to launch 950 nuclear attacks in a first-strike attack and a further 370 if the Soviets had tried to retaliate. It expected that ten million Americans would die but it also anticipated that far more Soviet citizens would not have survived radioactive poisoning, famine and the collapse of public health infrastructure. No scenario of nuclear detonation by a terrorist group such as the bomb that destroys the centre of Pittsburgh in Tom Clancy's novel *The Sum of all Our Fears* poses a threat of such magnitude.

What makes us so anxious is something else: it is the fact that many of the threats we face are *de-bounded*. Security has become 'three-dimensional' where it impacts most — our imagination. Risks are not always based on objective assessments that we find in physics; they are subjective and embedded in culture. They are not always open to testing or validation. They are not always calculative. And that is the challenge because societies, like people, are not easily argued out of their fears. Unlike fear, anxiety is grounded not in the immediate or the perceived, but the imagined. And the imagination can range far into the future. This is why we find ourselves living in what Tony Blair called a 'post-secure' world. The unmanageability of risks has diminished the authority of the nation state to which we once looked for our security. We find ourselves inhabitants of an uninsured society in which protection diminishes as the danger grows (Beck 1992:101). For that reason we are more anxious than ever. And the anxiety we experience is all the more pervasive because it is the product not only of the concerns that once haunted us such as the fear of unemployment or war. We live in a world where the risks we face are endless, global and potentially catastrophic.

It is because the risks we face are unbounded that we tend to *internalize* them. Take the first dimension, the spatial. Terrorism, climate change and transnational organized crime affects everyone, everywhere. We have nowhere to hide; distance no longer buys security. The Cold War era demarcated flanks and fronts and told as what was 'out of area'. The War on Terror recognizes no such frontiers. Nor does the spread of disease. First World societies may not produce SARS but an infected passenger boarding a Boeing 767 in Hong Kong can arrive in London eleven hours later, and start a pandemic.

'Terrorism respects no limits, geographical or moral; the frontlines are everywhere . . .' declared Colin Powell in May 2002 (Tilly 2007:152). The fact that terrorism is global adds to our insecurity because like many other threats it is too apocalyptic in scope to be comfortably contained within security regimes or even New World Orders. The anti-globalization movement in the US may fear a conspiracy on the part of big business and government, but even the alleged conspirators do not feel in charge. Instead, they too find themselves living in what President Clinton complained was 'a world in which risk is endless' (*New York Times*, 17 December 1998).

In the second dimension, the social risks have been de-bounded too in so far as it is becoming increasingly difficult to hold anyone or any institution responsible. The modern age put an emphasis on control; deterrence was grounded in attribution, apportioning blame and holding others accountable for their actions. But who is to be held to account for the collapse of financial markets? It is distributed networks that give rise to financial instability which in turn make everyday risks in the market appear so much more difficult to control than in the past. And who is responsible for the spread of disease? The H_5N_1 strand of the avian flu virus was called by the British Civil Contingency Secretariat in 2005 'as serious a threat as terrorism' to the British population (*Independent on Sunday*, 16 October 2005). Viruses are by definition silent and invisible killers which proliferate and survive by infecting the cells of a host organism by stealth. Often we don't know we are infected until it is too late. Viruses instil fear because they are so perfectly suited to their ultimate purpose of preying on other forms of life

Likewise, the security threats of the last century could usually be attributed to one country, such as the Soviet Union, or in the case of Hitler, to the ambitions of one man. Many now cannot be traced to source, and even if they can it is difficult to deter terrorists or hold them to account for their actions. Take, for example, the cyber attacks on Estonia in May 2007 which followed Russian protests against the closure of a monument to Red Army war veterans. These took the form of 'denial of service' attacks (which flooded targeted networks with bogus messages which caused servers to slow or shut down). Botnets (short for robot networks) were used for the first time. Some botnets are huge, using tens of thousands of computers around the world. They can be hired on the black market. Although the Estonian government knew the attacks were probably co-ordinated by Russian citizens (with or without the connivance of their government), because they originated from seventy-six different countries it was impossible to hold anyone responsible. Anxiety is the name we give to our uncertainty, to our ignorance of what the threat actually is and to incapacity to determine what can and cannot be done to counter it; indeed the measures we take seem calculated to deepen still further our sense of foreboding. As Bauman writes in his book *Liquid Fear*, 'among the mechanisms that claim to follow the law of perpetual motion, the self-reproduction of the tangle of fear and fear-inspired actions seems to hold pride of place' (Bauman 2006:137).

Beck himself eventually got around to addressing terrorism in the wake of the World Trade Center attack in a lecture which he was invited to deliver at my own institution, the London School of Economics, a year later. What made terrorism very different, he conceded, from many of the other risks he had identified in the 1990s was the fact that it was intelligently designed; it was not unintentional like the meltdown at Chernobyl. Al-Qaeda's attack on New York and Washington had replaced the accident with the principle of intention. Yet this only served even more to undermine confidence in the protection afforded by the state. 'The perception of terrorist threats replaces active trust with active distrust. It therefore undermines the trust in fellow citizens, foreigners and governments all over the world . . . [it] triggers a self-multiplication of risks by the de-bounding of risk perceptions and fantasies' (Beck 2004:44).

Terrorism also highlights the third dimension of Beck's de-bounded world – the temporal that makes us more anxious still. For in terms of time dangers are *latent*, as the consequences of actions can take a long time to work themselves through the system. The boomerang effect – backing bin Laden in the 1980s only to draw his fire in the 1990s – is not always immediate. It is the non-linearity of decision-making which gives rise to so much concern.

In the Cold War things were different – or appeared to be. The state could monitor the nuclear balance. It could identify 'missile gaps' or 'bomber gaps' and it had time to close them. A real increase of 3 per cent in defence expenditure, the Supreme Allied Commander (SACEUR) General Rogers assured NATO, could reduce the conventional military imbalance which had opened up in the 1970s. Now, no one knows how much is enough. We still aspire to make predictable the unpredictable, but our aspirations fall short every time. The need to categorize, regulate and monitor is still at the heart of the modern experience. Risk societies are preoccupied with controlling risks and uncertainties. At the same time, states can no longer order the risks which its citizens have to confront every day. Every attempt at control is of questionable value in an age that gives rise to global warming or terrorism, neither of which recognizes national boundaries. But the state cannot control them by anticipating what lies ahead. The old rules of thumb which permitted a measure of reassurance *over time*, such as statistical analyses, actuarial calculations, accident probabilities and scenarios, are no longer very convincing.

Case Study 1: the State's Structural Fitness for War

In the post 9/11 world threats are defined more by the fault lines within societies than by the territorial boundaries between them. From terrorism to global disease or environmental degradation the challenges have become transnational rather than international. That is the defining quality of world politics in the C21st . . .. In this sense, 9/11 has taught us that terrorism against American interests 'over there' should be regarded just as we regard terrorism against America 'over here'. In this same sense, the American homeland is the planet. (9/11 Commission, 2004)

De-bounding has many implications; perhaps the most immediate is that it robs us of the faith we once had in the capacity of the state to secure us against the multiplicity of risks out there. Once threatened by other states, the state is now more secure than ever before. The democratic peace hypothesis, though still open to empirical testing, is widely shared. Even the US faces no power or even combination of powers. Instead, it confronts two coalitions of non-state actors, the anti-globalization movement and al-Qaeda.

But the situation changes radically when it comes to the fate of its own citizens. Once the most formidable political unit ever designed to mobilize and send them into battle, it now can no longer secure them against other non-state actors, whether they take the form of fellow citizens at home who are intent on blowing them up, or foreigners based thousands of miles away but who have a global reach.

Security and the state are linked at the hip. After 1850, the security which the state provided the citizen was extended to include not only safety against external enemies, but also security against internal anxieties: the perennial insecurity which stemmed from falling ill or finding oneself unemployed or surviving into a destitute old age. The social contract into which the citizen and state entered was more Bismarckian than Hobbesian, for it was Bismarck who entered into the first 'grand bargain' – the state provided social security at home in return for the citizen's willingness to be conscripted.

The Bismarckian social contract was popular precisely because modernity made people particularly insecure. Industrial work also demanded a shared literary culture, as well as shared forms of social organization; it demanded a sense of community strong enough to offset the alienation which it produced. François Ewald has postulated that industrialization required the birth of something like the welfare state. He does not see the welfare state that emerged after World War II in terms of the capture of power by the social democratic or socialist Left. Nor does he see it as a project to guarantee social order after the war had exposed deeply entrenched social divisions. He sees it as the way by which the state eventually convinced the citizen that modernity itself was now safe (Ewald 1987).

The subsequent collapse of what he calls the 'provident' state has changed everything. It has robbed the citizen of the assurance that should he ever need help, a support mechanism will be at hand. Private and company pensions have filled the gap between what the state promises and what it can deliver. Private health schemes ensure immediate treatment. Private education promises better education for one's children. And, of course, private security companies are a much better guarantee than police forces that private property will be protected twenty-four hours a day. In the Western world private security guards now outnumber the police. The rich, and even these days the not so rich, increasingly focus their attention on what Anthony Giddens calls 'privatized survival strategies' (Mythen 2004:109).

The welfare state is in trouble on another front. It once was able to promise full employment. By the 1960s the unemployed masses of the Great Depression had become part of an unremembered past. This is no longer true in a world of 'downsizing' and corporate mergers. Our work regimes are no longer standardized, they are individualized. In the past, labour regimes were confined within state boundaries; today, they are global. Work goes to the places where labour is cheap and tax rates are low. In the past, business depended on the slow building of relationships. Now it has become transactional, involving a series of one-off encounters, contract by contract, deal by deal, which relies not on trust but the presence of lawyers (Sacks 2002:154). In their book *Re-engineering the Corporation*, the authors go to great lengths to defend 're-engineering' against the charge that it is merely a cover for firing people: 'Downsizing and restructuring only mean doing more with less.' But it is the 'less' which is the problem. Where do the rest go (Ellin 1997:62–3)?

Whenever workers are made redundant, they tend to be rendered obsolete. The labour force has discovered what Robert Reich calls 'the obsolescence of loyalty' (Sacks 2002:154). The workers can expect no help from their former employers, especially if they are too old to be re-tooled. Those who have not made themselves of value to others are condemned to redundancy. And as the economy requires fewer and fewer people to run it, so the moral distance between the mass and the elite continues to widen. The former are watched by the latter with the narrow compassion of a generation born into a hard and more restrictive world.

The gradual hollowing out of the social contract raises a question which is of acute importance to this study: is the nation state which even in the European Union is still the chief point of reference for the citizen's identity still *structurally fit* to undertake war? The term is a sociological one, and I owe my own interest in it to Ulrich Beck, so it is important to explain what he means by it.

Beck uses it to focus on the technological vulnerabilities which make the state so fragile. We live in a world of trans-boundary challenges and it is the trans-boundary nature of risks in the twenty-first century that bring into question the bond between citizen and the state. Even a conventional war between states is increasingly unthinkable because of the vulnerability of modern societies to the disruption of energy supplies and communications. Think too of the havoc that would be caused by detonating what Beck calls 'the industrial bombs' that lie at the hearts of our cities: the stockpiles and processing plants in the shape of nuclear power facilities, chemical plants, oil refineries and toxic waste dumps. Think Bhopal and Sevesco. The conclusion he reaches is that the danger the citizen now faces at home has begun to threaten the state's capacity to go to war against other states.

I would add that even when it goes to war against non-state actors thousands of miles from home the contract between state and citizen is being brought into question. The state can no longer ask for the sacrifices on the part of its citizens it once did. In that sense, Beck adds provocatively, perhaps it is time that we began to view the nation state, together with other categories such as class and even gender, as an increasingly redundant institutional form inherited from the nineteenth century which no longer resonates as much as it did in people's minds (Adam 2003).

Without necessarily accepting this claim, Beck does have a point. The nation state was grounded in the concept of society. One of the challenges it faces is that the 'social' has disintegrated into a competition between individuals. At the time of the bicentenary celebrations of the French Revolution there was a popular saying: '1789: the subject becomes citizen: 1989: the consumer becomes citizen.' The fact that citizenship has been redefined in terms of consumer choice is a cause for regret to many. The citizen increasingly thinks of security in terms of individualized safety and seeks to defend himself against anything which puts him personally at risk. As Mark Ritter, *The Risk Society*'s English translator, tells us (Adam 2003:37), the term Beck uses to describe the risks which the workforce has encountered since the introduction of more flexible patterns of employment is *Fressetzung*, a word which means both 'setting free' and 'dismissal' or 'redundancy', or even a 'free setting' – a place of no social obligation. For Beck this play on words (which cannot be replicated in English) has led to a 'de-traditionalization' of values particularly in the social relations they used to embody. The ultimate implication of this 'individualization' is that the individual him or herself becomes the reproductive unit of the *social* in the life-world.

Insecurity is thus not merely a reality of the environment in which we live; it has become an *existential* state. Wealthy individuals who can afford it will buy themselves out of dangerous environments. They move house in order to send their children to more secure schools. They move to gated communities. They prefer to wall themselves off, both figuratively and literally, from their fellow citizens. All of which represents a certain opting-out of the social order. As Bauman adds (Bauman 2007:11), those who can afford to do so fortify themselves against all visible and invisible, present or anticipated, known or as yet undefined risks. The very fact that urban life has become a risk and the city a battlefield has diminished the 'social' even further. The life project has become one of self-fulfilment. This 'inner development' does not have much time for the 'outer' disciplines or projects which once constituted the 'social', or the collective life of the citizens.

Individuals also secure their future in other ways that isolate them from the social world. The citizen is forced increasingly to ground his or her activities on his or her own efforts. Hence the growth of self-regulation, self-help and self-management which is demanded of us all, particularly in terms of health: we are expected to adopt the right lifestyles for a healthy life (Appadurai 2006:122). Even the 'civic' realm is becoming detached from the political. Many citizens in the West now have their own civic consciousness: their mosques and civic associations which often detach them from political life as traditionally understood. Indicative of the breakdown of the civic order is that we speak increasingly of communities: the 'black community' or the 'Asian community' or the 'Muslim community'. Governments enter into a dialogue with designated 'community leaders'. Even more bizarrely, we talk of 'community policing' and 'community care'. And then there are those outside 'the community' who live in a parallel world, independent of the world from which they derive their legal rights. Some, writes Appadurai, insist on the right to be un-American, or un-British, in matters of culture, politics and especially lifestyle. Some opt out and live the life of moral exiles; others opt into a counter-Weberian world of violence which strikes at the 'everyday' or 'normality' that constitutes the civic space – the space of peaceful association and debate. In the world beyond the nation state there is a global network of power, politics and violence which gives the alienated citizen full access to lethal technologies which can be directed against the state or one's fellow citizens at home (Appadurai 2006:122). According to the National Security Strategy of the United Kingdom (2008), at any one time the police and the security services have to contend with twenty plots, 200 groups or networks and 2,000 individuals who are judged to pose a terrorist threat to the state and citizen alike (National Security Strategy of the United Kingdom 2008).

Indeed, one of the principal challenges to the state is the increasingly networked nature of society. For the internet observes no fronts or frontiers. It can reach into every home. Instruction manuals on how to build a bomb are available to anyone willing to access the websites; bomb production is within the grasp of any citizen who has both the time and inclination to build one. The state, in other words, no longer monopolizes the *technology* of violence. In the Cold War it not only built the technologies of mass destruction, it also invested funds in various spin-offs such as jet transport, nuclear energy, space travel and virtual reality (VR). The extent of the state's investment gave governments some control over these technologies, many of which were also stored in highly specialized camps or bases which the public was forbidden to enter and which were secured by enhanced systems of surveillance. In the US the largest of these research establishments, Area 51, soon became a staple of conspiracy theories and spiced-up television programmes such as the *X-Files*. This era is now behind us. The twenty-first century will be that of the 'enabled machine'. Whereas the nineteenth century was steam-powered by experts and the twentieth electric-powered by the state, strangely, except for the car, the twenty-first century is likely to be digitally powered by the citizen. Early examples include the Sony Walkman, the first mobile phones, the computer/internet and VR travel. The portals to these machines now connect individuals across a network. It is 'personalized networking' that the state fears most (Urry 2003:126).

As a result, we have to live with two unappealing prospects which define the age. One is that some citizens may be monitored more closely than others. Ethnic profiling no doubt exists, even if governments deny it. The Hollywood blockbuster *State of Siege* took as its theme the mass internment of Muslims during a series of terrorist attacks in New York. This was fiction, of course. Real life one day could replicate it. An opinion poll conducted at the end of 2004 suggested that 53 per cent of Americans favoured restricting the civil liberties of Muslims (including their fellow citizens) in the interest of increased security (Stearns 2006:43).

The second challenge may arise from what demographers call the 'third demographic transition', the massive influx of immigrants into North America and Europe which, if current trends persist, will alter national ancestry, radically and even permanently. In combination with sub-replacement fertility and accelerated levels of emigration of the domestic population this is likely to pose one of the great historical challenges of the times. When a society is not reproducing itself, it needs a blood transfusion – it needs immigrants. Yet immigration adds to those many uncertainties that globalization produces; at the very least it tends to make us feel even more insecure.

The challenge takes different forms within the Western world. The US produces no suicide bombers of its own, although it has its fair share of home-grown terrorists such as Tim McVeigh and the Unabomber. Neither of these, however, were on the cast of the Long War. What worries Americans is the 'ethnic stranger', particularly those who are Spanish-speaking and deemed likely to bring with them in their suitcase the work ethic of the Third World. Despite the anxiety in Europe about asylum seekers and immigrants, it is not the ethnic stranger but the *ethical stranger* who is deemed to constitute the real danger. For the ethical tie between cit-izens which makes possible the civic order is ultimately far more important than ethnicity. Unfortunately, when the ethnic stranger becomes an ethical stranger (a stranger to the civic order of which he is part) and, more impor-tant, when he insists upon his own estrangement, then the state faces a dilemma. It is at that point that it confronts the threat of Rousseau's 'for-eigners among citizens', by which he meant the citizens opposed to the social contract that sustains civil society. For the ethical stranger, whatever his social or ethnic provenance, is by definition an antisocial citizen. And in Europe, writes David Selbourne, he has the advantage of living in a society which grants him rights without always insisting on the discharge of his duties. If duties without rights make slaves, he adds, rights without duties make strangers (Selbourne 1994:108).

The challenge posed by the 7/7 London bombers was that they saw themselves as members of an oppressed and humiliated body. In their mar-tyrdom tapes they claimed they were acting to revenge their Muslim broth-ers in Iraq and Palestine. They went about killing their fellow citizens to avenge 'brothers in faith' they had never met. Such is the power of one 'imagined community' (the Islamic brotherhood) over another (the United Kingdom). It would be a grim day, of course, were Muslims and non-Muslim citizens in Europe to understand opposition to each other as constitutive of themselves.

This is a risk many Western societies now run, and they are haunted by the fear that through their own actions they may even invite it. The link between British policy in Iraq and the London bombings (2005) was confirmed by both al-Qaeda's deputy leader, al-Zawahiri and Britain's Joint Terrorism Analysis Centre. It was in anticipation of such an attack that a year earlier the Foreign Office had set up a new programme called 'Engaging with the Islamic World', which included 'outreach' programmes designed to explain British policy to a domestic audience.

Only once before has the British state had to take into account the fault lines running through society when in 1919 London dockworkers refused to load a ship called the *Jolly George* with arms for Poland in its war against Soviet Russia. A threat by the Trades Union Congress to order a general strike forced the government to suspend arms shipments altogether. But class divisions, however real, were never translated into foreign policy choices. Is this true of the multicultural society we have become? Do the ethnic fault lines running through Bradford, Birmingham and Berlin now pose a danger to national security? Particularly worrying for the British government was the arrest in February 2007 of nine young British Muslims from the Birmingham area who were accused of planning to kidnap and decapitate British Muslim soldiers who had returned from Afghanistan.

There is a crucial difference between the 'ethnic stranger' that the US fears and the 'ethical stranger' that the Europeans may already confront, and it complicates state-building in Afghanistan and Iraq whether the Europeans like to acknowledge the fact or not. The Americans believe they are engaged in a war; the Europeans believe that they are trying to prevent one from breaking out at home. President Bush delivered a revealing speech in November 2005 in which he told the American people: 'Our troops are fighting terrorists in Iraq so that you will not have to face them here at home' (*The Times*, 22 November 2006). The Europeans cannot keep terrorism at bay in this manner. Its suicide bombers are already in position.

All of which translates back into a cybernetic feedback loop. Quite understandably, we may all fear stolen nuclear weapons, sarin gas and anthrax bombs, but it is the old-fashioned bombs in cars and trains, or what Mike Davis calls 'the brutal hardware and quotidian workhorses of urban terrorism' (Davis 2007), that do the most damage psychologically. For even the most law-abiding citizen is beginning to question whether his or her own government should actually be putting them at even greater risk by going to war. The social contract no longer offers the assurance it once did. The world is becoming so complex that it is calling into question the prevailing orthodoxies of the social contract which underpins the nation state.

Case Study 2: Anxiety and Disease

Let me take another example of how security has become 'de-bounded' in the risk age. Here we have another phenomenon at work. Once an issue appears on our mental radar as something that can cross boundaries, or infiltrate by stealth before anyone knows it is here, it tends quickly to become a security issue for the first time. Whether this should be the case is a moot question, but that is not the point. Disease is a matter that makes many of us feel insecure; and what makes the rest of us feel insecure in the risk age is inevitably of interest to the security community.

Discussing disease is particularly difficult, of course, for security experts – as it is for everyone else. To begin with, there is lack of perspective; we are too near to events to see their significance clearly. At the time of writing, SARS is only six years old; HIV-AIDS has only been recognized as a pandemic since the 1980s. A second problem is that of fashion. Does it really constitute a security problem at all? There are many others demanding our attention: global warming, climate change and energy security. There is always a temptation in these and other cases to mistake vogue for value.

But if we take a broad historical approach we can better appreciate how disease has tapped into the deep vein of anxiety which characterizes the risk age. For disease has a history (as has climate change and practically everything else). It was Nietzsche who claimed that every human emotion had a history. He was the first to suggest that we could write a history of mentalities – such as the history of greed, love, charity – and even fear. Some years later, Sigmund Freud suggested that fear could be divided into three historical eras: fright, fear and anxiety. Although we tend to think that they are synonyms of each other, they are not the same (Naphy and Roberts 1997:190).

In the pre-modern era, people were frightened of disease. Perhaps the key text here is Thucydides' *History of the Peloponnesian War* which tells us of the dreadful epidemic which carried off a substantial percentage of the Athenian population in the early years of the conflict, including most disastrously of all, the war leader Pericles. Thucydides himself caught the disease and gives us a pretty accurate description of its symptoms. His account is a pathology in a double sense: the pathology of the disease itself and of a whole society disintegrating under its effects. What really frightened the ancient Athenians was that they had no explanation for what had happened to them. By default their fate could only be attributed to the will of the gods. The Black Death which carried off at least one-third of the population of Europe in the fourteenth century was an even more destructive plague, and equally frightening, given that the Middle Ages too had no concept of epidemiology

The modern era, by contrast, was not so much frightened as fearful of epidemics and pandemics; it was fearful of diseases that it could explain medically but could do little to prevent or contain. The nineteenth century knew perfectly well that urbanization and associated overcrowding bred disease. And globalization, then in its early stages, increased the chances of exporting it. Take the cholera epidemic which broke out in Bengal in 1826 (the first global epidemic of its kind). Once it reached southern Russia the pace of infection quickened. Military movements connected with the Russian, Persian and Turkish wars were interrupted for a time. The Polish revolt in 1831 spread the disease to the Baltic. From there it arrived in England shortly afterwards. From England it travelled to Ireland, and via immigration to Canada and the US.

Later, the great influenza pandemic of 1918–19 killed nearly thirty million people. We still do not know whether it originated along the corridors of the rat-infested trenches of the Western Front or in an overcrowded army camp in Kansas where thousands of soldiers were waiting to embark for France. The pandemic was so virulent because immunity was so low. The Europeans were exhausted, both physically and emotionally, after four years of war. And Russia and China were crippled through revolution and civil war, as a result of which we still do not know the real casualty figures.

But if the modern world was fearful of disease, at least it knew how to combat it. The urban authorities, employing new sanitary techniques funded by public borrowing, were able to transform public health provision. Indeed, the medical provision was so good that it profoundly altered the face of war twenty years later. What makes World War II unique was that the armies were able to sustain themselves logistically in the field thousands of miles away from home without the fear that they would disintegrate as they had in the past. It was cholera, after all, which destroyed much of Napoleon's army on the march to Moscow, not its retreat from the city. In 1915, an outbreak of typhus in Serbia proved so virulent that it stopped the fighting for six months in the Balkans. Nothing like this was seen in World War II.

The culprit, of course, was the louse. The French novelist Fernand Céline recalls a conversation one evening in Paris with an SS major who asked him in his capacity as the Gestapo doctor why virulent epidemics seemed to have disappeared. The Allies had fought their way from the Middle East to Italy and seemed completely unaffected. 'A calamity, Céline . . . you saw the cables. Epidemics are washed up. . . .' Wearing his hat as a novelist Céline waxed poetic: the Allies, he suggested, had managed to abolish the fourth Horseman of the Apocalypse (Céline 1986).

Less poetically, we can attribute the success in combating typhus to the delousing station and the use of new chemical agents such as DDT.

Delousing was a special feature of the concentration camp system which prevented an epidemic from breaking out. There was of course a dreadful irony in all of this. The war continued, as did the Final Solution, because there was nothing to stop it except human goodwill. The Czech scientist and poet, Miloslav Holub, wrote a bitterly ironic poem which captured this all too well. His subject was Josef Meistner who as a boy was bitten by a rabid dog in Alsace on 6 July 1885. Meistner was the first patient to be saved by Louis Pasteur with quinine. He was also the first janitor of the Pasteur Institute. He committed suicide fifty years later when the Germans occupied the Institute following the fall of Paris in 1940. As Holub concludes ruefully, 'only the virus remained above it all' (Holub 1984:73).

Still, the modern age has one thing going for it. Even given human perversity (the will to destroy), the twentieth century lived in the hope that disease could be eliminated. Smallpox was the first disease to be eradicated, in 1976. In other words, although the century was fearful of disease, it could look forward to the situation contained in President Roosevelt's promise in 1940 that one day the world would know freedom from fear. Roosevelt took the phrase from Thoreau, and if we go back to the original speech we will see how persuasive was the vision: the world could be spared fear itself – 'nameless, unreasoning, unjustified terror which paralyses needed efforts to convert retreat into advance' (Bauman 2006:137).

And so we come to our own age, which for want of any better description, might be called the post-modern. Our age is not frightened of disease, much less is it fearful. But it is terribly anxious. And what makes us anxious is the knowledge that disease will never be eliminated. More depressing still, we now know that even diseases we had largely eliminated, at least in the Western world, such as tuberculosis, are set to return. TB has now become a growing infectious threat with the arrival of new immigrants from the Third World. Even smallpox may be reintroduced into the community by terrorist cells generating the virus in their laboratories. We are made more anxious still by the appearance of a stealth virus like HIV-AIDS which can incubate over a long period. And we are especially worried by diseases such as SARS which can speed across the world in days, courtesy of international travel. As Aldous Huxley asked in his novel *Brave New World*, 'What hope can we have in the future if the anthrax bombs are on their way?'

Max Weber had asked a very different question in the 1890s: 'What hope can we have if the Cossacks are coming?' We still fear political events, although this time we are often more anxious about the intentions of non-state actors rather than those of states. This was anticipated in a short story by the science-fiction writer H. G. Wells called 'The Stolen Bacillus'. Written in 1895 it describes an anarchist who injects himself with the bubonic plague so that he can secretly infect the population around him. Wells put his finger on the problem. It is not the virus which is the danger, it is human behaviour, active in the case in the terrorist, passive in the case of behaviour which opens people up to catching the pathogens lurking out there.

And our anxieties are addressed to the future, rather than the present. In one of the preambulatory clauses of Security Council Resolution 1308 – the first resolution ever to be passed on HIV-AIDS by the UN – we learn that 'if unchecked (HIV-AIDS) *may* pose a *risk* to stability and security' [my italics] (Elbe 2008b:178). As usual, our anxieties are cast in the subjunctive mood. Frustrated with the speculative nature of many such arguments, a number of social scientists working on the disease were moved to insist that 'those who write on AIDS and security are advised to avoid, if at all possible, using the word "may" or at least to note that whilst the epidemic may do X it may also not do X.' If they did, adds Stefan Elbe, the securitization of HIV-AIDS would probably have to stop dead in its tracks, for it works mostly on the basis of the precautionary risk logic in which a future which may never transpire is permitted to determine actions taken in the present (Elbe 2008b:179–80).

So what is the real risk of disease, and should it be treated as a security problem at all? Disease now accounts for 26 per cent of all global deaths per annum, and is the second largest cause of death on the planet in any given year. Death from war, by comparison, accounts for an average of 0.4 per cent of global deaths, possibly the lowest figure in history. War, in other words, is less problematic for most people than ever, and disease in war less problematic still. But disease itself has now become a security problem as was not the case in the past. And the reason why has to do with globalization itself. As Beck insists, our world is de-bounded; it has become three-dimensional for the first time.

In the *spatial* dimension, terrorism, like climate change and transnational organized crime, affects everyone, everywhere. So does disease. In nineteenth-century London, at least at the time of the last cholera outbreak in the 1840s, it was possible to identify the areas where it bred and to avoid them. The outbreak claimed the lives of more poor people than middle-class citizens. Now disease can attack any social class or any age group at any time. Add to this the frequency and scope of global travel. Asked to reflect on HIV-AIDS, the UN AIDS Executive Director responded, '[the] virus has made optimal use of let's say communication networks and contact among people' (Elbe 2008b:181). A virus caught in Hong Kong can be carried to Southeast Asia in four hours, to Europe in twelve and to North America in eighteen. Nearly 1.5 billion passengers travel by air every year. At the height of the SARS scare, the air industry was badly affected by the outbreak. People stopped travelling, but not for long. Nothing seems capable of changing our deep-rooted desire for mobility.

In terms of the second dimension, *time*, disease makes us anxious because it is a latent. This connects disease to a space–time continuum. More than 140 million people, for example, enter the US every year. The flight time between points of departure and arrival is seldom more than twenty-four hours, yet some diseases have a long incubation period. Symptoms may not manifest themselves for months, or in the case of HIV-AIDS for years. Just as we have stealth weapons and smart bombs, AIDS is a stealth virus. It is also smart like a computer virus: both can remain dormant for months and if the latter is programmed with evolutionary algorithms, it too can mutate just as fast. Even in the case of plague, symptoms do not manifest themselves for three days; in the case of smallpox it is two weeks. We screen passengers to ensure they are not carrying weapons or explosives; we cannot screen them for infectious diseases, whether they are aware of being infected or not.

Finally in the *social* dimension, the risk of disease is de-bounded too. It is difficult to hold anyone responsible for its spread, except in terms of vague lifestyle choices – such as in the case of HIV-AIDS, homosexuality, or intravenous drug use, or cultural lifestyles such as polygamy and prostitution in Africa. But that, of course, is the point. Whenever we discussed threats in the past, we were able to attribute them to intentions, mostly those of states. Now many of the risks we face come from non-state actors, or in the case of disease, arise from the life choices or social behaviour of the population at large. And no one intends to catch AIDS or TB or SARS. The fact that disease spreads in a non-linear fashion, horizontally, not vertically, is what makes us more anxious than ever. Pervasive anxiety is the mark of the post-modern age. And societies are not easily argued out of their anxieties (as opposed to their fears), which is why Freud tells us anxiety and fear are very different.

Unlike fear, anxiety is grounded not on the immediate or perceived, but the imagined. And our imagination these days ranges far into the future. That is why we find ourselves looking at what Tony Blair calls a 'post-secure world'. We live in a world in which diseases such as SARS and avian flu are global, and therefore potentially catastrophic, which is why we try to master our anxieties by telling ourselves stories. In the absence of a 'clear and present danger' social narratives are more important than ever.

But how much do we actually know? The risk age encourages us to 'securitize' everything, but we often do so in the absence of reliable information. We are forever drawing up lists of probabilities. Our scenarios and predictions are a bit like Plato's Forms in that they offer a world 'beyond' the real, the immediate or what can be seen (Bauman 2004:53). This brings to mind Donald Rumsfeld and his definitive way to categorize risks — his famous unknown unknowns. There are risks we know about, and risks we don't know we are running, and finally there are things we don't know we don't know. In the case of HIV-AIDS all three categories apply.

For we do know something, though not as much as we think we do. We know that twenty-five million people have died since we identified the virus in the early 1980s. We know 3.5 million victims die of the disease every year, and that twenty million are infected. And we now talk of the 'second wave' of countries — Russia, China and India — that may surpass Africa in the number of people who could succumb to the virus. If this happens the impact is likely to be much greater, for all three are aspiring Great Powers, not marginal countries representative of what some analysts like to call 'the African condition'. But even these figures must be treated with caution. We mostly have data not on men, but on women, and mostly pregnant women at that. And they are self-selecting — they choose to be tested.

We can guess what the impact of the virus has been on some of the indices of 'human security'. We know that HIV-AIDS targets primary-school teachers, and thus has a knock-on effect on education. We know that in terms of public health it targets the most productive part of the population, those aged between fifteen to forty-five. And we anticipate that the millions of children that have become orphans may one day form the foot soldiers of the feral gangs roaming the city streets. Our imagination can run riot, and usually does based on what we think are the 'known knowns'.

But there are also 'known unknowns'. Take state collapse. The World Health Organization (WHO) prefers to see the pandemic as an economic disaster. According to the US Census Bureau's *World Population Profile*, 30 per cent of the population of Botswana is HIV-positive. In other words, within twenty years a large percentage of adult males alive today will be dead. For its size, Botswana is one of the richest African countries, as well as one of the few that is genuinely democratic. But now that the life expectancy of the average male has gone down from seventy-three ten years ago to thirty-four today, its future is uncertain. In the years ahead it may become a society with at least one feature of the world portrayed by William Golding in his novel *Lord of the Flies*. It may be run largely by very young people with little access to their elders or the collective wisdom of the tribe.

But we don't really know whether any society will implode. Historians tell us that there must be a 40 per cent mortality rate before a society comes near to collapse. This was last seen in the Middle Ages. Even the cholera epidemic of the 1820s, the first global pandemic, killed only 15 per cent of its victims. HIV-AIDS has killed less than 3 per cent, which is historically insignificant.

Another 'known unknown' is the prevalence rate in African militaries. In some armed forces the prevalence rate is suspected to be as high as 60 per cent, which, if true, would have a decisive impact on combat performance. HIV has particular implications for peacekeeping, since in the case of Cambodia in the early 1990s, the armed forces served as a vector for the illness when they were first deployed. Croatia would not even let in the UN because of its fear the troops would bring the disease with them. HIV-AIDS, in other words, is not in itself a security problem. It becomes a problem when the collective impact of the disease undermines a country's political self-belief or confidence in external intervention. And in the case of the Democratic Republic of Congo where up to 2.5 million people have died in recent years, there is even a suspicion that the six armies that trashed the country were partly deployed so that their members could pay their medical expenses. In many African countries most anti-retrovirals are given almost exclusively to members of the armed forces. At $15,000 or more per year, the medical bills are way beyond the means of most African soldiers. Looting a country is one way of paying the bills. It is all a very ironic intimation, to invert Clausewitz, that war is no longer only a continuation of politics by other means; in some parts of the world it is also becoming a continuation of medication.

But all the studies we have should be treated with caution. Many African militaries do not test their personnel. The estimates we have are based on selective data. And the data we have for soldiers who test HIV-positive is not necessarily significant in terms of operational effectiveness. A soldier could serve for years before he develops AIDS; he could keep the peace perfectly well before he is posted back home.

In terms of Rumsfeld's third category – the 'unknown unknowns' – the picture is very different. For here we have indeed entered uncharted territory, and we have been led there by specialists who have their own agenda. The World Bank's 2004 report *Breaking the Conflict Trap* sees the pandemic as part of a larger picture: a crisis in development. 'Many of us', the President of the Bank pointed out some years ago, 'used to think of AIDS as a health issue. We were wrong . . . We face a major development crisis, but more than that, a security crisis' (Elbe 2008b:179). From an observation by Carl Menninger (cited by Susan Sontag in her memorable book *Illness as a Metaphor*) we can see where this is likely to lead: 'Illness is only in part what the world has done to a victim – in larger part, it is what the victim has done with his world' (Sontag 1979). Illness, in other words, is conditioned by lifestyles (think of the Western obsession with smoking and cancer); by human habitats (infection spreads in the teeming cities of the Third World); by human action such as global warming which is becoming especially important in the spread of infectious disease. Illness is not merely a matter of biology; it is also explained by human behaviour.

Accordingly, the world has begun to insist on changes in social practices. Development agencies are involved in monitoring those practices. Surveillance, as we shall see in chapter 5, is at the heart of risk management in everything from policing to arms control. Development itself has become a strategic tool of conflict resolution, as well as a medium of social reconstruction. And development agencies, whether they like it or not (and most do not), find themselves transformed into security actors, at least in the eyes of other states. Some of them are willing to abet this particular discourse because it brings in funds. Governments, after all, spend more on the War on Terror than the War on AIDS, although the US is now spending $50 billion on HIV-AIDS programmes because it has identified the virus as a national security threat.

The stories we tell are important, of course, for they provide us with an illusion of being in control. If we understand the meaning of a fast-moving situation we may be better placed to tackle the problem, or to anticipate the problems that may arise in the future. But there is also a case, of course, for not making disease into a security issue at all. To Rumsfeld's list the philosopher Zizek added a fourth: there are things we once knew but have forgotten. And what we have forgotten is that disease is largely a matter of poverty, not security. And what connects SARS, HIV-AIDS and avian flu is the world economy. What is the primary culprit is not the H_5N_1 influenza virus itself, but the destiny of the human race, including overseas tourism, wetland destruction, Third World urbanization and international travel. What makes the impact of disease all the more pronounced is that for the first time the majority of the world population now live in cities.

Unfortunately, we spend more and more time policing our societies against enemies redefined as 'risk groups' who constitute a danger both to us and to themselves. The risk age encourages us to criminalize more and more groups all the time and at the same time to ascribe blame. Perceptions of risk, in other words, tend to reinforce existing social divisions. This may even be a general trait of human society, speculates Mary Douglas; fear of danger tends to amplify social divisions. And in a world in which the pre-vailing ideology is one of competitive individualism 'it is easier to write off the unsuccessful as human derelicts' (Douglas 1992:34, 41).

And most of them are to be found in the cities where disease breeds rapidly, especially in the 200,000 shanty towns that dot the troubled landscape of the globe, today's foetid, densely packed slums. Twelve million live in the slums of Mumbai, the largest of all. Nine-tenths of urbanized Ethiopians know only slum life. To describe this as urban life is not strictly true, or at least not in the sense we understand. Many cities are a frontier land in which lawlessness prevails and murder is an everyday fact of life. In the late 1980s, in Bogotá so commonplace was murder that the city fathers encouraged the drug cartels to be environmentally conscious and bury their victims outside the city limits. 'Don't dump your dead bodies here', demanded a poster that was strung across the intersection of a major urban highway leading out of the city. In Bogotá the city fathers' concern for hygiene was apparently greater than their concern for human life. Indeed, since the death toll also included victims of police death squads who tended to target slum children, murder could even be seen as a perverse case of 'urban renewal'.

The cities of the future, writes Mike Davis, instead of being made out of glass and steel, will be constructed out of recycled plastic, cement blocks and scrap wood (Davis 2006:19). These urban sprawls will become what Bauman calls 'waste disposal units' for a vast mass of unemployed, unem-ployable people, largely the cast-offs of late modernity. They will be the dumping grounds for the 'collateral damage' of capitalism (Bauman 2004). What accounts for the Malthusian trap in which the poor now find them-selves caught is that the new shanty cities offer no secure source of liveli-hood. The peasants who migrated to the great North American and European cities in the nineteenth century were pulled in (not pushed). They soon found work as the cities rapidly industrialized. A booming city such as Manchester was a great 'job machine' which, not without immense human suffering, of course, and certainly not immediately, eventually pulled urban migrants out of the poverty trap through industrialization. Unfortunately, there is no similar historical process at work today, or none that can be readily discerned. The historical experience of Victorian Manchester, or twentieth-century Seoul, or even twenty-first-century Los Angeles (an ethnically diverse heteropolis, the ultimate 'capital of the Third World') affords no useful perspective on the reality of urban life for those experiencing it for the first time.

Not enough money is being spent on the eradication of disease where it hits hardest. The prevention of disease is massively underfunded. The

WHO budget is $1 billion, compared with IMF loans of $35 billion. At the same time private foundations, rather than states, are making much of the running. The Gates Foundation is committed to eradicating malaria where governments failed in the 1960s, and is already responsible for more vaccinations for children against childhood diseases than all the governments on the planet put together. All of which, claims Elbe, is to argue that the emergence and spread of global disease is less a result of evolutionary bad luck than of our own behaviour. As Pasteur famously remarked, 'the microbe is nothing, the terrain is everything.' It is the cultural context which is often more important. It was not the microbe but the cultural context which led Josef Meistner to take his own life in 1940. In other words, writes Elbe, there is a distinct epidemiological imprint that our societies are leaving on the planet. In environmental studies we talk of such an imprint: the ecological impact on, and sustainability of, human consumption patterns. Equally important is the epidemiological footprint generated by the contemporary world economy – though it is much less discussed (Elbe 2008a).

To call it an existential threat to national well-being is scare-mongering. It is not a positive response to the outbreak of the disease itself. It tends to privilege the short over the long term. It identifies symptoms, not underlying causes. In the case of disease it may be more sensible to return the problem to the doctors.

The Problem of Expertise

Yet there is the rub. For doctors are experts, no longer guardians of knowledge. The distinction is made by Anthony Giddens who reminds us that medicine too has a history. Traditionally, doctors were guardians of a knowledge that their patients found arcane; they neither had access to it, nor did they understand it. Doctors stood between the civilian world and access to medical understanding. They were not experts as we understand the term today. They had status, not competence. It was not possible to acquire their knowledge without a 'vocation' – that is what conferred status upon them. Their knowledge was not communicable to the outsider. The skill of the doctor was a craft taught by apprenticeship in the field and experience, plus intuition (the doctor was ultimately not a healer but a diagnostician) and the knowledge claims he incorporated were protected as arcane and esoteric (Giddens 1994:63).

Today, medical authorities observe the principle of concordance: they work with their patients; they even take patients into their confidence; they know those whom they treat, at least in the developed world, will have unprecedented access to information about their condition on the internet, as well as unrivalled access to support groups, and in some cases even unprescribed drugs. The stories we tell about disease lead us to trust some authorities more than others. In an age of risk all knowledge is corrigible; all treatment is highly contested. We live in an era of second opinions, in a competitive marketplace of diagnoses.

It is particularly ironic, of course, in the wider world the more we rely on experts in all fields the less we tend to trust them to get it right. Unfortunately, one of the things that has been much diminished in recent years is the trust we once invested in the traditional structures of knowledge. It matters a great deal that, as we have noted about the Cold War, we have been denied those mathematical models that once allowed us to quantify the dangers we faced and thus to some extent insure ourselves against them.

Casinos deal with risks every time a punter plays a roulette table, but they know the odds. And while they cannot predict the outcome of a particular whirl of the roulette wheel, they know that in the aggregate they will make a profit (there is no system that has yet been devised to beat the house). In the Cold War it was possible to measure the military balance in true number-crunching style which allowed the punters, the superpowers, to calculate risks with some certainty. It was possible to count the number of Soviet missiles or conventional forces, and to establish whether or not the Soviet Union had that 3:1 advantage which soldiers were taught at military academies was essential if the attacking side were to have any confidence of success. And although the Western Alliance was frequently plagued by long and often acrimonious disputes about whether military assessments should measure not only crude capabilities, but also the intention or not to use them, intentions too could be assessed with some accuracy by diplomats or academics who visited Moscow. The Cold War gave birth to a new academic community of Kremlinologists who considered that they were uniquely qualified to advise policy-makers as to whether the 'doves' or the 'hawks' were in power.

Risk assessment, in short, was a question of mathematics irrespective of whether the risk was explicitly or implicitly calculated. As such, the risk calculus was part of an instrumental world, a realm that provided clear distinctions between safety and danger, truth and falsity, past and future (Adams 2003:7). We could build in margins of safety, distinguish between real and hypothetical dangers and draw a line between the present and the future. This is no longer true, which is why the politics of security, at its most basic, has become the politics of insecurity. There is no escaping the fact that we are never likely again to feel as secure as we once did thanks to threat assessments and calculations. 'If knowledge can be shown as a sphere whose volume is endlessly expanding, the area of contact with the unknown is growing out of all proportion' (Virilio 2005:17). It is fear of the unknown, including the unknowable consequences of our own actions, that has brought the issue of fear management to the fore.

Rumsfeld's categories of known and unknown 'knowns' have attracted much derision but he was only echoing, if unconsciously, Aquinas's understanding of the ultimate unknown of the medieval world: the unknowable nature of God's intentions towards humanity. Human beings might try to understand God but they would never succeed. They would only find themselves entering into an area of greater darkness. Such questions could not be asked; humanity could only know that it only knew because it knew that it did not know.

The risk age is definable in terms of the limits of human knowledge not these days of the mind of God, but of the observable and quantifiable world around us. And what cannot be known is more revealing that what can be. There are boundaries that we cannot cross, limits that cannot be transgressed with any confidence. When life reaches a particular critical limit of complexity it becomes impossible to understand it fully. The paradox that we know that we cannot know is a striking feature of our age, and one that gives rise, of course, to its prevailing sense of anxiety. Paradoxes are favoured by philosophers for the insights they provide; as Bertrand Russell once remarked, the work of good philosophy is to begin with a statement that is regarded as too obvious to be of interest and from it to deduce a conclusion no one will believe (Barrow 2005:22).

Where Rumsfeld erred was in not taking this paradoxical logic further. For if we don't understand what we don't understand (and if we are prepared to acknowledge this), then we have to accept that insecurity is our lot. The question we should then ask is not, 'What should I be?' but 'how should I be?' (how can we so constitute ourselves that we can adapt quickly when the unknowns become apparent?) (Luhmann 1998:43).

Our predicament is particularly acute because we no longer have actuarial measurements to hand even to assess the risks posed by terrorism. There would seem to be an inexhaustible supply of suicide bombers out there; how many, however, we can only guess. And the so-called experts (in this case the intelligence services) are not much help; indeed, many have a poor record of assessment. Terrorists also do not attend conferences. Few can be interviewed in the field. Most go to ground until they resurface years later. What terrorists 'intend' remains a matter of speculation, not all of it well-informed. But then it is difficult to be well-informed if there is so little hard information to hand, which is one reason why intelligence-gathering is being outsourced to the private sector, such as the use of commercial satellites to assess Syrian or Iranian nuclear facilities (www.globalsecurity.org).

Or take the case of discontented nationals at home which makes the state far less structurally fit to make war than it was before. Of the 101 Western Europeans involved in Sunni extremist violence in 2007, thirty-two travelled to Pakistan specifically to train in al-Qaeda camps. Of these, twenty-eight were being monitored by the intelligence services of Pakistan or the home country at the time of travel. One was Fritz Gelowicz, who was arrested in September for stockpiling explosives and planning an attack on US military targets and nightclubs in his home country, Germany. Yet the trend is towards sourcing explosives and other materials from the black market and criminal gangs. The problem of identifying and monitoring such groups goes beyond a failure of intelligence; it goes much deeper. We don't even know what intelligence we need to identify a threat that has not yet appeared. For over time the character of terrorist violence in Europe is likely to change too: it is likely to become more internet-based, and the locals will probably evolve their own style of videos, mixing *jihadi* rhetoric and video footage with religious themes and urban street culture. Sure, there are things we don't know; there are matters that have to be discovered; we are always encountering new risks. But for much of history, especially in the modern era, the challenge was to turn the unknown into the knowable (Furedi 2008:54). Now the state suspects that in some cases, including terrorism, this may be beyond it.

Or take the Iranian nuclear programme. In 2005 US intelligence agencies expressed 'high confidence' that Iran was still developing a nuclear weapons programme. Only two years later, citing improved intelligence but with the same degree of 'high confidence', they claimed that Iran had actually abandoned the programme a year before the first report had been submitted. This dizzying inversion of what we thought we knew is sadly of a piece with the track record of the intelligence services not only in the US but also, for that matter, many other Western countries. In the early 1990s most Western intelligence services were confident that Iraq was nowhere near to developing a nuclear weapon. When Saddam was finally forced to admit the UN weapons inspectors, the world found he was only a few years away from obtaining a nuclear bomb. Even after his fall the situation was not quite as clear cut as the critics of the invasion were wont to maintain. It is true that the Iraq Survey Group which was set up to find WMD concluded that there was no stockpile of weapons to find, but its final report also revealed that

Saddam himself had always intended to restart the programme as soon as he could, and that there were many avenues still open to him to acquire nuclear weapons from a damagingly large list of contacts ranging from France to North Korea. In other words, but for the final invasion the containment of Iraq might have continued indefinitely (Chatfield 2008:66).

The point is that there is only so much the world can know about what a secretive regime chooses to spend its money on, and all intelligence assessments have to be constantly revised and updated. Intelligence-gathering, unfortunately, is rather like weather-forecasting. It cannot be the basis for going to war or declaring 'peace in our time' – it can only be a guide to decision-making. The buck still stops with the politicians and their gut instinct whether to trust intelligence estimates or not.

Unfortunately, risk management requires us all to take decisions every day. Should we venture out to travel if the colour code at airports is 'high' (i.e. Red rather than Orange)? Should we venture out for gasoline with the Washington sniper(s) still at large? And every decision entails consequences for ourselves and others. We can no longer separate ourselves from the mass; our lives intersect more than ever. It is because we have to take decisions despite the uncertainties that we have come to rely so much on experts, and, as Giddens tells us, expertise is qualitatively very different from knowledge.

Baudrillard made the same point in a key passage from his book, *The Gulf War Did Not Take Place*: 'Just as wealth is no longer measured by the ostentation of wealth but by the secret circulation of speculative capital, so war is not measured by being waged but by its speculative unfolding in an abstract, electronic and informational space in which capital moves' (Baudrillard 1995:56). Information is now critical in determining whether we go to war; but it is highly speculative because we have no absolute, objective knowledge of whether it is actually true. As a result we find ourselves having to work on the basis of the worst-case scenario which disposes us, in turn, to take unnecessary precautions.

The sociology of risk is the science of what Max Weber called *Möglichkeitsurteile* (judgements about probabilities). It is a word unlikely to catch on in the English-speaking world. There is a lot of background noise in the risk age, not all of it easy on the ear. It is useful word, however, because it embodies an important idea: risk means something that 'becomes real' over time. Whether we think it will become real sooner or later, or indeed never, is a matter of mediation: scientific, economic, political or popular. We rely on experts to mediate the risks we face on a day-to-day basis. We rely on expert-systems to determine risk levels. And the

Department of Homeland Security relies on its own expertise whenever it issues its 'risk alerts'.

None of this reassures the average citizen, though the public distrust of experts runs much deeper than the suspicion that they may not know all that much. In the 1980s, 90 per cent of mutual fund managers underperformed. In the Wilshire 500 Index, a relatively low bar, the number for bond fund managers was similar (Surowiecki 2005:33). In other words, expertise and accuracy are unrelated. Studies have found experts' judgements to be neither consistent with the judgement of others, nor internally consistent with their own. Experts are just as likely to disagree as they are to agree. One study found that the internal consistency of medical pathologists' judgements was just 50 per cent, meaning that a pathologist presented with the same evidence would, half of the time, offer a different opinion. Despite this record, experts are given to over-estimating the likelihood they are right. A study found this was true of 70 per cent of foreign exchange traders. In other words, adds Surowiecki, it is not just that they did not have any idea that they were wrong. They also did not have much of an idea how wrong they were (Surowiecki 2005:34).

To add to the problem, experts are always disagreeing with each other. Biogenetics, engineering and nuclear power, indeed all the Big Science issues, bring experts into conflict with each other in public debates more than ever before. Experts win government contracts and business consultancies by challenging other experts on contract to other government agencies or NGOs. Knowledge has become corrigible. All experts, by definition, are specialists, some of whom, in the words of Giddens, are intent on trying to 'colonize a personal future' (i.e. to make their names and with it their fortunes) (Beck 1997:88). Many experts (to quote Jan Myrdal) have become the 'whores of reason' – expertise itself has become a commodity to be bought and sold like everything else.

This is even true of knowledge for the public good, and to return to my point of departure it is even true, surprisingly, of medicine. It is not only the pharmaceutical companies that make money out of curing human distress. Today, universities are also trying to maximize profits by conducting more and more commercial work themselves, thus making their products more valuable to them when they are fully licensed. If they think they have a new drug they will do the FDA testing themselves. Scientists who once felt a humanitarian calling are now often businessmen concerned with the same logic of profit and loss as any other business venture.

Add to this, expertise is becoming increasingly transient or ephemeral. Experts are proved wrong in shorter and shorter time-frames, as knowledge about the side-effects and consequences of their recommended options bring them into question. Knowledge is on the move all the time. It is accumulating at a frightening rate. Sometimes it confirms the experts in their opinions, but it can also challenge their professional credibility. Many forms of knowledge, of course, are still secure, writes Giddens, 'the shifting sand is leavened with a measure of concrete.' But all knowledge is open to question, and a puzzling diversity of rival claims is to be found in those 'moving' areas of knowledge such as intelligence assessments, those that involve the 'unknown unknowns' to which Rumsfeld famously referred (Beck 1997:88).

The Precautionary Principle

> What we establish mathematically is 'objective fact' only in small part; in larger part it is a survey of possibilities. (Werner Heisenberg, *Dialectica*, 1948)

Speculation about the unknown is an exercise of the imagination. Let us return to Donald Rumsfeld's unknown unknowns: 'the ones we don't know we don't know' has entered the language. His reflections were treated with derision by sections of the press, yet the formulation, however infelicitous semantically, has been widely employed by environmentalists since the 1980s without inviting much criticism.

Given that we really are confronted by the unknowable, it is not especially surprising that we are always wanting to take precautions. We do so in everyday life so why not in international relations? The precautionary principle was adopted in international environment law in 1992 on the grounds that 'the absence of scientific proof of cause–effect relationship . . . should not be used to justify inaction.' The risk society was born from the environmental movement in the 1970s, when for the first time states publicly admitted that there were hazards in the use of any technology, however beneficial. Pollution, for example, is the price we pay for progress. Even so, pollution levels can be reduced.

The European Environmental Agency adopted the precautionary principle in January 2002, insisting that disasters could only be forestalled if actions were taken before there was strong proof of harm (Furedi 2008:71). The US may not have signed up to the Kyoto Accord, not so much because of the science but because of the costs, but it is a risk society too. The White House Declaration on Environment and Trade in 1999 stated that precaution was 'an essential element' in US regulatory policy. And the Bush administration has merely extended precautionary principle thinking into international security, especially the principle of regime change.

Anticipatory self-defence was its official legal justification for attacking Afghanistan in 2001. The political reshaping of societies most at risk of fostering terrorism is deemed by some to be a sensible precautionary measure.

In justifying the invasion of Iraq the President invoked the principle, though not by name. For the invasion was justified by reference to uncertainty: 'If we wait for threats to fully materialize, we will have waited too long.' He also added, 'I believe it is essential that when we see a threat we deal with those threats before they become imminent' (Sunstein 2005:4). This way of thinking is very much central to the philosophy underpinning environmentalism: that action is the only sensible course in the face of reasonable doubt.

'Absence of evidence is not evidence of absence' was Rumsfeld's famous response in the run-up to the war whenever he was asked by reporters what proof he had that Saddam was about to obtain nuclear weapons. The Americans insisted that they could not wait for conclusive evidence of his WMD programme. They aspired to translate their ignorance into impatience. And impatience produced a logic of its own: it translated ignorance into knowledge – in this case knowledge that waiting was no longer an acceptable option because knowing would come too late, if at all. Stated rather reductively, if we wait too long for conclusive scientific evidence of global warming, it will be far too late to act.

One often hears the argument, of course, that the Europeans are far more risk-averse than the Americans; that they are far more inclined to take precautions, though less willing to hazard all when it comes to the management of security. It is often added that they are far more sensitive to environmental issues. Such claims are certainly plausible in the light of the Bush administration's unwillingness to sign up to the Kyoto Accord or to address the risks of GM food. Beck even calls the US a 'surveillance state' to distinguish it from Europe which is far more interested in addressing the causes of terrorism and not just terror itself. But differences in the approach of the US and Europe actually throw light on the protean nature of risks themselves. They illustrate that risk management is highly *subjective*.

Risks are real but they are also social constructions in so far (and perhaps only in so far) as the categories we use to perceive them are distinctive (Lewens 2007:135). In thinking about a risk we apply certain heuristics, or rules of thumb. One is the 'availability' heuristic. We are inclined to compare one risk with another which throws it into perspective, and perhaps makes it less dangerous or time-sensitive. Salience is important too, the immediacy of an event in the imagination, for not every risk is at the forefront of our minds. And then there is the probability heuristic, or what

J. S. Mill called, 'learning by experience the tendencies of experience'. Have we experienced the risk before, or is it beyond the range of our historical experience? Is it off our mental map? And that is the point: experiences differ.

What one nation considers 'probable' as opposed to 'possible', let alone 'likely', will be informed by its own history. The events of 9/11 were bound to have much greater impact on the US than they did in Europe, not only because the attack involved two American cities. They immediately conjured up another 'stealth' attack on the US in 1941, which had provoked a long and costly war. And in trying to explain the significance of 9/11, the Bush administration chose to invoke the Cold War as a call to arms. Not only is the analogy more evocative for Americans than it is for Europeans, it is possibly more immediate because of the Cold War tropes that were always more real in the US than in Europe even at the height of the Cold War: the fear of subversion, the popularity of conspiracy theories and the formation of the infamous Un-American Activities Committee which sought to root out and punish subversive thoughts as well as actions.

For this reason the precautionary principle was bound to be highly divisive. The precautions which one person may think reasonable may appear unreasonable to others. The problem lies in ourselves, not in the world we are trying to analyse. We labour under a series of cognitive limitations and biases that hinder our ability to anticipate the unexpected. One is the confirmation bias: our tendency to look for evidence that confirms our pre-existing ideas and to ignore conflicting evidence, if of course it exists. Another is what Daniel Kahneman calls the 'narrative fallacy' – our preference for stories over truth and our propensity to compress a series of unconnected events into a single narrative. It is the narratives we construct that give rise to fear (Nuttall 2007:70).

The precautionary approach, in short, is not irrational but it is strategically incoherent. It purports to be a universal principle but it isn't really. Its incoherence stems from the fact that both action and inaction give rise to different risks, and hence the principle bans what it simultaneously mandates. At least as regards the environment, there is general agreement that carbon emissions need to be reduced, but little agreement on how we should live our lives differently so that we might become more eco-friendly. Securing ourselves against others presents us with a very different set of challenges. By definition the precautionary principle cannot be a unifying principle for going to war; it cannot unite the risk communities that alliances like NATO are in the process of becoming.

Conclusion

What I have attempted to show in this chapter is that the risk age has produced a much more explicit, long-term and risk-based approach to security
analysis which, unfortunately, has not made us feel any more secure.
Insecurity inheres in the age itself; all we can do is mitigate it by mediating
risks through the stories we tell ourselves and using force – in the case of
war or military intervention – to make the stories more plausible. The
problem is compounded by the fact that while immigration and disease,
like climate change and other issues, raise many hard security problems
they have no hard security solutions – indeed the harder the solutions the
worse the problem. We know so little. And even the worst-case scenarios
on which we often act depend on so many complex variables that they
render us particularly uncertain of what to do next.

Managing the risks of managing WMD programmes by using force (dis-
arming Iraq or Iran) requires an assessment of the cost of intervening pre-
emptively against those of not intervening in time; they also demand an
assessment of the cost of provoking the regime in question into retaliating
on other fronts (terrorism) which may further undermine confidence in a
government's judgement at home. Doing too little and doing too much can
both prove equally fatal.

While the risks of provoking a conflict by acting early can be assessed and
even measured they can never be known for certain – and experts will never
agree amongst themselves on final outcomes. There is a limit to the predictive ability of any analytical method; conflict and crisis feed off each
other. That much has always been known. What is new is that we know
much more. Any risk-mapping of the type that allows us to categorize
countries by the extent of the risk they pose – to identify them as 'rogue
states' or 'states of concern' – is unlikely to tell us what to do, for it is we
ourselves (or so we have begun to suspect) that may pose the greatest threat
if we get the calculations wrong, or if we intervene too early, or subsequently find that we need not have intervened at all. Consequence
management has become the demand of the hour.

4

Consequence Management

At the beginning of Shakespeare's *Henry VI Part 1* a messenger reports on the divisions among the English leaders that have resulted in the loss of Henry V's French conquests.

> One would have ling'ring wars, with little cost;
> Another would fly swift, but wanteth wings;
> A third thinks, without expense at all,
> By guileful fair words peace may be obtained.

In the run-up to the Iraq war the Bush administration faced a similar choice: 'invasion lite', or Shock and Awe, or the option of leaving it to the UN. As usual, Shakespeare's language is faithful to the real debates of high-level political discussion, however stylized it might be in this early play which probably was only partly written by Shakespeare himself. But with his 'unerring relevance' the playwright sets out the problem of choice that strategists face in many wars. Every decision is fraught with consequences and we are often as paralysed by the thought of those consequences as we are by the thought of the act itself (Nuttall 2007:29).

Some members of the Bush administration believed that they risked little in 2003 in invading Iraq; they expected that a weak regime would fall quickly and that they would be welcomed as liberators (as the American army had last been in Grenada in 1983). But it is also clear from the most recent literature to have emerged about the actual decision-making process that many in the military knew the risks from the first: the risk of not going through the UN; the risk of going in with light infantry, in the expectation of 'shocking and awing' the Iraqis into surrender; and the risk of finding themselves involved in a long-drawn-out counter-insurgency struggle.

The Americans were lucky in the conventional phase of the war. Iraq was so battle-weary as a result of twelve years of sanctions that the outcome was never really in doubt. Its army had no new weapons, or even spare parts for the old; its equipment suffered from indifferent maintenance, its soldiers from indifferent training. Even the suicide units which the Americans encountered in the dash to Baghdad forfeited the safety of urban terrain by engaging in head-on offensives which were ruinously costly in terms of lives. But it was at that point that the Coalition's luck ran out; almost within days of the fall of Baghdad the first fighting in the next phase of the conflict began as some experts had predicted. Iraq as a state might have been defeated, but as a society it proved stubbornly difficult to subdue.

In the risk age, uncertainties about the future tend to proliferate and intensify our preoccupation with 'aftermaths'. What seems to have come to an end is not war but the dialectic by which its progress has been articulated from time immemorial, that of 'before' and 'after'. For if the complexity of the world has made it increasingly difficult for states to go to war against each other, it has made it easier for 'wars' to degenerate into 'warfare', Hobbes's 'war of all against all'. 'Stuff happens,' remarked Rumsfeld of the looting that broke out shortly after the Americans entered Baghdad. It used to be that wars began with a declaration of intent and ended with a peace treaty. However sanguinary as episodes, wars did seem to end allowing for a period of grace in which victor and defeated could take stock. Now we seem to be permanently stuck in the 'after' mode, incapable of escaping from the present's unending rut. Nothing ends in a satisfying conclusion; it goes on and on, violently and frustratingly, and appears destined to do so for years to come. A major *structural change* would seem to have taken place in the rhythm of history itself.

I have quoted Shakespeare once, so let me do so again, this time from another of the history plays. In *Henry IV, Part 1* there is a good observation by the (anti)hero, Hotspur.

> Were it good
> To set the exact wealth of all our states
> All at one cast? To set so rich a main
> On the nice hazard of one doubtful hour?

Here, 'hazard' means both a doubtful outcome of battle and the game of dice so named, and 'exact' has the same sense as 'total' (all our wealth), but also of treasure exacted at cost from the conduct of wars. A 'main' is a winning throw by the banker at dice (and so a loss to the gambler). The passage captures one of the main risks in hazarding all in battle. It is not that we may lose, it is that we may win — and only then find out that not all conflicts are determined by battlefield encounters. Frequently they are determined off it.

The reason is to be found in another passage from the Shakespeare canon, this time from a speech by Macbeth, debating the wisdom of killing Duncan. It is one of the most famous passages in the play.

If it were done, when 'tis done, then 'twere well
It were done quickly. If th'assassination
Could trammel up the consequence, and catch
With his surcease, success; that but this blow
Might be the be-all and the end-all – here,
But here, upon this bank and shoal of time,
We'd jump the life to come.

The passage translates itself from the seventeenth-century to the twenty-first-century mind with relative ease because we find our own circumstances contained within it. It might even have been penned with us in mind. It is also a meditation on the time which inheres in every risk taken. For if Duncan's murder could prevent all that follows it, ruminates Macbeth, indeed if the king's death could put an end not only to him but to all that may follow his murder, then at this stationary moment in time he would 'jump the life to come' (i.e. he would risk the consequences in another life, including damnation). But as the Shakespearian scholar Frank Kermode adds, the key words in the passage are 'surcease, success', as well as 'be-all' and 'end-all', two terms that have passed into the common language. For what Macbeth is asking is impossible; if only time could be made to stop at the desired moment of the future, all might be hazarded with confidence (Kermode 2001:208).

Unfortunately, 'to be' and 'to end' contradict each other. The act of murder cannot be an end. Nothing in time, in that sense, can ever be said to be 'done'. Surcease does not imply the end of success (i.e. to be read here as succession – what follows from the deed). No act is without 'success' in that sense. Risk inheres in 'succession'. It is impossible to 'trammel up the consequence' of any act. Most of Shakespeare's heroes know this very well. They are fully aware that acts have consequences, even though some remain invisible for some time. Macbeth's dilemma is that he wishes for acts without consequences – the only real impossibility.

In war the problem is not primarily one of political judgement, though the fallibility of human understanding and the limits to human knowledge will always cast a permanent shadow over what the Pentagon calls 'decision dominance', the speed with which, on the basis of knowledge, the military can arrive at a decision (e.g. what to target) (Rasmussen 2007:122). The problem is much more profound. It inheres in complexity. In a networked world it is almost impossible to anticipate and therefore insure against all the effects of going to war. As a result we have become excessively preoccupied with the consequences of our own actions, the side-effects of our initiatives. Unpredictability is a product of every conflict but it has taken on an extra charge in the risk age because it is we ourselves that may be most responsible for the unfavourable outcome.

Cascading Effects

The word 'cause' is an altar to an unknown God (William James)

Now, all this has been known in war from time immemorial. But the risk age reinforces it by making the future even more uncertain. The modern age encourages us to think that we make the future ourselves: that belief after all is what makes us modern. We are not fatalistic about what lies ahead, and even less inclined to blame providence or God for events on the horizon. But the post-modern sensibility is somewhat different: we also know that the future makes us, for if we are anxious to anticipate consequences so much, we may be excessively cautious about the future we try to fashion, we may even be more modest in our strategic aims, especially if we suspect that linearity (cause and effect) is itself something of a historical construction; that just as 'before' and 'after' is a historical concept (or one we told ourselves was more rigid than it was precisely because we made our own history), predictability is a *historical* concept too. Like so many other 'eternal' values, has it passed its sell-by-date?

Nothing historians tell us is new, and one reason for that is that we can find practically anything in the past if we know what to look for – if we look for events that resonate with us more than they did with their own age. Take a new concept that we certainly take seriously – the cascading effect. We find it expressed especially graphically in Stendhal's novel *The Charterhouse of Parma* (1839), where the hero, Fabrice, is discovered at the Battle of Waterloo attaching himself to a series of leading figures in a vain attempt to see the overall pattern of the battle as it unfolds. The result is chaos:

> The sun was already very low and it was at the point of setting when the escort coming out of a sunken road mounted a little slope three or four feet high to enter a ploughed field. Fabrice heard a curious little sound quite close to him. He turned his head: four men had fallen off their horses; the general himself had been thrown off his horse but he was getting up again covered in blood. . . .
>
> The sergeant came up to Fabrice. At that moment our hero heard someone behind him say quite close to his ear: 'This is the only one that can still gallop.' He felt himself seized by the feet . . . he was lifted over his horse's tail, and then let slip to the ground where he landed in a sitting position.

The aide de camp took Fabrice's horse by the bridle; the general mounted and rode off at a gallop; he was quickly followed by the six survivors of the escort. Fabrice got to his feet in a furious rage and began to run after them shouting 'Laidi! Laidi!' (Thieves! Thieves!) It was rather comical to be running after thieves in the middle of a battlefield.

The passage, writes Paul Hamilton, sets out the chaotic and confusing picture that faces most soldiers on the field of battle. Fabrice ends up grotesquely out of place in a historical arena, proclaiming his own personal loss, his own 'curious little sound' (Hamilton 1996:16). Historians (*Pace* Tolstoy who claimed to have learnt all that he knew of war from Stendhal's description of Waterloo) have to make sense of events, but they run a serious risk whenever they try to do so. In downplaying the contingency of events they may mislead the public into thinking that a particular outcome was inevitable. Hence the recent interest in counter-factual history which attempts to tackle head on the pitfall of hindsight bias. As numerous psychological studies have shown, hindsight tends to distort human retrospection by portraying outcomes *ex post* as having been much more probable than they actually appeared *a priori*. We are strongly encouraged to rationalize events whenever we look back; the study of history almost demands that we devise chains of causation that were generally invisible to those who took part in the events that we try to make sense of with 20:20 hindsight.

The point Stendhal was making – and it is an important one – is that we must not mistake correlation for causation; we must not automatically assume that because one event takes place it must be the cause of another. And this is a challenge. We want events to have causes and in ascertaining them to establish a pattern sufficiently coherent to serve as a guide to action. Everyday life is grounded in causation. Karl Popper called causality 'a metaphysical hypostalization of a well justified methodological rule' (Carr 1972:94), which is merely a philosopher's way of saying that the idea that everything has a cause is a condition of understanding what is going on around us.

In the modern age, cause and effect ruled supreme. Our age, by contrast, is increasingly non-linear in the sense that we recognize that the future is as unpredictable as forecasting the weather. Meteorologists promise us that their forecasts are accurate, but concede that their accuracy cannot be guaranteed beyond a few days. It is still possible to offer yearly predictions, but it is never going to be possible to know with any certainty whether those predictions will be borne out on the day. Causality, in a word, is only partial. We can partially model, predict and control events; we can even make decisions according to a probability checklist. But a cause may not lead to an effect, and not every effect will have a discernible cause. Behaviour *emerges* like life. Indeed, life itself has been described as an 'emergent property' which arises when certain physio-chemical systems interact in certain unpredictable ways.

If we return to the example of the Big Bang to which I referred in chapter 2, we can add that all complex systems – whether the universe or human societies – exhibit elements of emergence over time. In other words, single-cell organisms had their potential emergence built into them from the beginning. They could and did lead to life as we know it today, but there were other possibilities. Run the tape again and you might well get a different outcome.

What everything needs is a 'gateway' event to get it started. The Big Bang was the most significant gateway event of all but every major historical episode, whether a war or a riot, can spark off a series of events that cascade towards unknown destinations, resulting in a wide repertory of behaviour. When the riots exploded in 2005 in the *banlieues* (the housing-estate cities on the outskirts of Paris) they were explained away as a protest by young, unemployed Muslims. At the height of the disturbances 700 cars were being torched every night. By the time the riots had petered out, they had developed a life of their own. Only 39 per cent of the rioters, according to the French government's final analysis, were Muslims; the rest were young white males who emulated the behaviour they saw on their TV screens every night (*The Times*, 7 March 2007). Television encourages exhibitionism. Activists often seek to outdo each other in violence. It is the way by which they win a reputation.

Some behaviour in other words *emerges* – it has no necessary rationale in terms of intent. Some social protests are like a computer virus which carry the instruction 'copy me', which is directed to a computer in its own language and is entirely invisible to the computer's user. What makes viruses so tenacious is that they have no purpose other than their own replication. They tend to travel light (without baggage quite literally) being nothing more than an information packet. They can even mutate in ways that cannot be predicted in advance especially if their programmers use evolutionary algorithms to help them to explore the adaptive landscape which they penetrate. Viruses can evolve, in other words, independent of their programmers; they can easily take on a life of their own (Dennett 2006:343).

What encourages events to cascade is the networks that characterize our world and make it so infinitely complex. For they produce what Howard

Rheingold calls 'smart mobs' – waves of violence made up of many individuals connected by text messaging. The rioters who almost derailed the World Trade Organization (WTO) meeting in Seattle in 1999 used 'swarming tactics', mobile phones, websites, laptops and hand-held computers. A year later thousands of citizens in the UK protesting against the sudden rise in petrol prices, used CB radios in taxicabs, email from laptop PCs and mobile phones to block fuel deliveries at selected service stations. And in the same year a violent political demonstration in Toronto was chronicled by a group of roving reporters who produced webcast digital videos of everything they saw. All these generated a critical mass which emerged from loosely linked networks (see Tilly 2005:156).

These spontaneous demonstrations had a political purpose, of course, even if the demonstrators themselves did not always share any particular ideology or advance a political programme. Today's activists pose a challenge to the state precisely because networked social action has no necessary cause, programme or even purpose. For that reason writers such as Alain Badiou consider it is non-political (a non-event), more carnival than demonstration. The demonstration was one of the features of the twentieth century in which the collective body was able to express its fraternity, whether in trade union demonstrations or peace marches or student protests during the Vietnam War. It legitimized collective action and it was always intended to make a difference (Badiou 2007:106–8). Today, we have to entertain the disturbing thought that causation as traditionally understood may not always be at work. In contemporary activism, ideas and behaviour can still spread vertically by descent from leaders but it may also spread horizontally by infection. Virtual revolutionary action is networked in a way revolutionary action traditionally wasn't. This would seem to have been the case in Iraq with the insurgency that broke out soon after the American army entered Baghdad.

The Dangers of Speed

the entire western world has lost those instincts out of which institutions grow . . . one lives for today, one lives very fast – one lives very irresponsibly: it is precisely this which one calls freedom. (Nietzsche, *Twilight of the Idols*, p. 90)

Cascading effects have made war more complex than ever. We have to entertain the possibility, as Nietzsche cautioned all those years ago, that we ourselves might stimulate them through our preoccupation with speed. Does our liquid world promote the process: is speed the problem, not the solution?

This is a difficult question to raise in the military because of what we have told ourselves for so long. As Clausewitz tells us, unlike the mechanical arts we direct force at an animate object that will react to a will opposed to its own. This reaction locks both wills into a feedback loop, and a positive feedback loop can produce runaway processes – Clausewitz's tendency for war to become absolute. The very nature of interaction is bound to make it unpredictable. 'The fundamentally complex and interactive nature of war generates uncertainty,' insists the US Marine Corps (1996). 'Uncertainty is not merely an existing environmental condition; it is a natural *by-product* of war' (US Marine Corps 1996:27). The italics are mine, for of course we hold all wars to be unpredictable in their outcome; the stronger side does not always prevail. But we now have to raise another question: does speed produce more uncertainty in a complex and interconnected world, and does it do so in the form of cascading effects?

The problem is compounded by the fact that for some time now there have been siren voices in the US military downplaying the role of chance and contingency, those chaotic elements which have been traditionally associated with war, by hyping up the value of speed. The US more than any other country has relied on the digital revolution to pioneer a new form of warfare in which speed is everything. It considers itself to be the chief beneficiary of Moore's Law (the observation that computer price/performance doubles every eighteen months). Bits can be copied and transmitted at almost no cost, in the process removing two of the main scarcity functions of traditional economics: the marginal costs of manufacturing and distribution. Similar abundance laws are at play in storage and bandwidth, and virtually everything else digital.

Since I have quoted Shakespeare, let me invoke him again to illustrate this contention. Everything Shakespeare wrote in a lifetime can be recorded with about 70 millon bits. If we employ the term 'shakespeare' as a measurement, like a gallon, one which refers to units of 70 millon bits each, then we can see what is involved in terms of data transmission. A laser beam can transmit 500 'shakespeares' per second over today's optic fibres. This capacity is extraordinary, but wavelength division multiplexing enables us to transmit more; the bandwidth of a fibre can be divided into many separate wavelengths and there is a separate laser beam for each. Thus 13,000 'shakespeares' per second can be sent over one very thin fibre, and some fibres can carry about a hundred laser beams simultaneously, each carrying tens of billions of bits per second (Martin 2006:66).

It is this revolution in the transmission of information which enables an army to advance further and faster than in the past very largely because it allows it to lift the 'fog of war'. It enables the military, in the words of one leading military thinker, to 'peer into tomorrow' (Leonhard 1999:130). In that sense, situational awareness in war may be more revolutionary than the introduction of gunpowder or even the internal combustion engine, for it has resulted in a tenfold increase in the speed of information-processing.

But it is at this point that we have to ask whether there is any real value in speed if it merely amplifies the unintended consequences of one's own actions. In many ways there is, in so far as it makes it unnecessary to pursue an attritional way of warfare – killing the enemy with battlefield force faster than the enemy can kill you. Situational awareness allows for precision targeting and the use of discriminate force. But leaping in the dark is not necessarily leaping into the future, let alone 'peering into tomorrow'.

When skating over thin ice, claimed Emerson, our only safety is in speed. In World War II both Germany and Japan found themselves skating over very thin ice indeed; the Japanese knew it when they went to war; the Germans found it out only later. Today, ironically, the US seems to be following suit. It took eighty-one days to force the Serbian army to evacuate Kosovo; two months to take out the Taliban government; and only three weeks to topple the Ba'athist regime in Iraq. Unfortunately, speed is often counter-productive. It is intended to undermine enemy morale as it did in the case of France in 1940. The same was true of Shock and Awe in 2003 which showed how much and how fast the US had taken war into the twenty-first century in one area, at least – the kill chain. In 1991 Desert Storm had started with a long-drawn-out bombing campaign and then a ground assault. In 2003 soldiers on the ground were able to provide bombers flying overhead with the co-ordinates for their bombs. The effect was devastating. In 1991 it had taken days of paper-pushing to assign a plane a target to hit. During Operation Iraqi Freedom it took under ten minutes. But for all that, the Americans found that they had only changed the dynamics of a networked-enabled process – killing. They had not changed the logic of war, even the network-centric 'upgrade' which is not about killing, but turning a tactical success on a battlefield into a decisive strategic result.

Unwisely, in Iraq the US traded mass for speed, not merely to seize and hold the initiative but to prevent its enemies from adapting to its own tactics. It also went in light to retain public support at home, to evade extensive political discussion of the conflict. Against the Iraqi Republican Guard small, fast-moving ground forces with massive stand-off firepower succeeded beyond expectation. Against the insurgents after 2004 the decision to trade speed for mass proved to have been downright foolish.

Warfare in the risk age does indeed centre around networks but the most important networks are social, in the case of Iraq linking clans and tribes, not just drones and tanks and special force units. Too little emphasis was placed in the early days of the campaign on securing key urban areas and government buildings which created security gaps filled by fire-fights and ambushes and extensive looting. The excessive emphasis on force protection within the US military (a feature of the risk age) diluted the security enforcement mission for the defeated society. Winning hearts and minds was often ignored. 'When we do operations, like when we do patrols,' observed one company commander, 'they are organised from combat patrols, they move like combat patrols and they have objectives like combat patrols. So, we really didn't change anything, we just can't shoot everybody' (Graff 2004:66–7). Another telling observation emerged from the *Army Lessons Learned Reports* from December 2003. It was found that the greatest intelligence assets were soldiers on foot patrol who were able to establish a 'ground truth' which often conflicted with the analysis of the commanders behind the lines. But the number of patrols was limited by the number of vehicles available in the task force. Force protection clearly took priority over effectiveness in tactical behaviour. As Anthony Cordesman remarked in his own analysis of what had gone wrong, troops were trained only to the point of dealing with a symmetrical war; they were not trained to deal with looting or to distinguish hostile and non-violent civilians from insurgents. In his own words, they were not trained to deal with *the consequences of victory* (Cordesman 2003:499).

It is a telling conclusion. The risk age may be conceivable as the compression of time, and history may have become the story of acceleration, but we must recognize that speed takes no account of complexity, which is why the direction in which the US military is taking war has proved so counter-productive. Virilio calls speed a 'negative horizon'. It produces sensorial privation because it obscures our perception of the world and blinds us to the consequences of our acts (Virilio 1986). Speed also deprives us of contact, or direct experience of the enemy, which is usually fatal when a war does not end in a formal cessation of hostilities. Speed is not a phenomenon in itself; it is a relationship in this case between ourselves and war. There is no reality outside this relativity. The reality of information about the enemy is contained entirely in the speed of its dissemination, and information is only ever the designation of the state that a phenomenon assumes at a given moment. In other words, its 'relief' which is why we talk of 'high definition; and 'high resolution' in relation to two phenomena: sound and the image (Virilio 1995:140).

In Iraq the US military soon found that tactical success gave it no 'high resolution' politically because it knew so little about the enemy or how it might react to its initial defeat. 'Speed kills,' writes General Franks in his memoirs. Franks had been a one-star general in Desert Storm, a campaign that ended in an inconclusive result. Next time new technologies would enable US forces to go in even faster, he concluded, and so indeed they did under his command. 'The victory in Desert Storm', he wrote, 'proved that speed has a mass of its own' (Strachan 2007:5). But Operation Iraqi Freedom proved even more inconclusive. Looking back, even George Bush lamented that the US had won too quickly. 'Had we to do it over again we would look at the consequences of *catastrophic success* – being so success-ful, so fast, that an enemy that should have surrendered or been done in, escaped to fight another day' (Buley 2007:123). Or as General Myers asserted, its victory in 2003 proved too 'elegant'. It allowed the Iraqi units to melt away, to fight on later under another flag. With hindsight, he told the Senate Armed Services Committee, 'we were probably *too gracious* in our victory' (Buley 2007:123).

The choice of words is striking. What both men meant is that a society is more likely to be reconciled to defeat after it has put up a fight (as Clausewitz tells us, a country only prevails in war when the enemy is ready to admit defeat for whatever reason). Defeat may even come as a welcome release, as it probably did for many Germans in 1945. Moreover, as long as a country has not disgraced itself, there is no shame in surrender. If an army collapses in three weeks or three months, demoralization may corrode the national soul. This may well have been the case in Iraq in the case of many of the young men who joined the insurgency, those who were referred to by the US military as 'POIs', an acronym for 'Pissed Off Iraqis'.

Honour must sometimes be won back. A crushing tactical victory on the battlefield which provokes an insurgency is no success at all. We now con-front a new paradox of war: you may arrive at your destination faster than ever, but at that point the problems begin. To quote Shakespeare for the last time, war can make even the victors 'the fools of time' (Sonnet 124). In Elizabethan English 'fools' can mean 'victims'.

Speed implies ease of movement. This is why it is a mark of our 'liquid times'. But when things are made easy our engagement with the task in hand usually becomes superficial. Speed is inherently paradoxical. It is meant to minimize risks: the risk of forfeiting public support at home if the campaign appears to be slowing down; or the risk of putting troops at risk longer than necessary. 'Von Clausewitz tells us that the longer a war lasts the sooner the enemy will learn what to do,' declares an officer in Robert

Redford's film *Lions for Lambs* (2008). But speed often poses a new set of risks: it increases the chances of failure.

In Iraq every obstacle to speed (such as the *Fedda'yeen* fighters, who appeared unexpectedly as the US Army advanced towards Baghdad) was seen as a temporary 'obstacle', to be bypassed or pushed aside as the army pressed on. And that is the point. Obstacles do not always go away; they are merely sidelined for the moment and are likely to reappear at unexpected moments later on. The obstacles we meet may, in fact, be the limits to military operations – the warning signs not to transgress the limits any further. Yet we tend to redefine them as problems which can be solved, if necessary later on. We have neither the time nor the urge, adds Bauman, to reflect on the darkness at the end of the tunnel. We tend to lock the stable door after the horse has bolted. Regrettably, in our race to get to the future, there is a constantly growing number of stable doors demanding to be locked. At the stage at which we have arrived historically – in these, our liquid times – a large part of daily progress 'consists of repairing the direct or collateral damage done by past and current efforts to speed it up' (Bauman 2007:116).

Unfortunately, speed often has no strategic significance and it takes no account of history. We can dispense with everything we have learnt in the classroom, of course, and gain all the advantages of travelling light. But efficiency in such cases is likely to be bought at the cost of emptiness – our victories may prove hollow. We may eventually be forced to recognize that tactical successes, however brilliant and admired by professionals as such, are not always translated into the political outcomes that matter.

Effects-based Operations

The fall-out of speed also takes another form: it can promote errors of judgement which may encourage young men to join an insurgency. Hence the need for restraint, or greater civility, in warfare. As Robert Kaplan reminds us,

> Because the battles in a counter-insurgency are small-scale and often clandestine, the story line is rarely obvious. [Interpretation] becomes a matter of perception, and victory is awarded to those who weave the most compelling narrative. Truly in the world of post-modern 21st century conflict civilian public-affairs officers must become war fighters by another name. (Evans 2007:29)

All wars involve the spinning of stories. The stories we tell ourselves and others change over time. In an age of risk we are obliged to recognize that the way war is conducted conveys a 'meaning' that is no less important than war itself. 'The medium is the message,' wrote Marshall McLuhan when he wanted to demonstrate how suspect the message was. Risk societies now acknowledge that the medium itself is no less suspect in the eyes of the rest of the world. The result has been to make it more 'humane'; it is part of the promise of what Western militaries call 'effects-based operations'.

Humanity is not something that has only recently been 'discovered'. Since the early twentieth century Western societies have attempted to remove some of the grosser forms of cruelty from the public space. But until recently it has been difficult to do this with war. Back in 1916, when the military in Germany were arguing for an unrestricted submarine campaign against Britain, they tended to dismiss civilian objections as *Humanitatsdusehei*, or mere 'humanitarian babbling' (Stone 2007:99). In fact, the debate whether or not to press ahead with unrestricted submarine attacks on Allied shipping went far beyond humanitarianism; it involved a discussion about the political consequences of being *seen* to be more inhumane than the enemy one was fighting.

The German Chancellor Bethmann-Hollweg was acutely sensitive to the costs of political misjudgement. He had been pessimistic about the war from the outset. In the summer of 1914 he told his son there was no point in planting elm trees along the drive of the family estate in East Prussia because only the Russians would profit. In the event they did not occupy the estate for another thirty years but when they did they stayed for fifty (Stone 2007:16). Likewise, he resisted the generals' demands for unrestricted submarine warfare against Britain, for fear that it would bring the US into the war. On both counts Clausewitz would have cautioned restraint. The principal object of the military art, he tells us, 'is to prevent the trembling balance from suddenly turning to our disadvantage and the half war from changing into a complete one' (Clausewitz 1982:401). Ultimately, both the decision to go to war and the decision to adopt unrestricted submarine warfare three years later represented a failure of political leadership for which Bethmann-Hollweg himself must be held partly responsible. It is the responsibility of politicians to foresee the consequences of their own acts; those like the Chancellor who did simply did not fight hard enough to be heard.

And the consequences of the submarine campaign were indeed devastating. Apart from the humanitarian concerns about drowning innocent passengers on ships like the *Lusitania* which had been torpedoed two years earlier – an egregious crime about which, alone among the German leadership, the Kaiser seems to have had misgivings (he called it a 'frightful thought') – it meant breaking international law (no small matter when the President of the US was a moralist like Woodrow Wilson). Wilson initially confined himself to breaking off diplomatic relations in the hope that this would bring Germany to its senses. The sinking of seven American merchant ships finally obliged him to summon Congress, which in early April 1917 approved a declaration of war. When it finally came, recruitment posters urged: 'Remember the *Lusitania*' (Updike 2007:471).

In a risk age, we are always enjoined to anticipate the negative effects of our decisions; we are urged all the time to bring the future into a calculative relation to the present. And this was also the dynamic of the U-Boat debate in 1916–17 – with a critical difference. The Germans externalized the risks, such as the response of neutral countries to putting their own shipping in danger by continuing to trade with the UK and, of course, the risk that the US would be bounced into war by public opinion. Today we *internalize* risks in the form of consequence management. And assessing the implications is made more difficult still by the multiplicity of actors we have to take into account. For the ones that count most are no longer always states.

The difference today is not that we have become more humane than the German High Command in 1917. The difference is not even the fact that the risks the High Command chose to incur were measurable in a way that many of the risks we run today are not. The real difference is that the costs of incurring them have become unacceptably high. We have become the *consumers*, not the *producers*, of risk and we have greater difficulty than ever in legitimizing the risks we ask others to take (including our own citizens, or fellow members of the alliances or coalitions of the willing to which we belong by virtue of the fact that they are implicated in every decision taken). No wonder the politicians feel under pressure, damned if they don't act, damned if they do.

Consequence management (as the internalization of risk) was clearly in evidence in Kosovo in 1999. Precision air strikes enabled the West to coerce the Serbian government without inflicting much direct damage on the population, although collateral damage could not be eliminated altogether. Over the course of seventy-eight days, allied aircraft carried out an estimated 37,000 bombing sorties. The initial targets were the Serbian forces in Kosovo, but as it failed to make any progress, NATO was forced to bomb economic and even civil targets in Serbia itself. Eventually 144 industrial plants were targeted. The most important was the Serbian power grid. Some of the bombs contained carbon fire spools which instead of destroying the generators themselves merely short-circuited the transformer yards, putting out the lights in the major cities for anywhere between eight and twenty-four hours. As soon as the Serbs managed to get the power working again, more air strikes would be carried out using non-lethal carbon fire bombs (Ignatieff 2001:107). Other non-lethal measures included electro-magnetic pulse and radio waves which were critical in disabling Serbia's air defence's electronic systems.

NATO was fortunate in its adversary. Serbia was not a totalitarian state; it was run by a comparatively weak authoritarian regime. Milosevic relied on a clientship network that had to be constantly rewarded. Once the West began targeting his clients, freezing their bank accounts in Western Europe, and preventing them from travelling abroad, as well as bombing their casinos and hotel chains in the last week or so of the bombing, they put pressure on Milosevic to give in. Few of his financial backers were Serb nationalists. Most were businessmen whose only interest was in making money, and in keeping Milosevic in power long enough to make as much money as possible.

As a medium-sized economy Serbia was also small enough to allow precision targeting to achieve its objectives without major damage, although the long-term consequences of the bombing campaign were much greater than NATO was willing to acknowledge, then or since. According to the UN, the percentage of the Serbian population living in poverty doubled in the year following the war to 63 per cent of the population. The World Bank and IMF reported that 250,000 people lost their jobs as a direct result of the bombing of the civilian infrastructure. In Pancevo and Novi Sad, two towns that vied for the title of 'the most bombed town in Serbia', the once thriving car factories which provided jobs were devastated (Coker 2001:152).

Since Kosovo, consequence management has evolved into a doctrine: 'an effects-based approach' to war. Effects-based operations is the name of a methodology in which the desired effect of any action, regardless of its scope, has to be identified first. In the air attack with which the invasion of Iraq began, the first concern of the Americans was to negate the effectiveness of the enemy's air defences without necessarily destroying Iraqi aircraft on the ground. The country's air defence system was rendered useless by a series of tailored actions including selective hard strikes against key command and control nodes (if pilots have no instructions, no radar to guide them and no communications, they are unlikely to be effective), as well as a series of 'soft strikes' (feeding false data into Iraqi information systems, and infecting them with computer viruses) (Stephens 2007:134).

In this regard, writes Alan Stephens, the term 'effects-based operation' has come to define a *philosophy* of war even more than a doctrine. The object is to achieve a specific effect, and to avoid both predicted and unpredicted consequences at the lowest affordable cost (Stephens 2007:133–4). But as a philosophy of risk management it also has its drawbacks. For the impact of an air strike, for example, is not always obvious at the time (Adam 2003:219); even more significantly, it is not even always obvious at the point of impact. The political fall-out is often latent, or in other words invisible to everyday perception. Hazards often externalize as symptoms only late in the day, and they often reach a critical mass before they are appreciated. It is the interval between action and impact (as a *latent* symptom) that is often critically important in determining whether public support for war can be retained.

The modern battle space is a fiendishly complex environment. At staff colleges soldiers are now taught that the more risks are unacknowledged at the time, the more likely they are to multiply (Adam 2003:220). And when they are latent, the cost is likely to be all the greater when the time-bomb finally explodes. This is especially problematic given the speed of modern war which brings us back to the fact that speed often takes no account of complexity. Targeting decisions have to be taken quickly. Whatever is effective in the medium term is usually preferred, whatever the attendant consequences. And immediate successes tend to result in complacency. Success on the battlefield is often taken to be its own reward.

War without Victory

The battlefield has been important because traditionally victory has been the objective of most military campaigns. In her path-breaking book *Between Past and Future*, Hannah Arendt invoked the Roman god Janus, the god of beginnings and endings who had two sets of eyes, one which looked to the past, the other to the future. By seeing simultaneously what mortals do not see at all, Janus was seen to connect the past to the future and vice versa. In the great days of the Republic the legions used to march out of the Forum through the gates of Janus to assure war's proper beginning, and to march through the gates at the end of a campaign which always ended either with victory or defeat (Arendt 1977:vii).

The pursuit of victory is still a canonical hypothesis of military studies. Indeed, Clausewitz encouraged his readers to see victory in terms of battle. In military academies soldiers are still taught that battle is the 'essence' of war, indeed its 'primary function'. Intense, limited and decisive, combat is what makes war politically useful.

War is a struggle between two wrestlers, each of them seeks to force the other to fulfil his will through physical force; his immediate purpose is to throw the enemy to the ground and thus make him unable to resist further. *War is thus an act of force to compel the enemy to do our will* . . . Force, that is physical force . . . is thus the means, and the purpose is to impose our will upon the enemy. (Heuser 2002:84)

And imposing one's will does not necessarily require extensive killing. Ever the realist, Clausewitz explained that the primary purpose of battle was psychological ('It is not mere mutual murder, and its affect is more the killing of the enemy's courage than of the enemy's warriors') (Heuser 2002:85).

Clausewitz's wrestling analogy is interesting because we still see war in terms of a sporting contest to be fought 'cleanly', 'decisively' and, especially, 'by the rules'. Many of us 'love war in strange and troubling ways,' adds the Vietnam veteran William Broyles. In his view it is men (not women) who love war because they love sport. 'War is a brutal, deadly game, but (still) a game, the best there is' (Kassimeris 2006:4). And as one delves further into the nature of games, so one quickly identifies a central principle: games establish the disjuncture between victory and defeat (Gelven 1994:93). We play to win and we generally derive most pleasure not from playing but winning. Though we may enjoy playing a game, even if we lose, it cannot be said that we play to lose without making unintelligible the logic of the game. Winning gives the victor an existential satisfaction. He counts for more than the loser (Gelven 1994:98). Treating war as a game turns the battlefield into a playing field and associates winning with the achievement of value and status. In their everyday speech most Americans still speak of 'fighting wars' for that reason; they are much more reluctant to speak of 'waging' war, and still more of 'warring'. They talk as though what distinguishes war from all other acts of collective violence is that decisive moment on the battlefield in which the dice are thrown and the issue determined once and for all.

All this is mirrored in the internal discourse that the US military conducts with itself. Today, it recognizes twelve principles of operation. Nine are the so-called traditional principles: objective, offensive, mass, economy of force, manoeuvre, unity of command, security, surprise and simplicity. Three others have been added which were originally developed for operations other than war: restraint, perseverance and legitimacy. None of the twelve actually amounts to a genuine principle of war, writes Antulio Echevarria, since they all pertain to the act of fighting or gaining a tactical advantage over an adversary, a critical task to be sure but one that is unlikely to be sufficient in itself to help the West prevail in the 'long wars' it will find itself fighting (Echevarria 2007:162).

The West now manages risks; it is for the long haul. And because this is the case it has to ask itself a question: is victory now out of reach, or even more to the point, is it even a useful aim? As traditionally understood, writes Rupert Smith, war can no longer deliver victory; it is no longer 'a massive deciding event in a dispute in international affairs' (Smith 2005:1). In the War on Terror, adds military historian Roger Spiller, 'victory [has become] an outmoded concept' (Spiller 2005:356). A report submitted to the EU defence ministers in October 2006 reinforced this conclusion, claiming that war has become so unpredictable in its consequences that the military should avoid the traditional concept of 'outright victory' and focus instead on promoting 'greater security' (*The Times*, 25 November 2006). Even Donald Rumsfeld, though arguing 'we don't have an exit strategy, we have a victory strategy', was the first to put forward a new template for assessing success in the Long War, as the War on Terror has been renamed (Hagan 2007:17).

Indeed, long before the end of the Cold War the changing security environment had led the US to recognize that war had developed an entirely new logic.

> In the future, 'winning' may be more amorphous than in the past. Winning may have to be defined in such terms as re-establishment of regional stability. It might also have a temporal component and be defined in terms of periods of relative quiescence, or a lack of hostile actions . . . Winning may be accomplished when an opponent meets specified demands, such as keeping its troops within designated boundaries, providing humane treatment to minority groups, or allowing economic trade to occur. (Alexander 1999:204)

In the case of the War on Terror the US has come up with a series of indices for judging success or failure.

- Are we tackling the root causes of terrorism?
- Are we winning the hearts and minds?
- Are we encouraging terrorists to defect from terrorist movements?
- Are we raising difficulties in recruitment?
- Are we cutting off financial funds?
- Are we ending state-support?
- Are we decreasing the military effectiveness of terrorist groups?

And then there are the notorious 'body counts' (the 'capture-kill kinetics' in today's military vernacular): how many terrorists are being killed every week, though even Rumsfeld conceded before leaving office that this might be one of the less significant indices of success. A central theme of the War on Terror, though it is rarely stated publicly, is that in an age of risk victory is no longer possible: all that can be pursued is the more effective management of the global disorder that obtains. Success now means reducing insecurity to more acceptable levels.

One of the toughest problems the military now faces, of course, is to convince public opinion both at home and abroad that the 'failure' to achieve a decisive result in a battlefield encounter – even the 'failure' to bring the enemy to battle – should not be seen as a setback, still less a defeat. This dilemma was brought home in August 2006 when the Israelis invaded southern Lebanon. It was a major undertaking. The Israeli military expended almost as much ammunition as it had in the 1973 Yom Kippur War, and it killed ten Hezbollah militants for every Israeli soldier killed, or some 25 per cent of the movement's front-line strength (which probably accounted for its near inactivity in the year that followed). The Israelis did not lose the encounter, but the world thought they had because the conflict continued. Nothing conclusive seemed to have been achieved.

What the Israeli military failed to grasp in 2006 was how much the conflict environment had changed. Hezbollah is not a state; it is a deeply entrenched, non-state entity whose logic of operations and concept of rewards and constraints differs radically from that of most states the world over. Hezbollah is not an army: it is a complex network which includes a sophisticated and well-armed military arm. But it is also a political movement, as well as a state within a state in Lebanon where it is now the country's largest real-estate owner. It is a social movement, as well as a Syrian and Iranian ally / proxy, and it has a worldwide visibility that ties it into other movements and interests across the world. It is the system which should be targeted if the Israelis are ever to weaken its hold on the imagination. And this calls for a quite different strategy, writes Orit Gal, from the one pursued in 2006, one which is attritional, evolutionary and adaptive; it calls in fact for something rather like Hezbollah's own strategy against Israel (Gal 2008:29–31).

Can a campaign against a non-state insurgency ever be judged in terms of 'decisiveness'? What would constitute 'victory' other than the movement's elimination? And what should be the tempo of military operations? None of these questions, adds Gal, were asked by the Winograd Committee that was set up by the Knesset to ascertain what went 'wrong' in 2006. Instead, the Committee's report talked of the outcome as 'a serious missed opportunity', a conclusion it reached in the mistaken belief that a 'clear military victory' had been possible.

Not all wars have been decided on the battlefield. Here is another case of where the risk age was historically foregrounded. Take the debate between two ex-World War generals during the Korean War. One, Douglas MacArthur, told Congress after being dismissed from his command that there was 'no substitute for victory'. He had incurred Truman's hostility for wanting to 'win' the war by a nuclear strike on China. Dwight Eisenhower, who succeeded Truman as President, settled for an armistice which left the contending sides at the 38th parallel where the war had broken out and where they are still to be found today. Later he confessed that the only thing that frightened him more than losing the Cold War was winning it. 'Victory' now meant ensuring that war never broke out.

Victory is not the characteristic of an organization but rather a result of organizational activity. Military outcomes alone are not always a useful measurement of effectiveness. Indeed, argues Rupert Smith, the aim of any military intervention must be to establish certain conditions on the ground from which political outcomes can be decided. In this context it is more useful to talk of success, a concept which also needs to be continually redefined. The British Chief of Staff speaking in 2007 spoke of achieving success in theatres such as Afghanistan, 'however we define success' (Dannatt 2007). The age of total objectives would seem to have passed; risk management requires a different framework of analysis.

A Mess with a Message: the Case of Operation Iraqi Freedom

Patrick O'Rourke observed of the intervention in Iraq: 'We blew the place to bits and left a mess behind . . . but it is a mess with a message – don't mess with us' (O'Rourke 2005). The best illustration of this thinking is the 'Surge' in Iraq, the decision in 2007 to deploy an additional 30,000 soldiers on the ground in the expectation of getting a grip on the insurgency, a strategy which met, at least for the first year, with some success.

Let us go back to the beginning. For the invasion was an example of risk management in one other critical respect. Operation Iraqi Freedom was a classic case of what the insurance industry calls a 'moral hazard'. People with life insurance policies tend to live life on the edge; they take risks they shouldn't. Racing car drivers also risk their lives because they are better drivers than the rest of us. In similar fashion, the Revolution in Military Affairs (RMA) encouraged the US to go to war in the first place (Rasmussen 2007:74). The US was never at any risk of losing a conventional struggle. One Washington insider famously pronounced that it would be a 'cakewalk'

(Adelman 2002). All the Jeremiads predicting close street-to-street fighting in Baghdad, or a refugee exodus to camps that were actually built for them in Kuwait, failed to materialize. But the US hadn't prepared for the aftermath; the post-victory phase and its failure to find WMD turned the US army from a liberating force into an army of occupation. Iraqi Freedom came to seem like a blatant use of force for no other object than itself. The US did it because it could. 'Just do it', proclaimed the logo on the sweatshirts worn by young Kosovars in 1999 as they urged NATO to intervene. 'Just do it because you can' might have been the catchword of the Iraqi mission.

Once a state decides it has the capacity to do something it often fails to ask *whether* it should do it, only *how* it should. The 'whether' should have included what might happen if an insurgency should break out. But as a risk society the US was not willing to commit. And it was its lack of commitment that proved so telling in the end. If you break it, you own it, Colin Powell had warned President Bush in the run-up to the invasion. 'You are going to be the proud owner of 25 millon people. You will own all their hopes, aspirations and problems,' he had warned (Ricks 2006:48). But it was precisely ownership that the risk society wants to avoid at all costs. As its troops took Baghdad twenty days into the campaign the US military commander attempted to establish martial law; the Pentagon immediately rescinded the order. The fundamental assumption of senior officials was that the US should not be labelled an occupier, as it had in Germany and Japan in 1945. Occupation, a term that has specific legal, political, moral responsibilities and obligations, would have required the US to provide long-term support to the Iraqi state (US Senate 2003). This was precisely what the US wanted to avoid; the risk society fears commitment at the very time that it is asked to assume greater responsibility than ever for the everyday lives of its own citizens.

It was to avoid any long-term commitment that the Bush administration overinvested in the belief that the US military would be operating in a permissive environment: that they would be welcomed by the locals with open arms. As Paul Wolfowitz stated, 'I am reasonably certain that they will greet us as liberators, and that will help us to keep requirements down' (Ricks 2006:98). Any prospect that this would be true, of course, was vitiated by the failure of the US military to provide basic services such as water and electricity.

In addition, the administration remained far too focused in the months that followed the fall of Baghdad on its main brief: the search for non-existent WMD. It made little provision prior to the invasion for dealing with the insecurity that rose as the state collapsed, producing a power vacuum that was quickly filled by criminals, insurgents and ex-Ba'athist party members. The main focus of post-conflict planning, according to one government official, was that the operations would be a 'patch job, not an overhaul' (Gordon and Trainor 2006:468). This is what risk societies prefer to do: to patch up, shore up or underpin. Risk management may be a long-term strategy, but it usually comprises a series of short-term measures, not grand projects such as the nation-building efforts of 1945–50.

So what of democracy? Here too the administration invested its hopes that the aspiration was universal; that Iraq was a state that could be kick-started into the democratic era. As the original viceroy for Iraq, Jay Garner, stated, 'We won't be here [long enough]) for bottom up democracy.' Democracy may have been one of the larger political motivations of the decision to invade Iraq but few resources were earmarked for promoting it in the immediate post-conflict period. Even here short-termism prevailed.

The growing crime surge which promoted popular insecurity owed much to the failure of post-conflict planning. The US did not seem to recognize that Iraq was already a criminal state; that under Saddam the country had become a family-party state dominated by close family members and local associates, and that the Ba'athist regime was more of an organized crime syndicate than a political organization. Unreconciled to its loss of power, it organized the initial uprising. In time, looters, ex-convicts and nihilistic jobless youths realized that banding together gave them a collective power to rob, mug and otherwise get 'a Darwinian foothold in the local economy' (Looney 2005:67). As the insurgency gathered pace, political actors like al-Qaeda used the crime wave to fund its own activities. The two biggest involved smuggling oil (often, to add insult to injury, reselling it back to the government) and kidnapping, which rose from 1 per cent of all crimes recorded by the police under Saddam to 70 per cent in 2004. In that year an average of two people were kidnapped every day in Baghdad alone. Although the insurgents often ordered the kidnappings, they outsourced them to criminal gangs.

There are three ways of looking at this phenomenon. The first is to see it just as a criminal activity, the regression of a society into a 'state of nature', the privatization of violence by other means. The second is to see the nexus between crime and political violence as a feature of a globalized age. Both groups increasingly feed off each other. This is not an old phenomenon; it is new, and it represents not the outsourcing of war, or the privatization of violence, so much as the degeneration of war into warfare. The third way of approaching the subject is to see it in *behavioural* terms. Insecurity proliferates in the risk age. Networks tend to produce 'emergent properties'. In a networked world, violence can become self-sustaining (it has no particular political rationale). In 2003 the Americans failed to prevent the conventional phase of the war from developing into an unconventional one and thus failed to manage the consequences of their own initial success because they failed to *network* security.

What makes war self-sustaining is that the transaction costs are so low. Networked insurgencies are a mark of a networked world, and a networked world is a historical transition to a new social landscape of war, just as after Westphalia the social landscape of war also changed, this time in favour of states and standing armies and decisive battles on battlefields that were quarantined off from society as a whole. As a result the state was able to claim the monopoly of violence.

One writer who has written about the networked society more astutely than any other is Manuel Castells in his seminal trilogy, *The Information Age*. Stated reductively, and applying his arguments to Iraq, we can make five claims. Power in the twenty-first century is embedded, not in any one agent, such as the state, or non-state actors, or NGOs, or even criminal syndicates. It is embedded in networks and when non-state actors (insurgents) co-operate with criminals they find their collective power to be far greater than the individual violence they could possibly produce on their own. Agents, whether states or NGOs, are merely nodes in a network and the number of agents tends to increase over time. Each of these agents is weak on its own but when networked their power increases exponentially. It is networking which accounts for the self-sustaining nature of war these days. It is not individual goals or objectives that are important so much as the critical mass (the critical mass that produces an emerging property, or behaviour). Such conflicts are difficult to bring to an end because networks are decentralized. There is not always a centre of gravity to attack, any more than there is always a political actor to talk to (Castells 2001). The good news is that there is an entropic principle at work. In the end everything burns out, even an insurgency. The trick is still to be there when it does. But it will only be possible to remain there to the end if one is actually producing a positive outcome: a lesser degree of insecurity for everyone else. It is a modest goal but an important one. Risk management is about minimizing insecurity, not providing a secure world.

In short, the insurgency that followed the fall of Saddam was fuelled by the Coalition's failure to provide any security for those they had liberated, the Iraqi people, whether in the form of electricity or jobs or personal livelihoods, the security that mattered most. The collapse of the formal economy forced thousands into an illegal economy of criminal extortion, kidnapping, smuggling and terror. In time, the Coalition was left 'securing' what it could: first, its own forces, and then the country's basic communications infrastructure and oil supplies.

And very soon it found itself relying on a multiplicity of 'security' actors who had not been in the frame before. Security forces began proliferating in bodies such as the Ministry of the Interior. As well as the regular police there was a Mechanized Police Battalion, a National Police Emergency Response Unit and three Special Border Police battalions, associated significantly with communities that straddled the Iraq border. Even though the list was long, it did not include eighteen provincial SWAT teams and the large, if vaguely defined, Facilities Protection Service. By October 2003 these totalled over 300,000 men, nominally trained and equipped. Once a state cannot provide security others will move in to fill the gap.

Quite what all these bodies were securing was never quite clear. It was not long before observers began to entertain the suspicion that they were securing the jobs or political positions of those who paid or penetrated them. Many effectively constituted private armies. Even the national forces were subverted by private interests. Most of them were involved in a long-term game in which they used violence (or its threat) to manoeuvre themselves into a position to negotiate access to power at a national or regional level. Each side sought to impress on the other that it could not take everything, that some kind of deal would have to be struck – as it eventually was. Once the Sunnis abandoned the contest for power in the summer of 2007 (80,000 were bought off with cash) the Shias initially had no more use for units like the Mahdi army. The Sadrist movement broke apart into feuding warlords and gangsters who were easily picked off by a resurgent Iraqi army – better armed, better trained and better led.

It had been a long road and it had involved a long learning curve and the journey isn't over yet. Iraq is likely to remain insecure for years to come, though it may not fall apart or export violence to its neighbours as was once feared. What the invasion of Iraq highlighted was one of the dilemmas of the risk age. The search for security impels us to act (in the case of Iraq the fear of Saddam's WMD); indeed failure to act may exacerbate the risks we have to run. There is no better breeding ground for risk than denial or inactivity. But if one is too fearful and tries to secure the future on the basis of incomplete knowledge or if everything becomes a danger that must be acted upon while there is still time, then risks may proliferate, making us all more insecure than we were before. It is called the 'risk trap' – doing too little or doing too much can both prove equally fatal (Rasmussen 2007:39). The trick is to do just enough.

The same logic applied once Saddam had been removed from power. Indeed, in retrospect we can see that the Iraq War was won and lost on the same day. The iconography of victory, writes Mikkel Rasmussen, was striking, but it was also carefully rehearsed. The President flew onto the *USS Abraham Lincoln* (the carrier from which the first cruise missile attack on Osama bin Laden had been launched in the late 1990s). Unlike President Whitmore in *Independence Day*, Bush may not have been a Desert Storm pilot, but he had learnt to fly in the National Guard – and he flew his own plane halfway across the Pacific (though he was not allowed to land on the aircraft carrier). 'Mission Accomplished', proclaimed the headlines, and the original speech had contained MacArthur's words when taking the Japanese surrender in 1945: 'the guns are silent.' At the last moment these were deleted because the guns were not. The war had not ended. In fact it had only just begun.

The victory, nevertheless, seemed total, and the US kept to this script for the next two years. The images broadcast on television even conjured up World War II. 'In the images of falling statues we have witnessed the arrival of a new era [of warfare]', proclaimed Bush on 1 May 2003 (Bobbitt 2008:208). The image of Saddam's statue being toppled recalled the iconic photograph of the Red Army soldier hoisting the Red Flag over the ruined Reichstag building in Berlin (a scene carefully choreographed by the Red Army) as well as Abe Rosenthal's shot of the US Marines raising the Stars and Stripes on Mount Suribachi on Iwo Jima, perhaps the best-known image of the Pacific War. And just as Germany was de-Nazified, Iraq was de-Ba'athized. The subsequent search for Saddam was important because his trial was intended to bring closure just as the Nuremburg Trials had provided an act of lustration, allowing the Germans to move on into the Cold War, this time as allies of the West in the next encounter against the Soviet Union.

The Americans had won decisively, or so it appeared, and this was the dilemma. Unfortunately, the US continued to keep to the script (the narrative of a conventional war with a neat beginning and a discernible end) long after the conflict had degenerated into warfare. 'Stuff happens,' remarked Rumsfeld of the looting which broke out in Baghdad shortly after Saddam had fallen. When the insurgency exploded in 2004 he continued to call the insurgents 'dead enders'. It was not they, however, but the Americans, adds Rasmussen, who had reached a dead end (Rasmussen 2008).

It was only in 2007 that the US changed the narrative. It was only then that it acknowledged that it was not involved in a war, but warfare. It was precisely at this point that victory was redefined: *damage limitation* under another name. It met with partial success. Al-Qaeda was finally wrong-footed. Some of the militias closed themselves down, at least for the duration. Baghdad and its environs did become more secure. But all this came at a price. The surge was highly kinetic; it was a military campaign, not a policing mission, even though it was sold to the public as putting more policemen on the beat. In 2007 the number of Iraqis in prison doubled to 30,000, and while casualty figures are sketchy, the number of insurgents killed was already 25 per cent higher than the year before. And while the new counter-insurgency doctrine had an anti-technology flavour that seemed to discourage the use of airpower, there was a five-fold increase in air strikes immediately after the Surge as compared to the previous year.

The Surge allowed the US to re-establish the control it had lost. Instead of talking of exit strategies it began talking of a long war which involved some unpalatable compromises, such as paying off 80,000 Sunni insurgents. The US is likely to have to manage the situation for some years to come. What it hasn't done is close the case. Even in the case of the Surge there is no such a thing as a risk-free victory. All it has managed to do is to apply a series of benchmarks: is the situation more or less secure, and for whom? Clausewitz would have been horrified because the war is apparently tactically driven. Tactical success on the ground is producing strategic outcomes that may or may not be satisfactory but it is hard to see a strategy in the traditional sense.

Yet there is a strategic logic if we look for it. The US has rewritten the script in order to adjust the consequences of its own failure. It has been forced to accommodate itself to the first-order consequences of its intervention: brokering a deal with Sunnis to fight a common enemy, al-Qaeda, in the hope of preventing a Sunni–Shia civil war. Of the second order consequences, none is more important than accepting the inevitable. Today Iraq is under the control of a few power blocs – Shias, Sunnis and Kurds – who can all challenge state power because they all have armed militias, illicit networks, cabinet positions and foreign support. The Bush administration gave many reasons for the invasion of Iraq but the independence of the Kurds was not one of them. Yet in many ways they are functionally independent already; the regional government has its own army, collects its own taxes and negotiates its own oil deals. Legitimized by two elections, each of the blocs has strength enough to veto progress if it wants to. They have become Iraq's problem, not its solution.

Success is now understood in the context of what we call 'wicked problems', which are part of the lexicon of the risk age. I will discuss these at greater length in the next chapter. The Surge bears out many of the features of wicked problems, of which I shall enumerate merely four. Firstly, understanding the problem one is trying to address is developed through the construction of the solution. Secondly, there is no solution to a wicked problem, only better or worse developments, in this case the avoidance of civil war and the disintegration of the country into its respective parts. Thirdly, solutions often generate other problems: no success, however qualified, or uncontested, is ever risk-free. Finally, since there is never an end result to a problem, there can be no definition of victory in the textbook terms of World War II which President Bush thought he could obtain when he declared 'Mission accomplished' on the deck of the *USS Abraham Lincoln*.

An Ethics of Consequence Management

Nietzsche's *Ecce Homo* opens with the disconcerting claim: 'We are unknown to ourselves, we men of knowledge.' These are also the first words of *The Genealogy of Morals*, a work which preceded it by barely a year. Starting from there, Nietzsche quickly arrives at the conclusion that we are 'necessarily strangers to ourselves'. Strangers or not, we have been interrogating ourselves ever since – it is the mark of the painful experience of being modern. It was Marx who made us conscious of the extent to which our values and beliefs are conditioned, in part, by our social position and economic interests. It was Freud who made us aware of our unconscious desires and impulses. Today, we are even more self-critical than ever: we feel especially guilty about the consequences of our own actions, and worried that we ourselves might constitute the principal risk we face. *Guilt in that sense is tied to compassion.* The two are joined at the hip.

Today, we have begun to acknowledge radically new responsibilities to those far from us, not only in terms of space but also time in what Beck calls our de-bounded world. There are new dimensions of responsibility which encompass nature (the 'greening' of morality). Rather late in the day we have discovered a responsibility to the non-anthropomorphic 'other': the biosphere, as well as the planet. As Hans Jonas reminds us, the concept of responsibility nowhere played a central role in the moral systems of the past (Jonas 1999:7). And there is an explanation for that. Responsibility is a function of power and knowledge. Until recently both were limited in time and scope. 'Right' action was restricted to the here and now. Today, by contrast, we have immense power and greater knowledge, though not necessarily greater wisdom.

And unlike traditional ethics which reckoned only with non-cumulative behaviour, we have to deal with uncertainties for which there is no historical precedent. We have to deal with the historically unbounded risks which include the consequences of our own actions. Consequences can snowball; risks can cascade. For that reason our risk societies deal with probabilities, not certainties. We are always estimating, measuring and anticipating the consequences of our actions in the hope of managing them as best we can. At this stage in history this is the shape of our ethical universe. It is what drives us to make war more 'humane' for ourselves and others.

Once a society starts to reframe the management of violence in this way, it is really bound to adopt a new moral heuristic. This moral heuristic does not rule out war. Indeed, risk avoidance can encourage us to use force more frequently. The invasion of Iraq was justified, after all, in terms of the precautionary principle; it was designed to purchase a margin of safety for the future – an Iraq without WMD. It was sold to the world on the promise that it would save future lives. As Cass Sunstein contends, such a moral heuristic can be defended, at least to the extent that it operates as a rule (Lewens 2007:168). It can be defended in the same way that all rules are, on the grounds that they are better than the alternative. Such a novel heuristic might even show a kind of 'ecological rationality' which works well in most real-world contexts, even if, he cautions, we must always bear in mind that the outcome might be far worse than the *status quo*: in this case continuing to manage Saddam Hussein.

But there are other ethical problems that inhere in risk management. We can take responsibility for the consequences of our actions but we will never know what those consequences are going to be, we can never anticipate all of them, and we can never calculate with any precision the cost of those that we can. We have to act in that knowledge. Of course, there are ethical dilemmas in not acting (in not going to war), and who else is going to take responsibility for the consequences of inaction, as the US is right to ask the rest of us? Ethics has never been able to provide any criteria for determining what risks to take. But morally speaking, we are usually only allowed to run risks on our own account, not for others. How are we to judge ethical claims when we are held to account by others for making the situation far worse?

If all sides had known what would be the consequences of going to war in 1914, they would probably have stopped in their tracks. If that is true (and there is no reason to question it) there is some hope for humanity. Possibly, George Bush too would not have invaded Iraq had he known what the invasion would cost. The risk age has thrown up a new set of ethical dilemmas which we are ill-placed to address, let alone resolve. At best, humane warfare can only be a palliative measure to reduce the risks of getting it horribly wrong.

5

The Geopolitics of Risk Management

In 1904 the greatest geopolitical thinker of his or any other age, Halford Mackinder, wrote a seminal paper, 'The Pivot of World History', in which he claimed that the decisive event of the modern era had been the colonization of the Americas by the Europeans and Siberia by the Russians. While the Europeans had sailed across the Atlantic and become Americans, the Russians had trekked across the Eurasian land mass. By the early twentieth century both had reached the Pacific Ocean. The political direction of the century would be determined by the conflict between the two (Zeman 1989:13).

This is the point about geopolitics. It tells a story. Mackinder just happened to get it wrong. The future of the world was determined not in the Pacific, but in Europe, as it had been the previous century, and the US and Russia did not find themselves in conflict until the second half of the twentieth century. The pre-eminent geopolitical narrative until the collapse of the Soviet Union in 1991 remained the recurring necessity of preventing the dominance of Europe by any single power. Europe, not the Pacific, continued to be the pivot of world history. The fact that it is no longer is probably the greatest change in recent geopolitics.

Modern geopolitical thinking has certain established ground rules. There is always an enemy. In the first half of the twentieth century it was Germany, in the second half, the Soviet Union. The identity of the enemy is not important for the cogency of the theory itself. What is important is the fact that conflict should be the motivating force in international affairs. Secondly, geopolitics assumes a permanent interest. The balance of power remained the principal concern of the Great Powers for almost a century, and the policy challenge for the liberal world was to form a coalition of like-minded societies against any country or combination of countries that challenged the liberal order.

Finally, to make sense of strategic history there has to be a major conceptual framework. In the twentieth century the framework was the New World Order which every President promised the American people would be the reward for their efforts. It is useful to remind ourselves that the very concept 'world' was a late invention. The first course in 'world politics' in the US was not taught until 1894. The 'world economy' was coined as a term to describe the international division of labour that had been forged by the Industrial Revolution. The first 'world power' was Great Britain, and geopoliticians were interested in which world order would emerge. What is interesting about George W. Bush, the first President of the new century, is that he has not promised a New World Order, only the more successful management of the present global disorder. When Bush told the nation that the War on Terror was 'unlike any other' (Furedi 2008:9) he was only stating a truth – the US does not expect to forge a New World Order even if it prevails; its political ambitions are much more modest now than they have been for some time.

It took September 11 to actually focus everyone's attention on the new realities. There is a nice passage in a short story by Don DeLillo which formed the basis for his later novel, *Falling Man*, his take on the attack on the World Trade Center. Looking at the televised images of the outrage the heroine at first thinks it is only a movie, and that everything will go back to being what it was. But then she thinks she might be wrong about what is ordinary. Maybe nothing is. 'Maybe there was a deep fold in the grain of things, the way things pass through the mind, the way time swings in the mind, which is the only place it meaningfully exists.' The camera, which had shown surprise at the first plane crashing into the twin towers, seemed to express no surprise about the second. By the time the second plane appeared 'we're all a little older and wiser' (DeLillo 2007:9). On this rather bleak note, the story ends.

9/11 did indeed force us to recognize that everything had changed. Homeland security is not national security; the defence of the citizen is much harder than the defence of the state. Unlike states, non-state actors cannot be deterred. We have also been forced to think seriously about pre-emptive strikes, for non-state actors may be more dangerous than states, and rogue regimes may be more dangerous still. Instead of a Cold War marked by armistices as well as periods of détente and co-operation, we have entered a world in which we may find ourselves permanently denied peace of mind.

A New Paradigm

The risk age, in short, asks us to address a new security paradigm. The term was first introduced into the general discourse in 1962 when Thomas Kuhn published *The Structure of Scientific Revolutions*, which may be the most influential treatise ever written on how science does, or does not, proceed. Kuhn employed the term to refer to the collection of procedures and ideas that instruct scientists in what they should believe, and how they should work. Most scientists, Kuhn tells us, spend their working lives solving problems and puzzles whose solutions tend to reinforce a belief in the prevailing paradigm of the day. Somewhat dismissively, he called this idea of research 'normal'. More dismissive still, he claimed that scientists were involved in 'mopping up' the problems others had not managed to resolve. But at certain moments in history, of course, paradigms change. New explanatory models are proposed. And the world changes accordingly.

Kuhn, who died some time ago, thought that social scientists should not use the word. He insisted it should be confined to the natural sciences. Science changes when scientists find that their existing model of the world has too many anomalies that either cannot be accounted for in the traditional framework, or that contradict the framework's main assumptions. When anomalies accumulate they will trigger a scientific revolution such as the Copernican in the sixteenth century or the Newtonian after that. We call this a 'paradigm shift' (a term not used by Kuhn himself). From time to time scientists are forced to abandon old ideas for new ones. Such was Kuhn's thesis, which interestingly enough has parallels with Hegel's dialectic which also depicted belief systems as generating 'inner contradictions' that could only be resolved by revolutionary change. When adopted, a new paradigm establishes particular ways of explaining phenomena which usually become established ways of thinking about the world. Take the classic paradigm shift, the transition from a pre-Darwinian to a Darwinian world. Creationism speaks of the world as adapted to man; Darwinian evolution by natural selection speaks of humanity as fitted for survival in the world. The two could not be more different (Burrow 2007:99).

In the social sciences, by contrast – and this is one of the reasons Kuhn felt social scientists had no business using the term – paradigms don't change as a result of internal contradictions. They change in response to external events. In the case of the last century they involved challenges from two major powers, Germany and the Soviet Union. After 1947 the only show in town was the containment of Soviet power, and the only puzzle was how best to manage it. What came to an end in 2001 was the 'Strategic Pause' which the Clinton administration had declared in the early 1990s in the apparent absence of any major challenge to America's position in the world. Rumsfeld never spoke greater truth than when he admitted that the intelligence services had acquired no additional information on Iraq's

WMD programme; instead the event had triggered the US to *re-perceive what it already knew*.

Today, the US has adopted a new security paradigm: risk management to address three very different challenges that have emerged in the first years of the twenty-first century: the rise of terrorism, the seemingly inexorable rise of China and finally the growing anarchy (often more perceived than real) on the margins of a de-bounded world. Risk has replaced threat as the centre of security studies. The *US Quadrennial Defense Review* (2001) describes risk as 'the single most important strategic tenet' of national security thinking. NATO's revised *Strategic Concepts* of 1991 and 1999 likewise identify the management of risk as the Alliance's central strategic purpose (Coker 2002:71–2).

Managing Terrorism

For the moment the War on Terror holds centre stage. Whether it is called a 'war' or seen as a policing operation is less important than the fact that we tend to apply to terrorism the same model that we apply in tackling domestic crime. Our societies now aim at modest improvements in crime prevention at the margins, as well as better management of resources, a reduction in the number and likelihood of criminal acts and, these days, greater support for the victims. These are all post-heroic objectives, in the sense that we no longer share the great Victorian hope that one day crime might be purged from social life.

Nineteenth-century societies which invented the first national police forces and regulated prison regimes signed up to a distinctly *heroic* idea of criminology. They believed criminals should not only be punished, but also rehabilitated and even redeemed. Once they began to think of criminals not only as malign but also as social deviants it became a moral duty to rehabilitate them. Prison became a reform school in which the criminal could be transformed into a useful citizen and then reintegrated into society on his release.

Since the late 1980s soaring crime rates and questionable results in rehabilitation (above all stubbornly high rates of recidivism) have predisposed states to adopt alternative strategies. As Tony Bottoms wrote somewhat despairingly in 1980, 'no-one now seriously pretends that . . . rehabilitation has any utilitarian value in the general reduction of crime rates or in the prevention of the recruitment of recidivists' (Rasmussen 2007:107). Nor should we be surprised that in the risk age rehabilitation can even backfire; the boomerang effect is present in every sphere of life including penology.

The complex issues of punishment were explored in a book called *Violent Offenders: Approaching and Managing Risk* (1991), a statistically rich broad overview of the problem especially as it concerned the rehabilitation of psychopaths. What the authors found was that their rehabilitation could have unforeseen consequences. Psychopaths who were given training in social sensitivity and interpersonal skills were more likely to commit violent crimes on release. 'We speculate then that patients learned a great deal from the intense programme but the psychopathic offenders put their new skills to quite unintended uses' (Dennett 2003:89).

Equally disturbing, a study of every British male born in 1956 found that a third had committed offences more serious than traffic violations, which was a surprisingly high number. This was the bad news; the good was that few of the crimes they had committed threatened social harmony, or even the quality of social life. Far more disturbing was the evidence that 5 per cent of males from the 1956 cohort had committed 70 per cent of all recorded offences as well as 70 per cent of all violent crimes. And a large number reoffended as soon as they were released from prison.

In the hard sciences information can be collected and recalibrated and then the dice thrown. If the results disappoint you can start again. In the world of punishment and rehabilitation you usually have only one throw of the dice. It is at this point that policy-makers and penologists find themselves linked together in a troubled marriage. Both parties like to promote the myth of a Cartesian dualism between the observer and the actor, between those who 'know' and those who 'do'. This distinction once even seemed to be a necessary condition for natural science. Since then scientists have found that natural science does not simply describe and explain nature but is part of the interplay between nature and ourselves (it describes nature as exposed to our method of questioning). So too, as in most other human enterprises, researchers and prison authorities are joined at the head and find themselves eventually sharing the consequences of failure.

At home, perhaps for this reason, we tend to play safe. We find it more sensible to sentence criminals to long terms of imprisonment; our prison populations have never been larger. *Three strikes and you're out* is now the slogan in the United States where, as of 2005, there were 2.2 million people incarcerated. This put the country at the head of the list of the number of citizens it imprisoned, ahead both of China (with 1.5 million) and Russia (with 870,000) respectively. The figure is extraordinarily high when one contrasts the population of China with that of America. On current projections there will be three to four million prisoners in American prisons by 2020, the great majority Hispanic and black.

Even when we do let prisoners out, we tend to monitor their movements. Britain now tags twice as many people as the rest of Europe put together. There is no longer any such thing as unsupervised freedom. We now accept (for the moment at least) that crime will never be eliminated, it can only be managed. And this is best achieved by reducing the opportunities for crime ('target devaluation') and by subjecting the general population to intrusive surveillance. We no longer treat individual offenders; we manage 'criminal environments' and criminal populations. We apply 'zero tolerance' policies; we move on suspected offenders from areas where they are deemed to constitute a risk, especially in the areas that matter most to us such as tourism and business. We quarantine likely offenders in ghettos or 'sink estates' where they are likely to internalize their violence (trashing their own neighbourhood which does no great damage to the economy).

In terms of surveillance, successful policing depends increasingly on information that provides the algorithmic methods of modern risk assessments. Crime control and policy are particularly connected with a 'culture of control', a term which was coined to describe a society in which the perennial desire for security, risk management and the taming of chance have been so magnified and reinforced that the regulation of every area of life has become a norm. In the UK the Home Office spends three-quarters of its crime prevention budget on CCTV cameras and face-recognition 'smart' technology. There is now one CCTV camera for every fourteen citizens in the UK. Londoners are now picked up 300 times a day by cameras gazing down on them from high-security buildings, or in department stores, or as they walk through main thoroughfares or housing estates, or catch a train back home at night. Corporations actively monitor consumer choice every time a credit card is swiped, or an internet site is visited, or an Oyster Card is used on the London Underground. Cars entering London are tracked by cameras operating a 'congestion charge'. The Global Positioning System can track mobile phone users, and the same, of course, goes for GPS systems in cars.

The British Ministry of Defence is investing in the development of neural network technologies for pattern-matching which can 'scan' faces in a crowd and cross-reference them to known troublemakers (Norris 1999:217). Pattern-recognition software in parking lots can now alert operators to suspicious behaviour before any crime has been committed. Very soon we will be able to programme computers to recognize patterns and relationships that we cannot recognize in each other – the body language, if you will, that betrays anxiety, even perhaps the intention to plant a bomb (Martin 2006:286).

Data-processing systems are also improving all the time. CCTV cameras can now be patched into information retrieval systems to facilitate a 'knowledge brokering' function which goes far beyond pinpointing people as they move about. We can now pinpoint the members of certain behavioural groups that we deem to constitute a risk to the rest of us. In the UK the Crime Net Management system which links together the police and local council-run CCTV networks can now track 'known' offenders with criminal records for shoplifting, car theft and vandalism. Local retail outfits have their own portfolios of top criminals and monitor their movements all the time. Even if they don't enter a store and pass by, information about them can be relayed automatically to other stores in the web.

In other words, the risk age requires knowledge of the people it seeks to control (Norris 1999:24). Surveillance enables the state to make biographical profiles of the population in order to determine what is likely to be their probable behaviour at some undetermined date. Thus not only is it possible to follow an individual as he moves through space, it is possible to assess his moral worth at the same time, using information contained on a database (Lyon 2007:107). It is called 'social sorting', an inclusive and exclusive process which is central to what the management of risk is fast becoming (Lyon 2007:106).

In the UK, the latest targeted group are children deemed to be 'at risk of criminality' – children whose parents are serving sentences in prison or who are among the 300,000 officially registered drug addicts. In both cases children will be actively 'case-managed' in future by social services staff. Regular 'up-dates' on every child through his or her development into adulthood will enable 'service providers' to identify those most at risk of offending. It doesn't stop there. Greater use of technology, including mobile fingerprint-readers and crowd-scanners, will soon bring thousands more into the police DNA database. Prolific offenders who account for 50 per cent of crime are to be placed 'on licence' for the rest of their lives. Essentially, there will be no 'Get out of Prison' clause. Once on the police database they are on it for life.

Given that regulation, inspection and control that have become such a central theme of social life at home it is hardly surprising that it has also become a central theme of international security. Back in the 1980s Gary Marx argued that the kinds of 'categorical suspicion' made possible by the new surveillance technologies were threatening to turn on their head the traditional idea of presumption of innocence. Zero tolerance policies introduced in New York at about the same time allow the police to identify 'potential' troublemakers and move them on. Mapping systems, video cameras, voice-recognition systems, still cameras and computer terminals in vehicles now enable the police to trace urban territory and those who populate it more comprehensively than ever before. Neighbourhood Watch schemes encourage neighbours to assist the police in keeping out of circulation specially identified groups. The state keeps sex workers and paedophiles and electronically tagged prisoners on probation inside security zones where they are most likely to pose a danger to those most at risk, such as children.

Now all of this is important because at the international level we apply much the same procedures to countries that we deem to be 'abnormal' – those who behave outside the accepted norms. At the very time that multilateral institutions, treaties and conventions are supposed to (and to some extent do) promote greater transparency and trust between states, international society is becoming increasingly distrustful of certain countries which it puts under surveillance twenty-four hours a day. 'Social sorting' applies to states as well as people. At home we distinguish good from bad: football supporters from hooligans; demonstrators from activists or troublemakers; the disenchanted from the dangerous. And dangerous states, like dangerous people, are designated by their risk profile too. They are first identified, then classified and finally managed according to the level of dangerousness they are deemed to pose.

Surveillance as a form of management takes many forms. Institutions such as the International Monetary Fund constantly seek greater surveillance capacity. Trade and environmental regimes increasingly arrogate the right to monitor the behaviour of their members. Intrusive verification is at the heart of many arms control agreements. The international community may have come to terms with proliferation among 'normal' states (Israel, India, Pakistan) but it is horrified at the thought that the 'abnormal' (North Korea, Libya, Iran) may go nuclear. In their case, risk assessment is probabilistic rather than deterministic (Lyon 2007:24). Offenders are classified as prolific rather than opportunistic (the latter will act badly only if encouraged to do so). Once designated 'proliferators' they are put under constant surveillance.

Surveillance has become crucial in obtaining the information that allows the international community to determine the scale of a risk and to shape the risk management strategies necessary to deal with it. It enables great powers like the US to systematically gather information to monitor the behaviour of certain risk groups that they identify as 'pariah states' or 'rogue states', or what the State Department more diplomatically chooses to call 'states of concern'. It enables them to apply a kind of 'moral 'mapping' which allows them to determine who is 'on side' and who is not in the War on Terror. 'You are either with us or against us' is very much the motto of the day.

Take the case of surveillance at sea. The US is promoting 'maritime domain awareness'; it is tracking shipping across the world and encouraging other governments to do the same. In 1993 the US navy stopped and boarded a Chinese cargo vessel, the *Yin He (Milky Way)* which was suspected of carrying chemical weapons components to Iran. So far the most extensive mission has been Operation Active Endeavour, an operation directed from Allied Naval Forces Command in Naples. By the end of January 2005 NATO had hailed approximately 59,000 vessels, and boarded eighty with the compliance of the ships' masters. In all a total of 488 vessels had been escorted through the Straits of Gibraltar (NATO 2005:4–5).

Once again the similarities are striking between policing at home and risk management overseas. At home, police forces go in for concentrated surveillance at high-risk locations and at high-risk times. Hence, for example, the rise in the UK of drink-drive blitzes and random alcohol checks at weekends and public holidays. These constitute a new *risk-focused pattern of policing* which is intended through reconnaissance to establish the extent of the risk that either criminals, or people involved in criminally negligent activity (drink-driving), pose to the rest of the community.

Surveillance is there for a reason: to identify a risk before it goes critical. To prevent it going critical the international community is encouraged to go to Step 2 – *target devaluation*. Just as we encourage self-help at home, so we encourage it internationally too. This is especially true of the international maritime industry which has expressed particular concern that a terrorist attack on a ship in a strategic waterway such as the Panama Canal, or Suez, or the Malacca Straits could result in massive economic damage to the global logistics chain. The Malacca Straits is perhaps most at risk. Each day 500 ships (approximately a quarter of all world trade) passes through its waters. In theory terrorists might be able to turn a liquefied petroleum gas ship into a floating bomb which could sink a container ship. As an attack it would be as devastating in its impact as the airliners of 9/11.

To counter the threat, shipping, insurance and oil companies are turning to the private security market. Pirate attacks are especially worrying because today's pirates, unlike those depicted in Hollywood blockbusters, tend to be well-armed militiamen equipped with rocket-propelled grenades, assault rifles, global positioning systems and high-speed motorboats. A pirate attack off the Somali coast on the passenger cruise liner *Seaborne Spirit* sparked off the interest as did the publicity generated by claims from a private security firm Top Cap Marine that it had been awarded a $50-million contract to tackle piracy in Somali territorial waters. ('US firm to fight Somali pirates', BBC News, 25 November 2005, http://news.bbc.co.uk/2/hi/africa/4471536.stm). Private security firms have been quick to market themselves as *global* security providers. Companies hired by shipping companies operate in extra-jurisdictional, international waterways. When the language of global security meets the discourse of risk the reliance on private security appears to be the logical option.

On land the situation is more complex. The role of the military is to fight and win war and to prevent war from happening in the first place. Draining the swamp of terrorists, President Bush claimed, was its first priority in the War on Terror. Prevention is better than punishment. Long before the first pre-emptive war in Iraq, Americans were talking about 'preventative defence', a strategy strikingly different from that of the Cold War. In the early 1990s the Nunn-Luger Co-operation Threat Reduction Program was intended to address the danger of 'loose Soviet nukes', a threat which had been brought home to Nunn during a visit to Moscow shortly after Gorbachev was released from house arrest. Who had control during the putsch? What if the coup had split the military, some siding with the President, others with the plotters? What if the Soviet Union itself had descended into chaos after 25 December when it was formally dissolved?

Some time before 9/11, in other words, academics and policy-makers had begun to turn their attention, not to threats that could be deterred (the most important from other countries), so much as risks that fell 'below the threshold' of deterrence. Two former policy-makers suggested that the US should identify three new categories of risk: an 'A' list of risks to America's survival; a 'B' list of regional contingencies in the Persian Gulf and Korea which might threaten US interests there; and finally a 'C' list of contingencies that might affect the US indirectly. Their preventive strategy addressed the concern that the 'B' risks , if mismanaged, might go to the top of the list.

Since then this has become a theme of American thinking. John Steinbrunner's book *The Principles of Global Government* begins with the premise that pre-emption may be necessary in circumstances yet to be determined. His is a world of diffused processes of insecurity involving everything from the spread of disease to environmental degradation. It is a world in which 'the surveillance state' reserves the right to monitor risks on behalf of the rest of us, and if necessary to intervene while there is still time (Steinbrunner 2000). This is not to deny that within the US there is profound disagreement between those who wish to attack rogue states when containment demonstrably fails and those who would prefer regime change as an instrument of first rather than last resort. But the right to intervene is widely accepted by most policy-makers.

This has been reinforced by American exceptionalism. The US, Colin Powell told a Senate hearing back in 1991 when he was still Chairman of the Joint Chiefs of Staff, was a 'power that could be trusted'. US military power we are told by the 2006 *QDR* is a 'force for good'. It is this moral self-belief that reinforces the stereotyping of 'rogue states' as 'criminal deviants' who like criminals at home have to be folded into a culture of control. These are the countries identified in the most recent *National Security Strategy* as being (if necessary) the target of pre-emption. Section 3 focuses on the defeat of terrorism; Section 5 on the proliferation of WMD. And in both cases the US reserves the right to intervene. 'The fight must be taken to the enemy, to keep them on the run.' Defeating terrorism, it is clear, marks 'a break with old patterns' (White House 2006).

This is exactly the language the Bush administration used to justify the war in Iraq and it is clear that the ensuing insurgency has had little influence on its subsequent thinking. 'The place of pre-emption in our national security strategy remains the same. We will always proceed deliberately, weighing the consequences of our actions. The reasons for our actions will be clear, the force measured and the cause just' (Williams 2006:40). Precautionary thinking will probably remain at the centre of Western strategic thinking for years to come. In their own *Security Strategy* of 2006, even the Europeans reserved the right to pre-empt if necessary. They prefer to call it 'pre-emptive engagement' and to talk of 'robust multilateralism'.

The problem with risk management, writes Beck, is that we can all agree on what we don't want (e.g. a nuclear Iran); we find it much more challenging to reach agreement on how to prevent it (Adam 2003:218). Doing nothing and demanding too much both threaten to transform the world into a risk trap. Iran is a typical case of this. Most governments accept that Iran wishes to become a nuclear power but they cannot agree on what to do next. Should they apply sanctions, or resort to military force? The US cannot predict the consequences of a military strike, though it can make a guess (increased Iranian support for terrorist groups overseas, increased intervention in southern Iraq and a rise in the oil price above $300 a barrel). If neither the optimism of the hawks nor the pessimism of the critics is based on knowledge, then what to do: hold back, or press ahead?

The Europeans, knowing that they are less powerful than the US are even more anxious when addressing a problem that it should not be compounded by acting too soon or needlessly. We tend to over-insure and over-insurance leads to over-extension: a bridge too far, a regime change too many. In avoiding the mistakes of our predecessors we must be careful not to make mistakes that no one has made before.

And risk assessments today are conditioned to a degree by how much the risk profiler feels at risk. Risk thresholds are highly subjective. Our fears are culturally constructed. What matters most is the *actualization* of risk as it is lived, imagined and acted upon in everyday life. The problem is that risk management makes us particularly accountable for our own carelessness. It plays up the principle that insurance companies call 'contributory negligence'.

Risk management revolves around probabilities: the probability of Iran going nuclear within the next five years as well as the probability that if attacked it will not passively accept its humiliation. These are not the probabilities involved in a game of roulette which merely reflects our *incomplete* knowledge of the game. For if we knew the speed of the roulette wheel, as well as the weight and balance of the white marble ball, if we could link into computers sufficiently powerful to do the calculations, we could probably beat the house every time. But gambling does not reflect any fundamental idea about how the world works. Assessing the probability of Iran going nuclear is very different. It is all a matter of political judgement in a fast-moving and confusing situation.

The threats of old were solid, grounded in geography, sometimes historically predictable, often mathematically quantifiable. The new risks are part of an environment which is a complex place when examined at smaller and smaller distances, and shorter and shorter timescales. Whether something appears simple or complex is usually a matter of the scale at which you are looking at it. Zoom in and almost impenetrable complexity is seemingly apparent; pull back and simplicity seems to hold. It is an illusion, of course, for at any other magnification non-linearity rules.

Hedging against China's Rise

The rise of China presents the US with a second geo-strategic problem. As the *Quadrennial Defense Review* 2006 stated, China is at a strategic crossroads. It can either choose to work with the US or against it (*QDR* 2006). Were it to heed the advice of Yoga Bera, the much-quoted American baseball player, it probably could do both: if you find yourself at a crossroads, he once said, you should take it.

Even if China is not strong enough to balance the US at present, even if it tends to be much less strident than other countries, including Brazil, in criticizing American actions internationally, it may be forced into a confrontation eventually. Yet there is also no immediate reason why the US should be unduly concerned at China's rise. Structurally, the US is likely to remain the Number One power until the mid-twenty-first century even if it is overtaken as the leading manufacturing nation by 2012, and the world's leading economic power by 2035. The one inescapable geopolitical fact – and it is a remarkable one – is that its share of global economic power has remained the same for a century and may remain the same for at least the next fifty years. Its share of world GDP may stay at around 27 per cent until 2050. Despite the disastrous war in Iraq it would be wrong to think that the US is over-extended. It is still spending only 3.5 per cent of its GDP on the military, compared with 35 per cent in World War II.

Yet it is a mark of its coming to terms with the risk age that the US has also come to the conclusion that it cannot contain a rising China; instead it is seeking to hedge against China's rise. Hedging has been a feature of market economics in the risk age for some time. The first hedge fund was established by Alfred Winslow Jones in the 1940s, though this historical provenance is not undisputed. Other economic historians trace hedging to the trading desk strategies practised within brokerage houses and investment banks, and still others to futures trading, particularly but not exclusively currency trading in the 1970s.

If there is no formal agreement on their historical origin, there is also no formal consensus on how hedge funds should be classified. Hedge Funds Research (HFR), one of the main hedge fund databases, lists thirty separate strategies with some overlap between them. In the 1990s some fund managers took the long-, others the short-term, view when investing in fixed income, equity or currency. Some fund strategies have a low correlation with overall market returns; others specifically gamble on market movements. Some are designed to enhance returns, others to reduce risks in the case of fixed income arbitrage and the long-term sale of funds. And some hedge fund managers prefer to focus on the securities of companies experiencing financial difficulties. The term 'distress security' broadly refers to securities issued by companies which have defaulted and filed for credit protection.

Tactical trading strategies also tend to differ significantly. Some hedge fund managers attempt to profit by forecasting the overall direction of the foreign exchange market and making bets on forecasts of major macro-economic events, such as changes in interest rates, currency movements and stock market performance. Other managers prefer relative-value strategies, designed to take advantage of mis-pricing among related financial assets such as company debt. As with the long/short-term investment approach, this class of strategies involves buying and selling two or more related securities. The risk involved depends on how closely related are the securities that are bought and sold.

In short, hedge fund strategies are extremely varied. Given this wide diversity we might not expect to find a common theme. But if we look closely enough we will find one. Hedge funds tend to capitalize on two things: *uncertainty* and *opportunity*. Take a company that has bought another company whose exports account for 75 per cent of its profits. If the dollar weakens it may run the risk of serious foreign exchange losses as a result of an unanticipated event such as a war. The uncertainty stems from the fact that it is impossible to predict what rate of exchange will apply when payment is made at the time the goods are actually delivered. One way of hedging is to insure against a falling US dollar. Companies that are most sophisticated in this field recognize that the financial risks that are produced by their business present a powerful opportunity to add to their bottom line while at the same time prudentially positioning the firm so that it is not unfavourably influenced by price movements. When dealing with a hedging strategy the core problem is to strike a balance between uncertainty and the risk opportunity loss to the firm's shareholders, some of whom may be excessively risk-averse. Setting a hedging policy is therefore a *strategic* decision whose success or failure can make or break the company concerned.

Now, we must be careful in the way we apply the hedging model because companies and countries are very different. Companies tend to take more risks than countries because they are always seeking to maximize returns. On the macro-economic level they achieve an efficient allocation of resources by such competition, at the micro level they create winners and losers. The whole system encourages a trade-off between risk and reward. It actively encourages risk-taking in a world in which winners are rewarded and losers punished. Secondly, countries do not compete with each other in the way corporations do. The main explanation for this is that the world is not as interdependent as we often think. The US is probably less dependent on the market than any other country, especially when it comes to trade, for it exports only 10 per cent of the value-added in the economy (which is equal to GNP). In other words, it produces goods and services largely for its own use. By contrast, even the largest corporations sell very little of their output to their own workers. The 'exports' of General Motors – its sales to people who do not work for it – represent virtually all of its sales (which are more than 2.5 times the corporation's value-added). In other words when a company competes for market share it competes directly with others. One company gains, another loses; the market can indeed produce a zero-sum dynamic.

In the case of most countries this is rarely the case. If the Chinese economy does well, its success is not necessarily at America's expense. Americans borrow from China $700 billion a year to finance their own excessive spending and to keep mortgage and house prices down. Conversely, by boosting American consumption, the Chinese make it possible for America to remain their largest market (Krugman 1998:9).

In that respect, nations do rise and fall, and certainly America's position vis-à-vis China can be expected to change to the latter's advantage. But neither country is involved in a 'race for the twenty-first century' as is often claimed. Companies, by contrast, often do find themselves competing for survival, especially when consumer demand collapses either because the goods they produce fall out of fashion or because they are rendered obsolete by technological change. Companies often go out of business. Countries rarely do. Yet, that does not mean, of course, that they do not compete. They still compete for power and the stakes are paradoxically higher. Great Powers wax and wane. No one really loses from the collapse of a company except its shareholders and employees, and even the employees can be re-tooled. But countries which fail to compete geopolitically can incur a cost, as can the rest of us when we can no longer rely on them for protection. When Great Powers forfeit their great power status they are sometimes missed.

Even so, the comparative decline in a country's global position can also work to everyone's advantage. The collapse of the Soviet Union gave rise to a unipolar moment for the US which was neither in its interests nor those of its allies. It encouraged an exaggerated belief in its own indispensability. The Bush administration came to conclude that order could be maintained only if the US behaved quite differently from others. 'American security, world stability and the spread of liberalism require the United States to act in ways others cannot and must not. This is not a double standard, it is what world order requires' (Jervis 2003:276). Looking forward to the future we may well conclude that the rise of India and China is not necessarily bad for America: it may force Americans to constrain their own exercise of power.

Hedging, in other words, has now been embraced by countries as well as companies. US policy is best described as 'engagement plus hedging'. The 2006 QDR acknowledged that China should be encouraged to play 'a constructive peaceful role in the Asia-Pacific region and to serve as a partner in addressing common security challenges'. But it also recognized that of all the emerging powers, the country had the 'greatest potential' to compete with the US in the future (*QDR* 2006:18–29). The reasons are set out clearly in the 2002 US-China Security Review Commission report which states that the two countries have 'sharply contrasting world views, competing geo-strategic interests and opposing political systems' (US-China Economic & Security Review Commission 2005). These differences are real; they cannot be papered over with joint communiqués, any more than eliminated simply by narrowing differences on specific policy issues. On the other hand, China is not perceived to be a revolutionary power like the Soviet Union. It is seen more as a late-comer in the Great Power game, one that is seeking to establish its position in a world that has been ordered strategically by earlier rivals.

The National Security Strategy in the same year accepted this analysis. '[We] seek to encourage China to make the right strategic choices for its people while we hedge against other possibilities' (Tunsjo 2007:42). In its annual report to Congress, the Defense Department insisted that the US must 'hedge against the unknown' (*US DoD Defense Department Executive Summary*) (in Tunsjo 2007:43). The unpredictable is now a permanent factor in international politics as was not really the case during the Cold War. And what is unpredictable, by definition, we must hedge against.

The main way in which the US is seeking to do this is to fold China into the existing security architecture; this was the logic behind 'fast-tracking' its entry into the World Trade Organization (WTO) a few years ago. Its intention is to create an interest in stability, to encourage China to become a responsible *stakeholder* in the international system. If, unlike the Soviet Union in the 1940s, it is more interested in securing a greater voice in the management of the system, and not challenging its fundamental operating principles or procedures, then containment is unnecessary. Stakeholders may not be allies but they have common interests.

And China has begun to participate actively in multilateral economic and security organizations such as the Asia-Pacific Economic Corporation Forum (APEC), the ASEAN Regional Forum (ARF) and the ASEAN Plus Three (APT). The ARF has drawn up a China–ASEAN 'code of conduct' in the disputed South China seas, while the APT provides a forum in which China, Japan and South Korea can discuss security issues. But China is hedging against the US too by joining the Shanghai Co-operation Organization (SCO) whose members include countries with which America may come into conflict in the future, such as Russia, Pakistan and Iran (the latter two not yet full members, only observers). The proliferation of such security organizations may set a pattern for the future: it may

establish a highly complex *network of networks*, each consisting of interconnected and partially interlocking organizations very different from the rival
systems of alliances and blocs that were so characteristic of the twentieth
century.

The problem is that there are as many different opinions in Washington
as there are approaches to China's rise – hence the need for hedging. If
folding it into the existing security architecture constitutes a hedging strategy, some experts have argued that China's actual integration into these
organizations has so far proved shallow or self-serving. Even if this changes,
they contend, China is a long way from becoming a cosmopolitan state
willing to acknowledge, let alone accept, any reduction of its sovereignty.

The point about hedging is that while it can reduce risks it cannot eliminate them. Companies attempt to hedge against risks that are peripheral
to their central business, such as currency fluctuations. Firms hedge in
order to improve or maintain their own competitiveness, but the competition between companies is generically different from competition between
states (Tunsjo 2007:107–19). When they fail to compete companies often
go out of business; countries rarely do so. And unlike the market, security
is subjective. Whether hedging policies are long-term or short, whether
they are prudentialist or opportunistic (whether they involve hedging
against the bad, or exploiting the unpredictably good), risk societies are only
as secure as they *feel* themselves to be.

None of which is to claim that risk management is only a Western strategy. Hitherto the West has set the pace in designing the normative framework of international relations. Now the Chinese are coming into the
picture and are anxious that the US should yield ground gracefully as it finds
itself unable to shape the system to suit its own purposes and needs. From
their own perspective as a rising state the Chinese are just as interested in
managing America's decline as the US is in managing their rise. The debate
began in 2006 with a private article by Wang Yiwei (a young scholar at
Fudan University) who asked: 'How can we prevent the US from declining
too quickly?' Given that the US is still the main 'service provider' in the
system and will continue to be so for some time to come, and given that no
other country at present can replace it (including China), few Chinese want
the US to decline too quickly. In a word, they too are interested in hedging
their bets by working with others (such as Russia). But their principal interest is to manage the risk of American decline until such time as they can
meet the demands of becoming the world's second superpower (Leonard
2008:116).

The Global Disorder

There is a quotation from Bill Clinton, regretting that there was no over-arching superstructure to 'regulate' the world, in default of which the neg-ative elements of globalization would outweigh the positive ones. It is rather depressing, of course, that we should feel nostalgia for the Cold War, but we do in part because it constituted a political order of a kind. In the global disorder that emerged after 1991 the West finds that the behaviour of many actors is considerably more unpredictable, and what is more important is that this uncertainty is not the outcome of defects in intelli-gence-gathering or political analysis. It is almost an organizing *principle* of the disorder, if this were not a contradiction in terms. Politicians have found that they cannot anticipate all the risks that may arise. It is trends that are most difficult to read; it is the concept of potentiality that has broken into international affairs. The global disorder is non-linear and therefore not open to actuarial analysis.

Today there is no world order, or even a semblance of it. Writing in the early 1990s, two respected analysts, Max Singer and the late Aaron Wildavsky, described the situation in their book, *The Real World Order: Zone of Peace, Zone of Turmoil*. Its premise was laid out starkly at the beginning of the first chapter: 'The key to understanding the real world order is to separate the world into two: a zone of peace, wealth and democracy, and a zone of turmoil, war and underdevelopment' (Singer and Wildavsky 1993:3). This presents us with an almost ontological rift in the human web; it also admits to a high degree of violence intrinsic to the life and experience of the Zone of War. People, claims Stephen Fry, can be divided into two: those who divide the world into two and those who don't. The same would also seem to be true of strategists – but the point is a little more subtle. For the question is not whether such divisions exist, the point is that we think they do, and we believe that violence tends to break out when the two zones intersect. 'The world is interdependent – to be engaged is only modern *realpolitik*,' remarked Tony Blair in August 2006 (*The Times*, 26 August 2006).

In dividing the world into different zones of prosperity and disorder, what makes us most anxious is the intersection between the two. Our polit-ical leaders now talk of living in a 'post-secure' world for that reason. Thus, Tony Blair addressing the US Congress in 2003: 'September 11 was not an isolated event, but a tragic prologue . . . our new world rests on order. The danger is disorder, and in today's world it can spread like a contagion (Mythen 2004:2). It is essential to ask, however, whether either Blair or Clinton (or many of the other world leaders for that matter) have actually grasped the reality of globalization. Globalization, writes the French social thinker Alain Touraine, does not define a stage of modernity; it does not even define a historical era. It should be seen for what it is: a way of *managing* historical change, or a way of looking at the world and solving some of its problems.

Touraine takes as his starting point the rupturing within the West of many traditional social bonds and the triumph of asocial individualism which I highlighted in chapter 3 as a major feature of the risk age. The decline of social classes and social movements as well as the traditional agencies of 'socialization' such as the school and the family is much discussed by sociologists. Politics is now determined by an aggressive individualism, or the rise of communitarian politics (multiculturalism) which challenges the state's structural fitness for war. So it should not be surprising that this is paralleled internationally too. There is no place in our imagination for great social discourses such as building a New World Order. At home the state negotiates with interest groups (religious or ethnic in origin); overseas the risk groups (terrorists / rogue states / risk factors such as SARS) have replaced the old social categories such as political ideas and ideologies (Touraine 2007: 19–32).

And war must be fitted into this picture too as an organizing or regulatory principle. The chief purpose of state power is management. The US often sees itself as a 'facilitator' of globalization; the EU actually claims to be a 'facilitator' of global civil society. Force can be seen as a facilitating factor too. It no longer has a political or social function. The West is no longer in the business of fighting crusades (such as the liberal world's crusade against fascism). War is no longer a means by which the US (or anyone else) can 'ride the wave of the future' (one of John F. Kennedy's favourite metaphors, lifted from the title of an earlier book by Anne Morrow Lindbergh in 1941). In the early 1960s Kennedy seized upon Lindbergh's vision of war: 'I cannot see this war', she had written, 'as simply and purely a struggle between the forces of good and the forces of evil . . . it is simpler to say that the forces of the past are fighting the forces of the future' (Lukacs 1976:514). Kennedy challenged the American people to ride the wave by seeing off the threat of communism rather than risk being pulled along in its undertow. Today there is no vision of the 'social' any longer; there is only a very utilitarian understanding of the future: the world is a dangerous place that needs to be policed against a range of enemies from terrorist movements to criminal syndicates and drug cartels.

What makes Touraine's argument so persuasive is that he claims that even terrorists tend to follow the same logic. They too have long since abandoned politics as traditionally understood (Iran is likely to be the first and last Islamicist revolution). Even radical Islamic states have abandoned war in its conventional (inter-state) formulation. Terror is not war; it is a tactic meant to derail, or slow down, the forces of globalization, in part by engaging in hit-and-run assaults on its 'facilitators', especially the US. Most terrorists are not animated by the vision of remaking the world according to a grand social vision. In that sense al-Qaeda is not what Lenin would call a 'revolutionary vanguard'; he would have seen the movement as an 'infantile disorder'. Globalization separates the social and economic; it puts paid to social visions by revealing all local action as meaningless in the face of global forces. Few of us define ourselves as social beings; instead we are products of an objective market, or a subjective culture that defines itself in terms of local or regional ideals. The world of organized political violence is no longer a *social* world at all. 'War is no longer the other side of social conflict' (Touraine 2007:2). Modern states were created through war and existed to pursue it in pursuit of a social vision; today's states wage wars which have no political or social function. For us war has become risk management in all but name.

And risk societies are much less interested in nation- or state-building as traditionally understood. The nation-building model is now out of favour, probably for good. The risk age is not one in which values or value-inspired strategies are rejected altogether. But interests count for much more than they did. One of the dynamics of strategic planning is a kind of fatalism, a rejection of ambitious projects with all their unanticipated consequences. Policy-makers exhibit a hardening of arteries as well as a hardening of hearts. We are much less willing than we once were to support people who are trying to shape their destiny rather than accept their fate.

Risk Management and Complex Adaptive Systems

For all the commitment of the neo-conservatives to nation-building in 2002–3, more sober American policy-makers – more in tune with the time – have begun to question whether in the risk age they should be attempting to reorder society at all. Is nation-building desirable, or is it part of the intellectual baggage of a previous era? Should it remain a canonical thesis of American foreign policy as it has since the time the US entered history to reorder the empires of central Europe following World War I?

In recent years a number of professions have been taken to task for continuing to be rooted to their own canonical hypotheses. One of the most persistent in economics, writes Robert Solow, is the concept of 'price equilibrium', a goal which is quite impossible in a capitalist economy whose very essence is change because it is the economic system itself which generates the forces which constantly transform it. Some economists now insist that all prices are disequilibrium-related for that reason. In any market information is discovered, adjustments made and resources shifted to try to keep up with changing conditions. Unless we hypothesize the existence of an omniscient auctioneer who controls the market and establishes the point of equilibrium, all transactions must take place inevitably at 'non-equilibrium' prices (Kamarck 2001:14).

Inflation, in other words, like all economic forces is driven from behind. In managing an economy we should only aspire to achieve certain outcomes, of which low inflation is one. At any moment, we can say that such-and-such may be an outcome. It would be deeply misleading to call low inflation an 'equilibrium' simply in order to maintain the canonical hypothesis involved. For this would imply that if a particular outcome does not come about that economic forces will continue to maintain it, or that if it should move towards disequilibrium other forces will restore it. And this all, of course, presupposes that maintaining equilibrium is necessarily desirable in itself (Kamarck 2001:189–90).

In the risk age a similar logic is beginning to be applied to security. If there is no possibility of building a New World Order then all attempts to 'restore' equilibrium (defined as permanent stability, order or even peace) through nation-building will almost certainly fail. An 'order' suggests that it can be enforced (pacification) or policed, or secured against external and internal threats. Risk management is much less ambitious: it involves managing disorder at levels of insecurity that are more acceptable to the international community until such time as an order of sorts can emerge (if at all). Security is not a project: it is a process in which solutions evolve over time. When intervening, all that the international community can hope for is a more favourable 'outcome' defined in terms of better behaviour.

When looking at any culture, wrote the late anthropologist Clifford Geertz, we should isolate its constituent elements and identify the internal relationships between them for it is these that produce specific outcomes in the form of specific behaviour. We should identify the core elements around which a society is organized and the underlying structures of which it is merely the surface expression. We should try too to identify its principal ideological beliefs. In Afghanistan we can analyse the key actors – the drug barons, the warlords, the tribal leaders, the local politicians – we can analyse the relationship between them, especially their role in the coalition that sustained Taliban in power after 1994; we can look at the country's underlying social structures such as tribalism with its honour codes, and its principal belief system, Islam.

But as Geertz reminds us, such a hermetical approach is in danger of locking cultural analysis from its proper objective – identifying the informal logic of actual life. What anthropologists should be looking at is *behaviour* because it is through the flow of behaviour (or more precisely social action) that cultural forms find articulation. They find it as well, of course, in various forms of consciousness (in the way a society regards the world) for these too draw their meaning from the role they play in the ongoing pattern of life.

To change the behaviour of any system, we need only change some of the rules at the local level. As Geertz contended, this is what politics is actually about (Geertz 2000:27). It is largely local – the trick is not to spend too much time shoring up central government but to try to improve the local quality of life. Service delivery should be the goal. In the development community this has been recognized in recent years. Development economists have tried to gain a deeper appreciation of the 'political economy' of the local environment. The *World Development Report* in 2004 pointed clearly to the importance of the local in the virtuous circle of social service delivery, noting that small changes can produce large effects, while large changes (such as a change of regime at the centre or the introduction of democracy) can make little difference (World Bank 2004). We call this non-linear behaviour because cause and effect do not always work as we expect. Small changes can generate surprises; they can produce emergent properties (such as greater stability) once a critical threshold has been crossed. The study of emergence in all its forms is one of the most important scientific enterprises of the age.

Much of the new theoretical work in economics takes the concept as its starting point. The Sante Fé Institute's researches on complexity, non-linear dynamics, evolutionary games theory and inductive rationality, all focus on achieving economic outcomes by treating each agent, whether an individual, a company or an industry, as part of a complex-adaptive system (the economy). Each is constantly reacting to what the other agents are doing. As one opportunity is grasped and exploited by one particular agent, so new opportunities will arise for others as competitors, partners, parasites or predators (Kamarck 2001:19).

The key to producing change in any complex adaptive system is to discover what the economist Herbert Simon calls 'meaningful simplicity in the midst of disorderly complexity' (Buchanan 2002:214). Let me cite a very old example, the introduction of democracy in sixth-century Athens.

The West is still formally in the business of making the world safe for democracy but it has an imperfect grasp of how history's first democracy came into being. It is an instructive tale. The reforms introduced by Cleisthenes are usually credited with democracy-building but this was not his mandate. He was charged by his fellow citizens with producing a specific outcome: changing the behaviour of a system in which family and dynastic conflicts had become so ruinous that they were in danger of destroying city life. His solution was brilliantly simple and quite ruthlessly ambitious at the same time. He decided to suppress identity with family, neighbourhood and local clan chiefs altogether by slicing up the country-side into 150 separate districts. It was from these *demes* and no longer from their families that the citizens of the state were obliged to take their second names. This created a remarkable sense of civic identity. Under Cleisthenes' reforms a young man when he came of age could only become a citizen by enrolling within a *deme*.

Cleisthenes' re-organization of the citizenry transformed the *polis* from a political framework into a political body. Its unity was reinforced by the participation of its citizens and became meaningful only through citizen input (Maier 1993:160). And Cleisthenes successfully introduced stability into the system by marrying political reform to an ancient past. And since the Athenians were nothing if not traditionalists, the tribes were all given the names of ancient heroes. Cleisthenes, in short, not only invented his city's future. Quite as crucially, he also fabricated its past.

Finally, each of the ten new tribes with voting blocks presided in rotation in the Council of Five Hundred which ensured that no single pressure group could dominate civic affairs. Compromise accordingly became less a procedural obligation than a social habit. By changing the behaviour of the system he found, Cleisthenes made possible democratic political life. Democracy was the outcome, not the project.

Like sixth-century Athens, Afghanistan too can be seen as a complex-adaptive system consisting of many different political actors each obeying certain rules that govern its behaviour. The units include drug barons and local politicians, warlords and revolutionaries. As one opportunity arises (the collapse of the Taliban) so other actors, such as the Northern Alliance, or the thirteen different warlords, or the groups with private armies (some 4,000 in all at the last count) interact as partners, predators or parasites. The behaviour of the system is the product of the collective result of each actor using his own initiative in the context of established rules. By attempting to change the system, in this case by democratizing the country, the West hopes to change its behaviour. Unfortunately, it has found that is has much less knowledge than the locals of how the system works. And in such an aggressively Darwinian environment it is knowledge which enables groups to adapt faster. Darwinists these days no longer talk of the survival of the fittest, so much as the survival of the best-informed.

Instead of trying to democratize Afghanistan, the West should perhaps be trying to engineer a particular outcome: greater stability, something which is best obtained not by reordering the country but by changing the behaviour of various social groups. If the study of complex-adaptive systems shows that many types of change have remarkably little effect on behaviour, computer modelling also reveals that a very small change in the rules can produce a significant change in behaviour. The task is to find the right *leverage* factors. In other fields examples include anti-trust laws which tend to curb the market's tendency towards monopolies, and vaccines which when injected into the bloodstream can trigger a patient's immune system to fight a particular disease. Let me cite one further example from the field of development. Within a decade the provincial government of Kerala had achieved a literacy rate as high as that of the developed world. The leverage factor that the state authorities identified was a notion popularized by the Brazilian educator, Paulo Freire, who claims that immediate problems in people's lives usually provide the best teaching materials (Martin 2006:61). The solution in Kerala was to give the peasants readings that related to their immediate situation such as hunger, poverty and safe drinking water.

Military force can act as a leverage factor too, but only if it is recontextualized to fit the risk age. And it can only promote greater stability (or lesser insecurity – stability for the international community and security for the locals) if the objective, changing the behaviour of a complex-adaptive system, is seen for what it is – a 'wicked problem'.

Wicked Problems

The concept was first defined by two urban planners at the University of California, Berkeley in 1973, H. W. J. Rittel and M. M. Webber, in their paper *Dilemmas in the General Theory of Planning*. The classical scientific method, they wrote, while supremely well attuned to the solution of 'tame' problems did not lend itself particularly well to the solution of wicked ones (Blockham 2007). The problem with the modern age was that it believed that every problem was 'tame', that every problem could be solved given enough time and resources. Our age, by comparison, manages problems that do not lend themselves to solutions. This is a particular challenge for the military profession which is by nature problem-solving. Soldiers are trained to think logically: they are supreme instrumentalists; they think in terms of solutions, programmes and projects. They are not so good at thinking 'outside the box'. And whenever they encounter the unfamiliar they tend to translate it into a format which fits the existing analytical structure. Soldiers are usually most happy when addressing the traditional concepts taught at staff college: the idea that wars have definable beginnings and ends.

As a wicked problem, war is resistant to traditional military thinking. The problem has been expressed very well by John Nagl, a member of the writing team that produced *Field Manual 3-24 Counter Insurgency*, the US military's latest take on the War on Terror. Counter-insurgency is often counter-intuitive, which is why he describes as 'Zen-like' some of the very first chapters which turn conventional military doctrine on its head (Nagl 2002:15). Nagl is particularly critical of the US military's obsession with bringing the enemy to battle. Officers are still taught at staff colleges that war is a clash of wills, a contest between equal or unequal forces. It is a tradition that dies hard.

In their landmark article Rittel and Webber did not mention war, but they did claim that there are numerous other policy problems that are impervious to the usual analytical, linear approaches of politicians. Tame problems are not necessarily simple; some can be very complex indeed. But they can more easily be defined, and are therefore are more open to definitive linear solutions. Wicked policy problems such as climate change are not. Unlike tame problems they cannot be defined definitively. Those who have a stake in the outcome usually have radically different worldviews and thus employ different conceptual frameworks in analysing what makes a situation 'problematic'. Because the experts disagree on causes there can be no conclusive 'best solution'. Climate change is a vivid case in point; it is a highly complex policy issue involving multiple causal factors and high levels of disagreement about the nature of the problem and the best way to tackle it. The motivation and behaviour of various actors, such as energy-intensive industries and energy-wasting consumers, and new emerging powers like China, are a key part of the solution.

The same is true in the field of security. In Afghanistan the Coalition powers do not agree on a definition of the problem. Some feel they can talk to the Taliban, that the movement has to be part of the solution. Others think that it is the problem. Some countries question the wisdom of trying to eliminate opium production, and denying many farmers a source (possibly their only source) of income. Others claim that it is the criminalized economy that feeds instability and corruption. None of these views is mutually exclusive, of course, and none of them is necessarily wrong. It is the interdependencies and internally conflicting goals (opium eradication programmes drive farmers into the arms of the Taliban) that make wicked problems hard to define. Every objective that is set tends to produce a range of new problems. Welcome to the risk age.

Sometimes indeed, as Dr Johnson warned, things get darker through attempts to define them. Modern physics now admits that many important factors in the universe may not be open to clear definitions; all scientists can do is to define them with respect to their *connections*. These relationships are of primary importance: just as no 'fact' can stand alone apart from its association with other facts, modern physics now tends to divide the world, not into different groups of objects, but into different groups of connections (Lukacs 2006:66). And the main point about relationships is that they are complex as opposed to complicated.

A wicked problem, in addition, cannot even be understood until a solution has been formulated, and formulations will differ because we cannot realize goals so much as seek them. Goals have to be reset as the situation evolves and as unforeseen consequences move centre stage. In a wicked problem the situation on the ground is never stable, which is why the definition of the problem may change as the situation evolves. In that sense, what makes a problem 'wicked' is that it can never be 'solved', only managed until someone finally decides to stop managing it, or the managers run out of resources, time or money. At that point they may choose to abandon the project because their understanding of the problem, and hence the working formulation of it, changes. Perhaps, other challenges are considered more pressing. In other words, when a problem ceases to be problematic, the problem goes away (Schmidtchen 2006:186).

Finally, in managing wicked problems the most important challenge is one that is central to an age of risk: consequence management. Every solution is one-shot because each intervention changes the context of the problem. Every solution can be considered as a symptom of another problem waiting to crop up. Niklas Luhmann puts it very well: 'We no longer belong to the family of tragic heroes who subsequently found that they had prepared their own fate. We now know it beforehand' (Luhmann 1998:74). We now recognize that we can be the instruments of our own undoing.

None of this is to suggest that there is nothing that can be done to improve the situation in a country like Afghanistan. One writer has come up with three possible strategies for tackling wicked problems. One possibility is to mandate one particular country to tackle the problems, and for the others associated with it to abide by its decisions. But there is no guarantee that even within the policy-making community of the country concerned there will be broad agreement on the definition of the problem, and even where this may not be the case the policy-makers may be unable to break out of their own narrow experience. Even with the tame problem of the Cold War the Europeans were not always prepared to abide by the decisions of the US, or its definition of the problem. Frequently the allies disagreed on their analysis of Soviet intentions – though less so on Soviet capabilities – but the main disagreement emerged from the emphasis that some wanted to put on deterrence and others on détente. In the end, of course, the Cold War was a tame problem; it had a resolution and it could easily be defined. For though the allies fought many bitter battles about burden-sharing and attached different importance to détente and trade, and though they especially clashed over 'out of area' questions – they debated endlessly whether the main threat was to be found on the Central Front (Europe) or the killing fields of the Third World – they never disagreed on the most important question of all – who was the enemy.

A second strategy is more competitive. Members of a coalition of the willing who put forward different analyses of the situation may produce better ideas; they may become more innovative. But equally they may pursue different ends and spend too much time undermining each other's initiatives, and when they cannot agree to disagree they may opt to impose national caveats (as they have in Afghanistan, over a hundred of them, fifty-three of which are operationally significant). It is the third strategy that tends in principle to be most effective and it is essentially the strategy NATO has tried to pursue: it has tried to produce a collaborative model involving not only its own members, but other stakeholders including NGOs. In setting up Provincial Reconstruction Teams it has tried to get everyone to invest more in the outcome and to follow more comprehensive solutions. The problem is that collaboration can end in conflict – in hardened positions and mutual backbiting and increased transaction costs.

As one writer puts it, the whole point about effective collaboration is to create a shared understanding of the problem, and a shared commitment to possible solutions. Shared understanding does not mean that the various stakeholders will necessarily agree on the problem; it means that they will understand each other's position enough to have an intelligent dialogue about the different interpretations of the problem and to exercise collective intelligence about how best to deal with it. 'Because of social complexity solving a wicked problem is fundamentally a social process'

(Australian Government 2007:28). It is a socialization process involving collective learning through shared experiences; the problem is that none of this is happening either in the ISAF HQ or in the field. It is certainly not happening fast enough to make an effective difference on the ground. Wicked problems are 'solved' when the managers persuade the local actors to behave differently, but that also requires them to behave differently themselves, and NATO has not persuaded its various national contingents to behave differently; some remain excessively risk-averse. Other powers (especially the US) are thought by some to be far too kinetic in their approach to the conflict. And NATO has failed signally to convince every member that they are in for the long haul; there is no long-term focus that can be discerned, only a preoccupation with immediate risks.

I hope that my discussion of 'wicked problems' is not the attempt of an enthusiastic political scientist to hitch his wagon to a new star, or to jump on a bandwagon – a bandwagon for 'wicked problems' can hardly be said to exist. It is the philosophical aspects of the concept which I find of most interest because the concept seems to meet a demand of the risk age – that we recognize that victory as traditionally defined is no longer a realistic objective. Peace cannot be an objective either, defined that is in terms of building a stable, functioning democracy. Progress rather than success, adds one writer, may be the best means of evaluation (Talentino 2004:54).

'We are Local'

In the end, wicked problems highlight the seminal importance of the local: tame problems can often be tackled from the centre; wicked problems rarely can. Perhaps, it has always been the case. Let me recount an anecdote involving Arthur Ransome (the author of *Swallows and Amazons*, a typical English story of children messing about in boats). Ransome was not only a popular author, he was also a Foreign Office official who in 1919 was to be found touring Galicia in order to ascertain the ethnicity of the peasants, committed as the Allies were to the principle of self-determination. Coming across a group of peasants working a field, he found that they were unwilling to identify themselves as belonging to any ethnic constituency. Again and again on asking them to what nationality they belonged, whether Russian, Little-Russian or Polish, he heard the reply 'Orthodox', and when pressed to say to what actual race they belonged he heard them answer safely, 'We are local' (Zeman 1989:21).

Ransome thought this was a telling example of what Marx and Engels called the 'idiocy of rural life'. Isn't the local always resistant to change, reform or improvement? Or was there a more prosaic interpretation: isn't the answer one gives to a question often dependent, not only on the time at which it is being asked, but also on the identity of the questioner? In this case, uncertainty as to national identity was likely to have been genuine, rather than the result of proverbial peasant guile. The 'local' tends to be particularly persistent when the coincidence between nation and state cannot always be taken for granted. And it can't be taken for granted today in Afghanistan where the West is involved in stability-enabling.

Throughout the Greater Middle East, local power networks give the region its identity, as well as its cohesion. A technical term for them is 'micro-societies' and though often difficult to identify from the distance of London or Washington, or for that matter the UN, they are part of the complexity of political life. In much of the world power is not centralized in the state; it is decentralized in distributed networks which are often tribal. Anthropologists call them 'solidarity networks'. Sometimes they can be broken down further into clans or 'local mutual-aid associations', as the anthropologist Ernest Gellner called them. In the absence of a strong state these clans are stubbornly resistant to change.

At the same time, it is the very persistence of the local which accounts for the absence of strong government. Tribal power comes from the tribesmen themselves, and as such cannot be used against itself to maintain a structure they oppose. Government is more a coalition of interests which strong leaders have to manage as best they can through patronage networks. And what makes distributed network systems even more stubbornly resistant to change is Islam. For Islam generates networks of its own – an *ulema* (a religious network) made up of people with a similar education (in madrassas) and interests. When the existing order is under challenge *jihad* is an effective response. But *jihads* against that order are extremely uncommon. Islam legitimates the system; it rarely aspires to transform it.

Even the Taliban discovered this quickly once in power. The young Taliban recruits were certainly religious. But many had been educated outside the country in madrassas in Pakistan. Others had leaned their fundamentalist ideology in refugee camps, in an environment largely alien to traditional Afghan norms. Their subsequent attempt to transform Afghan society made them deeply unpopular and is likely to make them unpopular once again should they ever return to power. For their attempt to create a theocracy did not go very far where it mattered – deep down in the structure of local life – which is why the regime fell from power within a few weeks in 2002.

Is it possible, one must ask in conclusion, to devise a strategic plan for a wicked problem like Afghanistan? It is certainly highly difficult and it may well lie beyond the ambition of coalitions of the willing called into being to address them. If progress is constantly being redefined and success is indefinable at any one time the West runs the risk it did in Kosovo, where, to quote Rupert Smith, there was no strategy. Smith should know; during the war he was deputy SACEUR. At no point before or during the air campaign, he writes, was there any clear expression of a long-term political purpose: was the war intended to create an independent Kosovo, or to depose Milosevic, or to change the regime in Belgrade to one that would continue to govern the province but in a manner more acceptable to international opinion (Rupert Smith 2005:291)? But then the campaign had only one real purpose – to make the problem less problematic for the West.

Perhaps Smith's account suggests that risk coalitions are driven by tactical imperatives, not strategic concerns, and that to imagine things could be different is simply not yet to have come to terms with the imperatives of the risk age. Are there any 'ends', or is everything a matter of 'means'? 'The Iraq war will be won when Americans feel more secure again,' Rumsfeld insisted (Morgan 2004:6). How can such a war ever be won if 'feeling secure' is a matter of subjective response and entirely unquantifiable? Like progress and success, security is a matter of perception.

This is the case when the main objective in war (to quote Smith once again) is to sustain the mission. 'We fight so as not to lose the force rather than fighting . . . at any cost to achieve the aim' (Rupert Smith 2005:17). In a situation where the world has to be policed, and the problem constantly redefined, the mission must indeed determine the alliance, not the other way round. Coalitions of the willing are tactical by definition because their ultimate objective is not to 'win' wars, but police the wild frontiers of a globalized world.

The Policing Model

At the Marine Corps University at Quantico, particularly popular with the cadets is a novel by Robert Heinlein which forms the basis of Paul Verhoeven's film *Starship Troopers*. The film exploits almost every Hollywood war movie cliché down to the parody documentaries within the film based on Frank Capra's 1940s series *Why We Fight*. It also conjures up an early era of Indian wars in the West which resonates with the space troopers who find themselves engaged in an Indian-style war of the future, 'the Great Bug War'. In the same mould the television series *Above and Beyond* follows the exploits of a company of Space Marines in their unending quest to prevent the alien 'Chigs' from overrunning the galaxy.

Heinlein's book is popular with the Corps because it emphasizes the importance of 'distributed operations'. But its relentless emphasis on body counts as the main measure of success hardly meets the requirements of a successful counter-insurgency campaign. During the Cold War making the world safe for democracy at times might have seemed like squashing bugs, for instance the carpet-bombing of North Vietnamese cities in the 1960s. But if the body count rises relentlessly even Western public opinion might be prompted to ask a disturbing question: can democracy still be made safe for the world?

In recent years the US military has begun to adopt a more appropriate policing model of military operations in line with the new strategic objective: promoting greater 'progress' however progress is defined. 'Stability-enabling' may require terrorists be killed but it requires a great deal more, like 'community policing' at home. And like domestic police forces, foreign militaries may have to maintain a long-term presence. A report published in the summer of 2004 by the influential Defense Science Board argued for a change of mind-set in the military that would permit it to put together a post-imperial constabulary force: 'To be fully effective the United States will need to have some of its people continuously abroad for years, so that they become familiar with the local scene and the indigenous people come to trust them as individuals . . . tours of duty we imagine will be far longer than traditional assignments today' (Buley 2007:133).

The US military is already being radically restructured in keeping with this vision. The army is currently modularizing its force structure, moving from ten divisions up to forty-eight stand-alone brigades comprising up to 4,000 men each who will be quickly deployable, self-contained and self-sustaining. Pride of place is going to Special Forces who are likely to find themselves in the front line of operations, replacing the large-unit combat forces that hit the Normandy beaches in 1944 and served as far afield as the Gulf in 1990. They may yet be transformed into a fifth branch of the armed forces, just as the Air Force only became a distinct service in 1947. Steps in this direction have already been taken with the designation of an Assistant Secretary of Defense who is now tasked with co-ordinating Special Force requirements (Hart 2006:166–9).

The Marine Corps is also experimenting with 'infestation' tactics that might radically change the face of ground warfare. The Corps calls it 'plug in and play', a concept that involves rotating units in the field for months or even years at a time as autonomous nodes in a larger network. Others have proposed establishing 'pop up units'. Like landmines, you only discover that they are there when you tread on them, by which time, of course, it is far too late. Even technology is catching up. Instead of the grandstanding weapons systems deployed by army divisions, the military is now investing in electronic shields and signal jamming devices, hand-held drones for reconnaissance, robotic remote-control bomb-disposal units and unmanned aerial vehicles (UAVs) to help track individual enemies and even individual vehicles. Persistent area denial systems (PADs) employing robotic sensors may be particularly useful in providing security for small units (Evans 2007:23).

Times are changing. Military forces increasingly look like police forces. 'Snatch squads' in the Balkans have brought over fifty war criminals to justice at The Hague. In 1997 US Special Forces mounted two major operations involving up to 3,000 operatives in that year alone. Two years later the British Special Air Service (SAS) captured General Stanislav Galic, the Serb commander who besieged Sarajevo. In the period up to 2000 the SAS conducted eleven such operations in the British sector of Bosnia which resulted in the arrest of fifteen suspects and the death of two others while resisting arrest (Brailey 2006:22–3). Perhaps, it is a sign of the times that police forces increasingly look like militaries too, with their armoured cars, water cannon and SWAT teams.

The global nexus between crime and war is creating a grey zone where the two services are required to interlink, exchange information and carry out joint operations. In the British Sector in Iraq the Royal Military Police were inserted into Iraqi police stations to identify not only members of the Shia militia but also criminals who had no particular political agenda of their own (Steward 2007:10). In Afghanistan, British, Canadian and US Military Police units have been deployed to gather information in twenty-five villages surrounding Kandahar. Their presence represents a temporary stop-gap until such time as Special Forces can perform a 'pseudo-combat role' and patrol the criminal networks which run the drug trade and help finance Taliban operations.

Nevertheless, we must always remember that the aims of the military and the police are very different, and the differences are worth highlighting. The aim of intelligence-gathering in the military is to promote what Rupert Smith calls 'evidential information' that will legitimize in the eyes of the local community as well as public opinion at home the need to take out an adversary, rather than bring him to book (Rupert Smith 2005:42). Pinpoint accurate targeting, he writes, allows the military to kill the enemy in the right place and at the right time, and in such a way as to exploit the result. It is intended, in the jargon of the day, 'to network the effects of our actions' (Rupert Smith 2005:42). The intention is still to kill, but in a way that does not detract from the legitimacy of the mission. In that regard, Smith is quite right to insist that information is the life-blood of risk management. For it permits the more effective use of firepower with the promise of minimal collateral damage. It is there to avoid what John Gentry calls, 'risk-rebound' (Gentry 1998:145).

And the policing analogy runs deeper still. Just as the police try to separate criminals from the local community which may be harbouring them, so the military do their best to persuade the locals to provide information about insurgents and their movements and, if possible, their intentions too. In that sense there is a *diagnostic* operational rationale at work here. Surveillance at home is intended to establish the extent of a risk in the absence of any concrete data, and the same is increasingly true of military operations overseas. In a fast-moving, cascading environment, soldiers are becoming information processors.

The point of all this, Smith reminds us, is simple: 'We must capture the narrative.' Just as the tactician has always sought to understand his ground, the modern commander needs to understand the popular environment in which he now operates (Rupert Smith 2007a:40). Unless one understands the people, how can one decide on the right mix of forces and even how best to deploy them? One of the persistent complaints of more thoughtful military commanders such as Anthony Zinni is that Western politicians have a 'simplistic view of what is actually out there; they lack understanding of the complexities, the fine points, the subtleties of conditions on the ground' (Zinni and Koltz 2006:223). The narratives we spin are important because in a counter-insurgency campaign the central struggle is often over control of the story – and the story we tell ourselves is no less important than the story we tell others. Being seen as a winner by the locals is more crucial than ever.

It is the perceived importance of the local, of course, that has boosted the anthropological approach to war in the West. Successful risk management, like successful policing of the streets at home, requires the managers to be well informed. Cultural competence is now a buzz word in the US military. The army's new counter-insurgency field manual mentions 'culture' eighty-eight times, while the adjective 'cultural' appears ninety times in its 282 pages (US Department of the Army 2006). The change is a response to a demand of the times. More concretely, the Americans have set up a new project with the quintessential Pentagon name Cultural Operations

Research Human Terrain, which began life in Iraq by analysing the eighty-eight tribes and sub-tribes in a particular province. Since then it has been extended to include 'five person single terrain' teams that are now serving as cultural advisers with twenty-six different combat brigades on six-to nine-month tours of duty.

Western militaries, in short, find themselves operating in a grim Darwinian environment. Darwinism, however, has evolved since Darwin. We see evolution itself as a form of information-processing which allows those species that can process it more quickly than others to survive and thrive. In cybernetic terms information-processing can be seen as a form of feedback.

This is at the heart of complexity theory and its focuses on the behaviour of complex systems called networks. The first and most obvious property of any network is that its relationships are non-linear. The message we want to send can travel along a cyclical path which may become a feedback loop. The concept of feedback, therefore, is intimately connected with network patterns. A related concept is that of *emergence*, the process by which complex structures are organized on the basis of simple rules. As the scientist Stephen Wolfram has put it: 'Whenever you look at very complicated systems in physics or in biology, you generally find that the basic components and the basic laws are quite simple; complexity arises because you have a great many of these simple components interacting simultaneously. But complexity is actually in the organisation – the myriad possible ways that the components can interact' (King 2000:132).

Thus genes in an organism form a vast interconnected network, rich in feedback loops in which they directly regulate each other's activities. The genome should not be seen as a linear array of independent genes (manifesting as traits), claims Francesco Vearela, but a highly interwoven network of multiple reciprocal effects mediated through repressors and depressors, exons and introns, jumping genes and even structural proteins. Nevertheless, complexity remains within the information paradigm since these non-linear interactions do not have to be physical; they can also be thought of as the transference of *information* (King 2000:76–7).

In a sense this is what Rupert Smith means by war as narrative. It is the narrative that helps militaries to manage complex-adaptive systems. They themselves are required to respond on the basis of information far faster than they have before. And although the military forces deployed by risk societies are not entirely risk-averse, they are being asked to take risks in a more informed fashion.

Adapting in the Field

There are two kinds of risk: risk as a product of a probability and the likely impact of an event once the probable actually happens, and risk as a necessary gamble for an immediate gain. In terms of the second definition risk is central to life. If we are not willing to take risks we would face a real problem. Capitalism requires all of us to bet on the risks we take. A company can only make a profit, after all, by successfully calibrating opportunity costs.

Armies too are being challenged to be more competitive in risk-taking. To be competitive they have to react faster. I have said that speed is often dangerous. It has predictable limits and produces diminishing returns (Campen 2000:68). It deprives us of contact and direct experience of an enemy. But speed is essential in information-processing, which has been speeding up all the time. There is a curious dialectic at work here. Wars are actually slowing down; they are becoming more protracted. In Israel the intifada has lasted twenty years. In Northern Ireland terrorism continued for over thirty. But the longer conflicts continue so the more innovative the insurgents become. It counts for much that they are no longer the national liberation armies familiar to us from the Cold War. Instead, they are more open-sourced and decentralized and organized around distributed or quasi-independent groups. In Iraq they engage in distributed swarms, learning from each other's experience, sharing information and responding quickly to change. In the early days their innovation cycles were often faster than those of the Coalition forces.

They also differ from the old national liberation movements in another critical respect. They are interested in outcomes, not order-building. What gives them the advantage is that, unlike the old national liberation movements, they are usually not interested in holding territory, though they may be ready to lure the enemy to fight for it as the insurgents did in Fallujah on two separate occasions in 2004. They are not usually interested in building schools (though like the Taliban they may empty them, especially of girls). They are not even interested, unlike the criminal cartels in Colombia, in creating social welfare nets to legitimize their presence. Some like Hezbollah resemble the old national liberation forces; others, however, thrive in the *lawless* spaces created by the collapse of law and order. They don't construct anything, or take responsibility for anything they do. As a result, writes John Robb, they are hard to take out (Robb 2007).

And the outcomes they produce can lead to significant returns. In one case in Iraq an insurgent group spent $2,000 to blow up an oil pipeline that cost the Iraqi government $500 million in lost revenue. This represented a staggering return on their investment of 25 million per cent. This evolutionary leap in methods of warfare is being exported around the world from Pakistan to Nigeria, creating a new class of insurgents that Robb calls 'global guerrillas'. The West is staring at a future where defeat may not be experienced immediately, but as an inevitable withering away of military, economic and political power through wasting conflicts with minor foes (Robb 2007).

Western militaries are in for the long haul. Wicked problems are always changing, and those on the ground have to be able to adapt quickly, and to process information about the changing situation faster than ever before. In a recent British Cabinet Office study of 'Better Policy Delivery and Design' it is argued that 'past experience has shown that delivery is rarely a one-off task. It is best understood not as a linear process – leading from policy ideas through implementation to change on the ground – but rather as a more circular process involving continuous learning, adaptation and improvement with policy changing in response to implementation and vice versa.' Of equal importance is the organizational culture of shared learning.

The merits of networks over hierarchies is to be found in the superiority of distributed information-processing. Hierarchical structures are effective at managing large-scale operations, but much less efficient in managing conditions of high complexity. 'Hierarchical command systems are designed for the largest-scale impacts and thus *relatively* simple warfare. Indeed, traditional military forces and related command control and planning were designed for conventional large-scale conflicts. Distributed control systems, when properly designed, can enhance the ability to meet complex challenges' (Bar-Yam 2003:1).

The real benefits of the network are to be found in its capacity for distributed computing.

> The key to this understanding is that each individual has a limited complexity. In particular, an individual is limited in ability to process information and to communicate with others (bandwidth). In an idealised hierarchy, only the single leader of the organisation can co-ordinate the largest organisational units whose commanders are directly under his command. The co-ordination between these units cannot be of greater complexity than the leader. More generally, we can state that to the extent that any single human being is responsible for co-ordinating parts of an organisation, the co-ordinated behaviours of the organisation will be limited to the complexity of a single individual. Since co-ordinated behaviours are relatively large-scale behaviours, this implies that there is a limit to the complexity of large-scale behaviours of the organisation.

Thus, using the command hierarchy is effective at amplifying the scale of behaviour, but not its complexity. By contrast, a network structure (like the human brain) can have a complexity greater than that of an individual element (neuron). (Bar-Yam 2003:8)

While the logic of this argument is sound, different organizational arrangements may suit different types of war environments. One of the criticisms of the Revolution in Military Affairs is that in privileging technology it has taken human beings out of the loop. 'A new human understanding of the environment', writes Ralph Peters, would be of far more use than any number of brilliant machines. 'We have fallen in love with the wrong revolution' (Peters 1999:30).

Yet, ironically technology may still help restore the advantage to Western militaries in what has been called the new 'counter-revolution in military affairs' prompted by the comparative failure of the mission in Iraq. In an environment as fluid as Iraq, junior officers have come to trust the experience of their peers more than that of commanders behind the lines. And these days they can connect with each other horizontally as never before. They can share information and learn from each other's experiences through the web. It is not that the soldiers on the front line have lost confidence in the judgement of their leaders. It is merely that they know that a hierarchical system is slow to adapt to the situations they face every day. Soldiers may well express confidence in the formal hierarchy that governs them, but they tend to trust their own experience and that of their peer group much more. The figures tend to bear this out. In 2004 the registered membership of the website companycommand.com in Iraq doubled (Schmidtchen 2006:290).

No less important, worldwide web-based peer-to-peer information-sharing services such as companycommand.com and platoonleader.org tend also to foster *social capital*. Social capital is the term we give to trust, and trust is different from confidence. Military organizations use standard operational procedures and competency-based training to build workforce confidence. Confidence depends on routine, unlike trust which emerges out of actions which, in the case of a military operation, can put at risk soldiers' lives. Confidence is usually risk-averse. When standard operational procedures are found to be flawed confidence can be lost quite quickly. It is trust which inspires risk-taking. If confidence, writes Schdmidtchen, depends on routine, trust depends on being able to deal with the unexpected, and even turn it to one's advantage (Schmidtchen 2006:289). Trust educates us to take sensible risks, and encourages us to defy the risk-aversive dynamic which these days is to be found at the heart of most organizations, including or even especially the military.

In terms of problem-solving, James Surowiecki cautions, the performance record of experts behind the lines is quite dismal. What counts for most is experience at the front line. Aggregation, he adds, is central to successful decentralization. Decentralization is a great strength in that it encourages independent specialization on the one hand, whilst still allowing people to co-ordinate their activities and solve problems on the other (Surowiecki 2005:171). Decentralization, however, can also be a weakness in that there is no guarantee that valuable information which is uncovered in one part of the system will find its way through to the other parts. This is where the new technologies offer a way through the puzzle, or fog of war.

A decentralized system can only produce genuinely intelligent results if there is a means of aggregating the information to everyone in the system. One advantage of a decentralized or distributed system is that it offers an incentive to share information. It creates an incentive for soldiers 'at the edge' to come up with the right solution because there are no bureaucratic filters or political factors that are likely to influence the processing of information. Soldiers at the edge don't have to tell others what they really want to hear (as they often do the high command). Those who find themselves 'at the edge' are less likely to tailor their opinions to fit the political climate of the day, or to satisfy the internal demands of the organization.

In short, a military can overcome excessive risk aversion by adapting fast. And this still calls for co-ordination. Imitation can be a powerful tool for spreading good ideas fast, and blogging helps them to spread faster than ever. This is only true, of course, as long as the process allows you to learn for yourself: to stop following the lead of others when experience demands it. This is why Surowiecki insists that 'intelligent imitation' is the key, not slavish following. Intelligent imitation demands an initially wide array of options and information plus the willingness of some people to put their own judgement ahead of the group; this is the reason why leadership is important, especially in the military, whose best leaders still tend to emerge from the field. We should draw comfort from the fact that collective learning is better because it is based on what we all do naturally – mimicry. Mimicry is so central to the way we live, suggests Herbert Simon, that humans are probably genetically predisposed to be imitation machines (Surowiecki 2005:59). And the leaders we tend to follow are the type of people who lead with their gut.

All great commanders, wrote Clausewitz, have acted on instinct and the fact that their instinct was always sound is partly the measure of their innate greatness and genius. The reason why Clausewitz emphasizes intuition rather than conscious thought is because he was fully aware that problems are real-life problems, not mathematical equations. For the same reason cognitive science has taken a renewed interest in the untapped possibilities of intuition. '[Intuition] is good at uncovering non-obvious relationships between areas of knowledge; at seeing "the pattern that connects" experiences that are superficially disparate. Intuition proves its worth in any situation that is shadowy, intricate or ill-defined' (Claxton 1998:56). The unconscious realms of the human mind tend to recognize patterns which the normal consciousness cannot see. They help to make sense of situations that are too complex to analyse logically. They enable us to get to the bottom of certain difficult issues much more successfully than the questing intellect.

Some design researchers, adds Gary Klein, may advocate a combination of intuition and analysis but they really aren't very comfortable with intuition as such; they would rather leave everything to computer modelling. But keeping intuition under control doesn't work. Only intuition can often give us the big picture (Klein 2003:54). Even in the risk age the big picture is important. If we are not to be overwhelmed by complexity, if we are to make the decisions that risk management demands, we might trust to it even more.

Risk-taking

Wicked problems are a useful way of thinking about one's objectives in a risk age. What risk management requires of the great powers is that they assess the risks they are willing to run in intervening and whether they are appropriate to the level of responsibility they wish to assume for their actions ('if you break it, you own it', as Colin Powell warned the President in the run-up to Operation Iraqi Freedom). And it also demands they ask themselves whether as political actors they have an *appetite* for risk. Intervention will always produce risks. It is the management, not reduction of risk, that should preoccupy the best political minds, as it does the best minds in business, and success will depend ultimately on the geo-political narratives we construct.

The stories we tell structure our everyday lives. They invest it with meaning. We spend a phenomenal amount of time, in fact, telling stories, listening to them, reading them, as well as watching them being enacted on screen or on stage. Our history books are largely made up of stories (the historical experiences that shape our view of the world are informed by narrative themes). The news we imbibe from television or newspapers is invariably in the form of stories; those structured sequences of images are the way by which we make sense of almost everything in our lives. So it is not surprising that the same is true of war. Strategic narratives are vitally important: we ask what any particular war is about; what is its subtext, or its principal theme. Strategic coherence is narrative-based which is why in an age of blogging, twenty-four-hour news channels, digital media, global TV stations and the internet, it is particularly difficult to control the story being told. 'The worst intel in history and bad PR [Abu Ghraib]', claims Senator Jasper Irving in the movie *Lions for Lambs*, who blames both for his country's setbacks in Iraq.

In the risk age, coalitions will always be ambushed by unforeseen events (stuff happens, and always will). But we must also make sense of what happens as it happens. We must be prepared to readjust, or readapt. We must be willing to tell a different story, to make sense of the narrative for others as well as ourselves. There is a line from Shakespeare's *Henry IV, Part 2* that comes to mind: 'When first we mean to build we first survey the plot, then draw the model.' When we talk of scaling down our strategic ambition we mean telling a more modest story, and constructing a more modest model, a story above all that is more plausible in the telling.

If even victory is not risk-free, if the management of risk is our principal objective then there is no inherent sanctity to any strategic objective such as democratization or nation-building. It is not that the model is wrong, only that once we become part of the reality on the ground (part of the political landscape in Afghanistan) we find ourselves part of someone else's story. We become part of the problem and must be prepared to change tack accordingly. When drawing up a strategy we must be willing to change the story as the situation develops on the ground; this is the logic of wicked problems. We cannot impose our own reality on the situation because we are part of the reality we are observing.

Our understanding of what is real, indeed, is a cultural construction like any other. The neo-conservatives' view of the Greater Middle East as a *tabula rasa* that awaited reshaping was an inflexible story which trapped the narrative in what Wittgenstein called a 'picture' – an ideological construction of an ideal world, something whose shape was not perceived but which conditioned the way we thought, inferred, experienced and argued. Thus in the run-up to the Iraq invasion it seemed obvious to the Americans that their soldiers would be welcomed as liberators. It took three years for the administration to re-perceive what was happening. The enframing constructions were only really challenged when the primary agents lost their jobs (Rumsfeld, Wolfowitz, Feith, Bolton). In order to reframe a story quickly there can be no closed world-ordering; the risk age demands our view of the world must be open-ended so that many stories can be told, not one (Taylor 2007:566). To say that there are many stories is not to adopt the post-modern fallacy of arguing that all stories are equally plausible. In order to be believable the stories we tell must be open to reason. But some of them will be more plausible than others.

The problem with the neo-conservatives is that when they did change the script in the hope of making the best out of the mess they had produced in Iraq, the stories they told were simply unbelievable. 'Bring them on' was President Bush's challenge, the idea being to reduce Iraq to a 'Terrorism Superbowl', an apocalyptic struggle in the desert in which the US and the terrorists could engage in a final struggle. Later, in the dark days of 2006, some Pentagon officials drew bizarre consolation from the prospect of a Sunni–Shia civil war spreading from Lebanon to Iraq; at least this seemed preferable to the otherwise 'inevitable' clash of civilizations between Islam and the West. In all story-telling, but especially in war, the old British army adage applies: 'when you're in a hole, stop digging.' Sometimes it's more sensible to cut and run though the risk age, ironically, suggests that this is usually the worst option – management requires commitment which is likely to be long term.

Conclusion

War is indeed a continuation of politics by other means but politics itself is always changing. In the twentieth century its main aim was to rationalize life. Politicians set out to reorder society; to make everything uniform by applying a single model in order to eliminate 'anomalies' as well as to ratio-nalize social life in Weber's double sense. Politics not only involved the increasing use of instrumental rationality in the sense that its only purpose was political (the existential world was bypassed – that is what made life, in Weber's words, so 'disenchanting'); politics was also bound by rules, and at the same time it was rule-making.

In the risk age, by contrast, life is too complex to be reordered, and even if this were not the case, war is too imperfect an instrument to do the reordering. As Rupert Smith insists, war is no longer a problem-solving device that can be applied to any complex issue. He takes a very risk-age view of politics. Politics isn't about order (either New World Orders or orders on the ground), and it no longer involves utopian projects of social engineering. For most of us no longer believe there is a perfect society.

Politics is now about purpose. And in the risk age our purposes are different from what they were fifty years ago. We are now in the business of 'managing' insecurity or 'enabling greater or lesser stability' or guaranteeing better 'service provision'. We have these particular vocabularies because we have such a multiplicity of purposes. As history evolves so new vocabularies come on stream but none of these vocabularies or purposes is more or less 'superior' to any of the others. Our own management of security is not necessarily better than the nation- or state-building of old. It just happens to be more relevant for us. It is all that we can aim for though we must hope, of course, that the purposes served may be better.

Clausewitz's seminal definition of war is important because it is dialectical. If war is a continuation of politics by other means, it must also change politics as long as politicians still rely on war as a political instrument. We recognize that complex systems hold surprises; our experience of them is that they display a tendency to organize themselves into critical states that cannot be predicted with any certainty – 'whether it is sand grains or thoughts that are being self-organised their next move is always a surprise' (Barrow 2005:251). This reinforces Clausewitz's insight that war too is inherently unpredictable, more so perhaps than ever. Our age is so much more complex that we have to acknowledge that there are limits to human actions – this understanding is a feature of the times. So if politics and war are still joined at the hip, are both condemned to produce ever-diminishing returns?

This, it seems to me, is the nub of the matter. At this stage in history we have to ask whether our awareness of the dialectic is beginning to paralyse our freedom of manoeuvre, as well as reduce our ambition. As we confront a rising tide of uncertainties and a depressing record of mistakes, should we entertain an even more radical thought? Is war becoming a template of politics? Do we talk the language of ultimate causes but practise the art of minimum risk? The words are not mine but Michael Ignatieff's, writing of the Kosovo War (1999) and American perceptions of their European allies (Ignatieff 2001:155). But the same these days could be said about other peoples' perceptions of the West. If this is the case, is there any hope that the Western world will one day escape from the risk age?

6

The Risk Age and its Discontents

In the course of writing this book I kept in mind a telling creation of the risk age, a creation of the American novelist, Don DeLillo. 'It is axiomatic', remarks the Professor of Latent History in his novel *Great Jones Street*, that history is the record of events. 'But what of latent History? We all think we know what happened. But did it really happen? Or did something else happen? Or did nothing happen?' (DeLillo 1978:74–5). His own subject, the professor continues expansively, deals not with what did happen but with events that almost took place, with events that definitely took place but remained unreported and with events that probably took place but which unfortunately no one at the time saw fit to chronicle. The latent, of course, is a feature of the risk age, the delayed symptoms that alert us to the fact that we can fall ill long after we have contracted a disease; that even the effects of 'effects-based operations' do not always become clear until it is too late.

Is there latent in our own age a tendency or set of weighted probabilities that are taking us beyond the risk age? We would have to abandon the study of history if we sought to eliminate all surprises. Can we assume, for example, that there will be no major inter-state wars in the future? Or is the risk age just another first draft of history?

Books such as this demand a lot of their authors – the times enjoin us to be equally wary of claiming too much, as well as too little. Indeed, we could question the whole endeavour of dividing history into eras and subdividing them once again. Freezing time into conventional periods is often problematic (Cornfield 2007:202). Historians tend to compartmentalize eras of history, giving them a special character they may not have, and then to evoke them to explain everything within the period, which is a circular argument. Periodization, nonetheless, is one of the ways by which we can make sense of the times in which we live. In the case of war it is the only way we can discover its particular 'cultural grammar'.

In the risk age inter-state conflicts are so few probably because they are so costly. This view is endorsed by a wide spectrum of opinion; it is no longer as it was in the age of William James and Norman Angell merely an academic hypothesis. In the 2006 US *Quadrennial Defense Review* we read that traditional inter-state threats are giving way to decentralized network threats emanating from non-state actors (*QDR* 2006:24–5). A recent study on strategic affairs by the leading defence analyst Lawrence Freedman, similarly suggests that the world is witnessing a rise in complex irregular conflict alongside the 'demilitarisation of inter-state relations' (Freedman 2006:7–9). In short, the trend in strategic affairs seems to be moving away from the discussion and planning of large-scale warfare between states, and instead towards a spectrum of conflict in which forms of both regular and irregular warfare may well interact.

We have been remarkably fortunate that none of the conflicts we have fought so far have resulted in high death rates. The Gulf War tally was amazingly low given the number of troops committed. Kosovo saw no fatal casualties and Operation Enduring Freedom very few. Subsequently, the West may have been corrected of the mistaken impression that the ability to destroy its enemies by stand-off precision has made close combat casualty-free. Even so, the death toll incurred at the time of writing (2008) – almost 4,000 – is historically small. Add non-fatal casualties and the picture changes. The official figure of American soldiers wounded in Iraq is 30,000 which is still lower than the death toll of an average Napoleonic battle.

Reference to the Napoleonic wars reminds us that our own experience is not untypical. The generation of 1788 also looked back on a world in which war seemed to be more risk-free than ever before. Today, argued an essayist of the period: 'War is waged . . . so humanely, so deftly and with so little profit, that it could be compared without paradox to civil trials' (Bell 2007:48). Another writer, blithely unaware that the French Revolution was waiting in the wings, felt moved to write that war had become increasingly risk-averse: 'Wars are like games of chance in which no-one risks his all: what was once a wild rage is now just a folly' (Bell 2007:49). Armies, he added, now slaughtered each other 'politely'. All this was to change when the French Revolution ushered in almost twenty-five years of uninterrupted conflict which produced the horrific killing grounds of Eylau, Borodino and Waterloo.

As David Bell reminds us, it is impossible to extrapolate from any period of history into the future and assume that things will be the same (Bell 2007:315). As the most unpredictable of all human activities, war is particularly unsuitable for the sort of trend analysis in which so many people put their faith. A graph of eighteenth-century combat deaths would have given no hint of the slaughter that was to come. A similar exercise carried out in 1910, the year in which James published his essay, *The Moral Equivalent of War*, would have been similarly pointless. What we can assert is that history does appear to move in cycles and that our age is one that is structurally predisposed to limited war – or in this case risk management.

In trying to explain the risk aversion of eighteenth-century conflict we have to look to sociology as I have tried to do in this book to explain the risk society at war. One explanation for the comparative 'humanity' of the eighteenth-century battlefield was the decline in religious fervour. The horror of the Thirty Years War was still etched in peoples' minds. Killing in the name of God always produces high casualties. But in the course of the eighteenth century states had begun to test each other's strength in battle against each other's soldiers, not civilians, and to abide by the results of the encounter. The growth of state power also witnessed the disappearance of private armies, the last to go being the Highland clans who were disarmed after 1746. Interestingly, Adam Ferguson was one of the army chaplains appointed to report on their political loyalty after they had been incorporated into a famous British regiment, the Black Watch. It was his own work on 'civil society' that did so much to define the mid-eighteenth century as a period of 'polite' conflict.

But perhaps, the most important explanation for the 'cabinet wars' of the period, was that societies were largely aristocratic. The aristocracy had been tamed: the eighteenth-century nobleman was very different from his sixteenth-century counterpart. Limited war reflected the values which aristocrats now valued most: restraint, self-control and, above all, honour. All this was to be swept aside after the French Revolution displaced the old regime and ushered in an age of ideology.

But then again the breaks between periods of history are never as sharp as we tend to think. The eighteenth century had its own double standards. Every age does. If there was one rule for European warfare, there was another for colonial campaigns, and another still for counter-insurgency such as the war in Corsica where the French were involved in a particularly savage conflict that lasted nineteen years. And if religion was less of a political force in the eighteenth century than it had been before, the religious dynamic was not dead, but only dormant. It was de Tocqueville who later described the French Revolution as a form of 'religious revivalism'; it bred the first of the 'political religions' which were such a feature of the next century. Marxism owed a particular debt to the Jacobin regime (Bell 2007:9–11).

The French Revolution offers one other warning from history. It would seem that complex systems can tip over into systemic crisis quite quickly, and when least expected, as was the case in 1789. 'Look at the world around you', writes Malcolm Gladwell, 'it may seem like an immovable, implacable place. It is not. At the slightest push, in just the right place, it can be tipped' (Gladwell 2001:259). In 1914, the tipping point was the assassination of Franz Ferdinand. But then again who would have predicted in 1910, the year of William James's death, that World War I would give birth to a second, even more ruinous conflict, as well as indirectly to the revolutions and global pandemics that followed, which in total claimed the lives of 200 million people or one in eight of all the people alive on the planet in the last year of James's life (MacGillvray 2006:135).

The tipping point for us was 9/11, or so we believe. But we may await a more dramatic event, a more striking example of destruction that might take us beyond the risk age into something far different. The paradigm-shaking break which the risk age has ushered in may be only temporary. There is an age beyond this one, and there are certainly likely to be even more surprises in store for us in the years to come.

For in the event of a truly life-defining challenge that forces us to confront our own self-belief, then the contest might be joined on different terms. For that, it seems to me, the casualty list would have to rise significantly. The casualties of the global War on Terror (even factoring in 9/11 and the American soldiers who have not returned from Afghanistan and Iraq, as well as counting the victims of the US Embassy bombings in 1998), number far fewer than those of an average-size Napoleonic battle. A dirty bomb in Philadelphia or Pittsburgh or a concerted anthrax attack or a major inter-state conflict in the Middle East would constitute a different order of magnitude. War might be joined on other terms.

There is an even more sobering thought. For the attempt to manage risks may make the world a more risky place than ever. The authors of *Unintended Consequences,* one an Australian academic, the other an Adjunct Professor at the US Navy War College, insist that Clausewitz was wrong to posit that war is a continuation of policy by other means – a rational and legitimate means of furthering the national interest. On the contrary, war is so unpredictable that it often forces governments to adopt entirely new policies. Unintended or unforeseen consequences are invariably more long-term than intended outcomes. It was Hannah Arendt who reminded us that politics is the realm of unintended consequences. She was drawing attention to the distinction between the predictable world of mechanics and the world of politicians who cannot accurately predict the consequences of their actions. 'If this is true of politics, it is even more true of war, which is

why the notion that war is merely policy by other means is nonsense'
(Hagan and Bickerton 2007:10). It is a bold thesis, and one which is persua-
sively argued. If it rings more true today than in the past that is because
there is much evidence to suggest that war is far more indecisive than ever.
Whether we can infer from this that it is becoming obsolete is another
matter. My own opinion is that it is continuing to evolve and that the risk
society has reinvented it to suit its own purposes. It just so happens that risk
societies are not very good at it, but the societies that follow the risk age
may be better. It need hardly be said, many will disagree with this view.

The message of this book can be read two different ways. We may choose
to see an ubiquitous, all-pervading process at work, leading inexorably to
the inconclusiveness of war, its continuing lack of appeal and its post-heroic
nature. Other readers will conclude that this is not inevitable, and that is
even if it is a trend, it is one that could quite easily be reversed. It is only our
residual Enlightenment belief in progress that makes us so impatient to see
the back of it. The Western imagination is underequipped to cope with the
passions outside the narrow middle range of what the Enlightenment has
made familiar. Out there in the rest of the world there are still ancestral
voices summoning people to battle.

The Moral Equivalent of War

The final point I wish to make in this book is that the risk age is not a fixed
phenomenon like capitalism, it is merely the latest stage of modernity – for
some. It too in time will give rise to another stage, what Giddens might call
'third modernity', though there is always the possibility of regression, a
return to the first.

This brings to mind Rilke's claim that 'the future enters into us in order
to transform itself in us long before it happens' (Strathern 2007:1). The
future, in other words, germinates in the present, to be revealed to a privi-
leged few who have an ear attuned to its subtle rhythms. And the future
(short of some environmental or economic catastrophe) is going to be
more of the same increasing complexity but there will be dialectical turns
that may take everyone by surprise – I cite René Girard here (Girard
2007:261). It is even possible that some of these turns may emerge from the
existing dialectical tension between that part of the globe that has entered
the risk age, and the part that has not – between the globalized and non-
globalized, the post-modern and the modern – the terms vary according to
taste, but the phenomenon engages many observers of the contemporary
scene. A dialectic of sorts already inheres in the War on Terror and it may

even engage other players on a larger stage still, including China and India. Unless, of course, we conclude that once again the West has reached the future ahead of the field and that others will catch up later. Such a view would be somewhat dated but not intellectually unsustainable, if, by the risk age, we mean as I do one which enmeshes societies in ever more complex relationships.

We just don't know. We are condemned as Hegel told us to not knowing. Indeed, we can only fully understand our own age when it has passed. Our level of understanding does not allow us to peer too far into the future. But then why quote Hegel when one can quote Hayek (one of his great critics but a critic who was writing in an era when complexity was acknowledged as the main reality of life)? Managing change rather than avoiding it by perfecting society or human nature is what we now do – but successful management depends on the degree of complexity that we are studying. According to Hayek there is no chance that a human brain could understand a system that is more complex than itself but human society represents just such a system, which is why he later claimed that the only way we can bring order to chaos is to let it arrange itself (Hayek 1990).

But the human brain is important because the system is driven by human aspirations, as well as human needs. And one of the reasons why the risk age may not last much longer is that it is already provoking its own discontents. To put it bluntly, many find it unrewarding, if not boring, and others think it dangerous. War may adapt again, to something more primordial, or life-affirming.

'Our [own] ancestors have bred pugnacity into our bones and marrow and thousands of years of peace would not breed it out of us', wrote William James (Wilshire 1984:351). What marks James out as different from other contemporary pacifists was his acute understanding of war's enduring appeal. James clearly admired some of the qualities that war tended to bring out in the human species such as courage, stamina and physical endurance. Perhaps it would be more true to say he admired warriors far more than he did their profession. Similarly when discussing religion, he admired the qualities shared by saints and mystics about whom he wrote in his most enduring book, *The Varieties of Religious Experience*. He admired the process of conversion, the act of repentance and the stoicism of saintliness. What he most liked about religion was not the metaphysics, but 'the will to believe'. For religion not only encourages devotion, it demands it. It not only induces intellectual ascent, it enforces emotional commitment. In that sense, it has far-reaching implications for human conduct (James 2003).

As his fellow American philosopher Santayana once argued, religion offers visions and propounds mysteries that constitute another world to live in. 'And another world to live in — whether we expect ever to pass wholly over into it or not — is what we mean by having a religion' (Geertz 2000:87). And what belief in another world fosters is a spirit of sacrifice. War, in that sense, like religion defines our humanity because it demands of some that they surrender the instinct of self-preservation in the present to make life better in the future. It is the fact that we can imagine the world other than it is that marks us out as a species. No other species suffers such a capacity for thought, such a complexity of imagined but frustrated possibilities, such a troubling ability to question the biological and tribal imperatives that govern our lives. This also, of course, explains James's optimism. Violence, he supposed, was bred into societies as it was into humanity, and in true Darwinian spirit he believed that violence might one day be bred out.

In sum, it could be said (though James would have been unwilling to concede the point) that he saw both religion and war in Durkheimian terms as the idealized projection through ritual acts of our social solidarity, made manifest in a generalized notion of the sacred: both religion and war preach that whoever loses their life shall gain it. What James ultimately grasped is that war is very rarely about profit or plunder; it is about power. It involves a clash of wills, a willingness to hazard all on the spin of the dice. Would a world without war be a world without risk? For courage is demanded by many of our activities, especially politics. The market may reward risk-taking but only politics rewards sacrifice.

Indeed, for a society to be free and essentially equal, each individual must concede something, to sacrifice something *inside*, something traditionally constitutive of his or her authenticity as a person. Even tolerance, writes Julia Kristeva, implies 'internalised sacrifice' (Windsor 1995:433), for you have to live your life in the same civic space as others. There can be no total-izing project. 'We want everything' was the slogan of the students in 1968. The right to live and be all one wants to be is the extraordinary pretension of modern times. But modernity requires us to recognize that we cannot have everything, or be what we always want, without some form of inter-nalized sacrifice. Indeed, the social complexity of our societies requires us to make even more sacrifices than we did in the past, as well as to recognize the incompleteness of the internalized sacrifices we have already made, and might be asked to make in the future. The problem with fundamentalists of any kind is not that they are willing martyrs for their beliefs. The problem is that in terms of their beliefs they are not prepared to sacrifice anything *of themselves*.

James himself would probably find our age distinctly unattractive.

Though he could imagine a world without war, he could not imagine one without risk. Hence his urgent quest for a 'moral equivalent'. Whether something is good or bad, he insisted, should be defined by its utility, not some transcendent principle. The question is not whether war is good or bad for humanity but whether it is good or bad for those who practise it — what are its consequences? James was ahead of his time in 1910 in warning the Great Powers that it wasn't good for very much; that the world was too complex for the easy victories of old, that it was becoming too disruptive even for hope of plunder.

But when he argued that the good and the bad are instrumentally important he had in mind the interest not of states, but of society. What was most important about belief in God was not the pay-off in the afterlife but our own — did it serve to promote a 'larger, richer, more satisfying life?' For those who genuinely believed in God, James conceded that it did. What was important about the religious experience was its 'fullness' (Ford 2007:158). 'No criticism avails to cast doubt on its reality. They know for they have actually felt the higher powers in giving up the tension of their personal will.' It is the sacrifice of selfishness and self-interest, and even the most persistent instinct of all, self-preservation, that is demanded of every warrior, throughout the centuries. 'The operators in Delta's C squadron were borderline suicidal that they weren't in the fight yet,' claimed a US Army Special Operations source referring to the war in Afghanistan in January 2002 (Naylor 2005:37).

James held no brief for the individual who only though war can satisfy his own humanity. What moved him most was war's social pay-off: it provided the myths and heroic archetypes, the templates of courage which inspired society. But the sacrifice had to be useful. He would also have applied, one imagines, the same logic to today's suicide bombers. As of 2008, 1,300 have died in Iraq and achieved very little. Indeed, there is reason to hope that this particular madness is so pointless that it will soon exhaust its possibilities, such as they are, quite soon. Or there would be reason if we were entirely rational creatures. Unfortunately, the pointlessness of a venture is not always the point.

For people who take risks do not always weigh them. Thinking, James added, is all very well but we live also by sensation, passion and intuition. Thought 'deals solely with . . . surfaces. It can name the thickness of reality but it cannot fathom it.' Young people need a challenge which John F. Kennedy tried to give them by creating the Peace Corps, an organization James had even proposed (he called it the 'blood tax' the young owed their country). Of course, peace too demands we take risks. The beliefs that underpin that vision also demands courage, plus a willingness to live without guarantees and assurances. If we wish to make a difference, James tells us, 'we need to redeem our own hearts from fear' (Wilshire 1984:150).

What makes war so seductive is the risk-taking which still acts as a funnel for excitement and adventure for the young who constitute the foot soldiers in most armies, both regular and irregular. The urge to take risks is especially pronounced in young males. Risk-taking provides them with an opportunity to test their strength and display their credentials as alpha males. In recent years the connection between risk and excitement has been confirmed by the rise of some new, dangerous activities such as sky diving and whitewater rafting. Some of them even go 'ice surfing' – the latest craze in which water-borne daredevils wait for ice to break from glaciers and surf on the resulting twenty-five-foot high waves, an ideal sport in an age of unstoppable global warming. All this should tell us only what evolutionary psychologists have always known: some of us like the adrenalin rush of risk, even though most of us can live without it.

There is even a technical term for this coined by sociologists; they call it 'edgework' (i.e. living on the edge) (Mythen and Beck 2006). Edgework allows young people to conquer their fear, display courage and achieve a heightened sense of self-esteem. If anything, risk-taking is becoming even more pathological in youth subcultures in response, one suspects, to the excessive risk averseness of the life we all lead. Edgework is a vivid example of what Jeremy Bentham called 'deep play', of which he profoundly disapproved. In deep play the stakes are so high that it is irrational for anyone to engage in it since the marginal utility of what you stand to gain, a chance to test your limits, is grossly outweighed even in terms of self-knowledge by the disutility of what you stand to lose. Bentham couldn't imagine deriving pleasure from the experience of danger. Of course, the fact that something is deadly serious doesn't mean that it isn't pleasurable; on the contrary, it is the seriousness or the danger that constitutes the pleasure.

One writer in particular spent his last years warning us of what happens when deep play is banned. In his last novels J. G. Ballard depicts a world not too distant from us, caught in the grip of a boredom so intense that it can only be relieved by grotesque acts of violence. The profound ennui that inheres in Ballard's dystopian streets is that of a society out of the war business, entrenched in an aggressively risk-free comfort zone. What is remarkable about this vision is that the mood of social alienation is to be found at the top of society, not the bottom. 'Burn down the National Film Theatre', 'Blow up Peter Pan' are revolutionary slogans of the middle classes. Ballard had an instinct for the future of a society on the verge of a collective breakdown. Even our risk societies, if the circumstances were right, could come apart at their civilized seams (Ballard 2007).

One cannot help but be struck by the cultural appetite for war which is such a pervasive feature of the risk societies we have become. Take war-gaming at all ages and, even more, Hollywood's endless roster of war movies. The historian Omer Bartov has rightly noted the paradox of most anti-war films: the closer they come to representing actual battle (*Saving Private Ryan, Band of Brothers*) the less effective they are in evoking anti-war sentiments. Combat is reconstructed in such a realistic way thanks to computer animation and the leading characters are so sympathetic and usually heroic that we tend to empathize with them more than ever before (Bartov 1996:10). War on the screen brings out the best in life, the noble and heroic, the qualities we still find admirable precisely because we encounter them so infrequently in real life.

Elsewhere in the world others resort to violence precisely because it is still life-affirming. The courage to hazard everything including life still has an appeal for many. Terrorism, writes DeLillo, fills the void which is at the heart of the risk age. 'The danger they represent equals *our own failure to be dangerous*' (DeLillo 1992:157). The novel was published long before 9/11 and the observation I have just quoted is not about terrorism at all. It is offered as a critique of the post-heroic societies we have become which discourage us from putting ourselves at risk. DeLillo was writing about his fellow novelists, many of whom have surrendered the high ground or sold out by writing celebrity fiction. The terrorist too has become something of a celebrity, guaranteed his fifteen minutes of fame. It is unfortunate, of course, that he also kills the innocent but that is precisely what the language of terrorism has become – the art of being noticed. It is the only language the rest of us can understand.

What DeLillo raises is a disturbing question: are the fundamentalists of all persuasions at war not with us but the society we have constructed? Is their real enemy the risk society itself? Do they challenge its *humanity*? It is the non-instrumental nature of terrorist acts that makes us instrumentalists so concerned, for they are wholly beyond our understanding of politics, which has become one of management, not conviction. Hence our fear of the actions of jihadists which are more ethical than political in nature. What is distinctive about al-Qaeda, writes Faisal Devji, is the surprising disproportion between its limited means and seemingly limitless ends, which means that the local causes of its *jihad* from which it derives men, money, motives and munitions have vanished into the immensity of its own global effects. The *jihad* is global not because it controls people but for precisely the opposite reason: al-Qaeda is too weak to control its own followers. Its operations have taken on a life of their own which have exceeded its intentions. For that reason its operations have become gestures of duty rather than acts of instrumentality, properly speaking (Devji 2007:3–4).

This is asymmetry at its most profound. One world is obsessed with minimizing risks even when going to war; others are apparently willing to hazard all in battle. And the sides do not have to be political or religious, any more than the damage has to be inflicted by groups. Individuals have a tendency to spin the dice, too. The creator of the Sasser computer virus was an eighteen-year-old German, taking computer science as a part-time study. Yet the virus he produced penetrated millions of computers and was responsible for an estimated $4 billion worth of damage. Had he designed it to erase data rather than just stop and restart infected computers, the damage would have been five times greater. Hackers with a grudge against the world could do immense damage by infecting their viruses with genetic algorithms that will mutate in ways that not even the programmers can anticipate. The risk society finds itself at war with uncertainty every day, not all of it 'intelligently designed'.

Conclusion

In the end, the risk management model of war affords us only a partial and distorted vision of reality. We need to apprehend its limited vision, its severely restricted cognitive slant on the world. Our societies certainly seem to lack the self-confidence, even self-belief, they once manifested. Arguably, in the past they had far too much; they were insufficiently sensitive to the consequences of their actions and the cost of realizing their dreams. But do we still dream for others or only for ourselves? And is the risk society equal to the challenges of the future? Back in 2005, Tony Blair told an audience in University College London, that risk aversion was becoming a serious problem. In an attempt to eliminate risk, government bodies, local government authorities and public services were adopting measures that were out of all proportion to the potential damage the risks themselves posed (Truscott 2007:2). Blair's lament has been echoed by the philosopher Alain Badiou, who is wary of an age which is so fearful of 'events'. He has coined his own revolutionary manifesto 'the Idea against Reality, Freedom against Nature, the Event against the State of Affairs' (Badiou 2007:164). It is the 'state of affairs' to which the risk age is so wedded, a state that cannot be changed because it is change itself which is considered to put us at unacceptable risk. Few are likely to be inspired by the manifesto; we live, after all, in a post-revolutionary age. No man, Hegel told us, is a hero to his valet and when heroes are out of fashion it is the valet's point of view that tends to prevail.

Will we continue to live in such post-heroic times? Will we continue to live life not as a 'project' but as a predicament, to be experienced as a perpetual present not a movement towards a historical goal? Will we continue to engage in a series of lesser or more intelligent trade-offs between what are often incommensurable values and unknowable outcomes? The risk age has produced its own discontents; some regret that we lack ambition either for ourselves or for others; others are dismayed by our foreshortened perspectives on the future, while many are horrified by the deep scepticism it seems to foster. We await the future in the knowledge that much will change, and that when it does war will be governed by a new set of rules and a very different 'cultural grammar'.

Bibliography

Adair, Gilbert 1992: *The Post Modernist Always Rings Twice: Reflections in Culture*, London: Fourth Estate.

Adair, Gilbert 1997: *Surfing the Zeitgeist*, London: Faber & Faber.

Adam, Barbara (ed.) 2003: *The Risk Society and Beyond: Critical Issues for Social Theory*, London: Sage.

Adelman, Kenneth 2002: 'Cakewalk in Iraq', *Washington Post*, 13 February.

Alexander, John B. 1999: *Future War: Non-Lethal Weapons in Twenty-First-Century Warfare*, New York: St Martin's Press.

Anderson, Chris 2007: *The Long Tail: How Endless Choice is Creating Unlimited Demand*, New York: Random House.

Appadurai, Arjun 2006: *Fear of Small Numbers: An Essay on the Geography of Anger*, Durham NC: Duke University Press.

Aradau, Claudia et al. 2008: 'Security. Technologies of Risk and the Political: guest editors' introduction', *Security Dialogue* 39:2–3 (April), 155–73.

Arendt, Hannah 1977: *Between Past and Future: Eight Exercises in Political Thought*, London: Penguin.

Australian Public Service Commission 2007: *Tackling Wicked Problems: A Public Policy Perspective*, Canberra: Commonwealth of Australia.

Badiou, Alain 2007: *The Century*, Cambridge: Polity.

Bailey, Jonathan 2007: 'Strategy and Campaigning: Ends, Ways and Means', in Scott Hopkins (ed.) *Asymmetry and Complexity*, Canberra: Land Warfare Centre, Study Paper 308.

Ball, Philip 2004: *Critical Mass: How One Thing Leads to Another*, London: Arrow Books.

Ballard, J. G. 1995: *The Atrocity Exhibition*, London: Harper Perennial.

Ballard, J. G. 1997: *A User's Guide to the Millennium*, London: Flamingo.

Ballard, J. G. 2007: *Millennium People*, London: Flamingo.

Barrow, John 1996: *The Infinite Book: A Short Guide to the Boundless, Timeless and Endless*, London: Vintage.

Barrow, John 2005: *Impossibility: The Limits of Science and the Science of Limits*, London: Vintage.

Bartov, Omer 1996: *Murder in our Midst: The Holocaust, Industrial Killing and Representation*, Oxford: Oxford University Press.

Bar-Yam, Yaneer 2003: 'Complexity of Military Conflict: Multiscale Complex Systems Analysis of Littoral Warfare' http://necsi.org/projects/yaneer/SSG_NESCI_3_Litt.pdf.

Baudrillard, Jean 1995: *The Gulf War Did Not Take Place*, Sydney: Power Publications.

Bauman, Zygmunt 1997: *Post-Modernity and its Discontents*, Cambridge: Polity.

Bauman, Zygmunt 1999: *In Search of Politics*, Cambridge: Polity.

Bauman, Zygmunt 2000: *Liquid Modernity*, Cambridge: Polity.

Bauman, Zygmunt 2002: *Society under Siege*, Cambridge: Polity.

Bauman, Zygmunt 2003: *Liquid Love: On the Frailty of Human Bonds*, Cambridge: Polity.

Bauman, Zygmunt 2004: *Wasted Lives: Modernity and its Outcasts*, Cambridge: Polity.

Bauman, Zygmunt 2005: *Liquid Life*, Cambridge: Polity.

Bauman, Zygmunt 2006: *Liquid Fear*, Cambridge: Polity.

Bauman, Zygmunt 2007a: *Liquid Times*, Cambridge: Polity.

Bauman, Zygmunt 2007b: *Consuming Life*, Cambridge: Polity.

Beck, Ulrich 1992: *The Risk Society: Towards a New Modernity*, Cambridge: Polity.

Beck, Ulrich 1997: *The Reinvention of Politics: Rethinking Modernity in the Global Social Order*, Cambridge: Polity.

Beck, Ulrich 1998: *Democracy Without Enemies*, Cambridge: Polity.

Beck, Ulrich 1999: *World Risk Society*, Cambridge: Polity.

Beck, Ulrich 2002: 'The Terrorist Threat: World Risk Society Revisited', *Theory, Culture and Society* 19(4), 39–55.

Beck, Ulrich 2004: *The Cosmopolitan Vision*, Cambridge: Polity.

Beck, Ulrich 2005: *Power in the Global Age: A New Global Political Economy*, Cambridge: Polity.

Beck, Ulrich, Giddens, Anthony and Lash, Scott 1997: *Reflexive Modernization: Politics, Tradition and Aesthetics in the Modern Social Order*, Cambridge: Polity.

Bell, David 2007: *The First Total War: Napoleon's Europe and the Birth of Modern Warfare*, London: Bloomsbury.

Bessel, Richard 2004: *Nazism and War*, London: Phoenix.

Blair, Tony 2001: Labour Party Conference Speech, 2 October, http://www.org/newshour/bb/military/terroristattack/blair_10-2.html.

Blinn, James 1997: *The Aardvark is Ready for War*, New York: Anchor.

Blockham, Jeremy 2007: 'Dealing with Wicked Problems', *RUSI Journal* 152:4 (August), 88–97.

Bloom, Harold 1999: *Shakespeare: The Invention of the Human*, London: Fourth Estate.

Bobbitt, Philip 2008: *Terror and Consent*, London: Allen Lane.

Bordo, I. 1992: 'Ecological Peril, Modern Technology in the Postmodern Sublime', in P. Berry and A. Wernick, *Shadow of Spirit: Postmodernity and Religion*, London: Routledge.

Brailey, Matthew 2006: *Transformation of Special Operations Forces in Contemporary Conflict*, Canberra: Land Warfare Centre, Working Paper 127.

Bronowski, Jacob 1973: *The Ascent of Man*, London: Book Club Association.

Buchanan, Mark 2002: *Small World: Uncovering Nature's Hidden Networks*, London: Phoenix.

Buley, Ben 2007: *The New American Way of War: Military Culture and the Political Utility of Force*, London: Routledge.

Burrow, John 2007: *A History of Histories*, London: Allen Lane.

Bush, George 2003: 'Remarks at West Point, New Threats Require New Thinking', in Mark Safre (ed.), *The Iraq Reader*, New York: Touchstone Books.

Campen, Alan 2000: *Cyber Warfare 3:0: Human Factors in Information Operations and Future Conflict*, Fairfax VA: Afcea Press.

Camus, Albert 1978: *American Journals* (trans. Hugh Livick), London: Hamish Hamilton.

Carpenter, Ted 2001: 'NATO's New Strategic Concept: Coherent Development or Conceptual Model?', in Ted Carpenter (ed.) *NATO Enters the 21st Century*, London: Frank Cass.

Carr, E. H. 1972: *What is History?* London: Penguin.

Carter, Ashton and Williams, Perry 1999: *Preventative Defence: A New Security Strategy for America*, Washington DC: Brookings Institution.

Castells, Manuel 2001: *The Internet Galaxy*, Oxford: Oxford University Press

Céline, Fernand 1986: *North*, London: Bodley Head.

Chaisson, Eric 2001: *Cosmic Evolution: The Rise of Complexity in Nature*, Cambridge MA: Harvard University Press.

Chandrisekaran, R. 2007: *Imperial Life in the Emerald City: Inside Baghdad's Green Zone*, London: Bloomsbury.

Chatfield, Tom 2008: 'Whispers in the Desert', *Prospect*, April, 62–6.

Christian, David 2006: 'Progress: Directionality or Betterment?' *Historically Speaking* 7:5 (May–June).

Clausewitz, Karl von 1982: *On War*, London: Penguin.

Claxton, Guy 1998: *Hare Brain, Tortoise Mind: Why Intelligence Increases when you Think Less*, London: Fourth Estate.

Cockburn, Andrew 2000: *Out of the Ashes: The Resurrection of Saddam Hussein*, London: Verso.

Coker, Christopher 2001: *Humane Warfare*, London: Routledge.

Coker, Christopher 2002: *Globalisation and Insecurity in the 21st Century: NATO and the Management of Risk*, London: International Institute of Strategic Studies, Adelphi Paper 345.

Conklin, J. 2001: 'Wicked Problems and Social Complexity', http//www.cognexus.org/dnformp.2.pdf7.

Connelly, John 2006: 'Rampaging', *London Review of Books*, 22 June.

Cooper, Robert 2000: *The Breaking of Nations: Order and Chaos in the 21st Century*, London: Atlantic.

Cordesman, Anthony 2003: *The Iraq War: Strategy, Tactics and Military Lessons*, Westport CT: Praeger.

Corn, Tony 2006: 'Clausewitz in Wonderland', policy review, September, http//www.hoover.org/publications/policyreviews/4268401.html.

Cornfield, Penelope 2007: *Time and the Shape of History*, New Haven CT: Yale University Press.

Dannatt, Richard 2007: Address at the RUSI Land Warfare Conference on the Subject of 'Tomorrow's Army, Today's Challenges,' 5 June, http://www.mod.uk/DefenceInternet/Defence News/ DefencePolicyand Business (accessed 2 September 2007).

Davies, Norman 2006: *Europe: East and West*, London: Jonathan Cape.

Davis, Mike 2006: *Planet of Slums*, London: Verso.

Davis, Mike 2007: *Buda's Wagon: A Brief History of the Car Bomb*, London: Verso.

DeLanda, Manuel 1991: *War in the Age of Intelligent Machines*, New York: Zone.

DeLillo, Don 1978: *Great Jones Street*, London: Picador.

DeLillo, Don 1992: *Mao 2*, London: Vintage.

DeLillo, Don 2007: 'Still life' http://www.newyorker.com/fiction/features/2007/04/09/070409fi_fiction_delillo/?prin (accessed 12 April 2007).

Dennett, Daniel 2003: *Freedom Evolves*, London: Penguin.

Dennett, Daniel 2006: *Breaking the Spell: Religion as a Natural Phenomenon*, London: Penguin.

Devji, Faisal 2007: *Landscapes of the Jihad: Militancy, Morality, Modernity*, London: Hurst.

Doctorow, E. M. 2000: *City of God*, New York: Little, Brown.

Donald, Dominick 2006: *After the Bubble: British Private Security Companies after Iraq*, London: Royal United Services Institute, Whitehall Paper 66.

Douglas, Mary 1992: *Risk and Blame: Essays in Cultural Theory*, London: Routledge.

Echevarria, Antulio 2007: 'The Future of Military Theory: The Need for a Method of Verification', in John Andreas Olsen (ed.), *On New Wars*, Oslo Files on Defence and Security 4/07.

Elbe, Stefan 2002: 'HIV/AIDS and the Changing Landscape of War in Africa', *International Security* 27:2 (fall), 159–77.

Elbe, Stefan 2006: 'Should AIDS be Securitized? The ethical dilemma of linking HIV/AIDS and security, *International Studies Quarterly* 50:1 (March), 119–44.

Elbe, Stefan 2008a: 'Our Epidemiological Footprint: the circulation of SARS, avian flu and HIV/AIDS in the world economy', *Review of International Political Economy* 15:1 (February), 116–30.

Elbe, Stefan 2008b: 'AIDS, Security and Three Concepts of Risk', *Security Dialogue* 39:2–3 (April), 177–98.

Ellin, Nan 1997: *The Architecture of Fear*, New York: Princeton Architectural Press.

Elliott, Anthony 2007: *The Contemporary Bauman*, London: Routledge.

Euben, Peter 2003: *Platonic Noise*, Princeton NJ: Princeton University Press.

Evans, Michael 2007: *City Without Joy: Urban Military Operations in the 21st Century*, Canberra: Australian Defence College, Occasional Paper 2.

Ewald, François 1987: *L'Etat Providence*, Paris: Editions Grasser & Gasquell.

Ferguson, Nial 1998: *The Pity of War*, London: Allen Lane.

Ferguson, Nial 2006: *The War of the World: History's Age of Hatred*, London: Allen Lane.

Finkelkraut, Alain 2001: *In the Name of Humanity: Reflections on the 20th Century*, London: Pimlico.

Ford, Dennis 2007: *The Search for Meaning: A Short History*, Berkeley: University of California Press.

Freedman, Lawrence 2006: *The Transformation of Strategic Affairs*, London: International Institute of Strategic Studies, Adelphi Paper 379.

Furedi, Frank 2006: *The Culture of Fear Revisited*, London: Continuum.

Furedi, Frank 2008: *Invitation to Terror: The Expanding Empire of the Unknown*, London: Continuum.

Gaddis, John 2006: *The Cold War: A Brief History*, London: Allen Lane.

Gal, Orit 2008: 'Revolutionising the Concept of Victory', *RUSI Newsbrief* 28:3 (March).

Gallie, W. B. 1991: *Understanding War*, London: Routledge.

Garland, David 2001: *Culture of Control: Crime and Social Order in Contemporary Society*, Chicago: University of Chicago Press.

Gaskell, George, Rothstein, H. and Huber, M. 2006: 'A Theory of Risk Colonisation: the spiralling regulatory logics of societal and institutional risk', *Economics and Society* 35:1, 6–12.

Geertz, Clifford 2000: *Available Light: Anthropological Reflections on Philosophical Topics*, Princeton NJ: Princeton University Press.

Gelven, Michael 1994: *War and Existence: A Philosophical Inquiry*, Philadelphia PA: Penn State University Press.

Gentry, John 1998: 'Military Force in an Age of National Cowardice', *Washington Quarterly* 21:4, 179–91.

Ghamari, Tabrizi 2005: *Sharon, The World of Herman Kahn: The Intuitive Science of Thermonuclear War*, Cambridge MA: Harvard University Press.

Giddens, Anthony 1994: 'Living in a Post-traditional Society' in Beck, Giddens and Lash (eds) *Reflexive Modernization*.

Girard, René 2007: *Evolution and Conversion: Dialogues on the Origins of Culture*, London: Continuum.

Gladwell, Malcolm 2001: *The Tipping Point*, London: Abacus.

Gordon, Michael and Trainor, Bernard E. 2006: *Cobra 11 – The Inside Story of the Invasion and Occupation of Iraq*, New York: Pantheon.

Graff, Jonathan 2004: 'US Counter-insurgency Doctrine and Implementation in Iraq', MA thesis, Fort Leavenworth.

Gray, Charles Hables 1997: *Post-Modern War: The New Politics of Conflict*, London: Routledge.

Gray, Colin 2007: *The Implications of Pre-Emptive and Preventive War Doctrines: A Reconsideration*, Carlyle PA: US Army War College.

Greene, Brian 2000: *The Elegant Universe: Superstrings, Hidden Dimensions and the Quest for the Ultimate Theory*, London: Vintage.

Greenspan, Alan 2007: *The Age of Turbulence: Adventures in a New World*, London: Allen Lane.

Hagan, Kenneth and Bickerton, Ian 2007: *Unintended Consequences: The US at War*, London: Reaktion Books.

Hamilton, Paul 1996: *Historicism*, London: Routledge.

Handy, Bruce 1997: 'Acting Presidents', *Time*, 14 April.

Hart, Gary 2006: *The Shield and the Clock: The Security of the Commons*, Oxford: Oxford University Press.

Hayek, Frederick 1990: *The False Conceit: The Errors of Socialism*, London: Routledge.

Heller, Agnes 1999: *A Theory of Modernity*, Oxford: Blackwell.

Heng, Yee-Kwuang 2002: 'Unravelling the War on Terrorism: A Risk Management Exercise in War Clothing?' *Security Dialogue* 33:2 (June), 227–32.

Heng, Yee-Kwuang 2006a: *War as Risk Management: Strategy and Conflict in an Age of Globalised Risk*, London: Routledge.

Heng, Yee-Kwuang 2006b: 'The Transformation of War Debate: Through the Looking Glass of Ulrich Beck's World Risk Society', *International Relations* 20:1 (March), 69–91.

Heng, Yee-Kwuang 2006c: 'The Iraq Crisis: Intelligence-Driven or Risk-Driven?', in Eunan O'Halpin, Robert Armstrong and Jane Ohlmeyer (eds) *Intelligence, International Power and Statecraft*, Dublin: Irish Academic Press.

Heuser, Beatrice 2002: *Reading Clausewitz*, London: Pimlico.

Hills, Alice 2007: 'Looking Through the Keyhole: Future War in the City', in Scott Hopkins (ed.) *Asymmetry and Complexity*, Canberra: Land Warfare Centre, Study Paper 308.

Holub, Miroslav 1984: *On the Country and other Poems*, London: Bloodaxe Books.

Homer-Dixon, Thomas 2006: *The Upside of Down: Catastrophe, Creativity and the Renewal of Civilisation*, London: Souvenir.

Horgan, John 1996: *The End of Science: Placing the Limits of Knowledge in the Twilight of the Scientific Age*, New York: Little, Brown.

Howard, Michael 2007: *Liberation or Catastrophe: Reflections on the History of the 20th Century*, London: Continuum.

Hughes, Thomas 2004: *Human Built World: How to Think About Technology and Culture*, Chicago: Chicago University Press.

Hurd, Douglas 1967: *The Arrow War: An Anglo-Chinese Confusion 1856–60*, London: Collins.

Ignatieff, Michael 2001: *Virtual War*, London: Chatto & Windus.

Iriye, Akira 1985: 'War is Peace, Peace is War', in Nobutoshi Hagihara and Philip Windsor (eds) *Experiencing the Twentieth Century*, Tokyo: University of Tokyo Press.

James, William 2003: *The Varieties of Religious Experience: A Study of Human Nature*, New York: Signet.

Jenkins, Brian 2004: 'Redefining the Enemy', *Rand Review* 28:1 (spring).

Jervis, Robert 2003: 'Understanding the Bush Doctrine', *Political Science Quarterly* 118:3 (fall).

Joas, Hans 2003: *War and Modernity* (trans. Rodney Livingstone), Cambridge: Polity.

Johnston, Alistair 1996: 'Learning Versus Adaptation: Explaining Change in Chinese Arms Control Policy in the 1980s and 1990s', *China Journal* 35 (January).

Jonas, Hans 1984: *Imperative of Responsibility*, Chicago: University of Chicago Press.

Jonas, Hans 1999: *Mortality and Morality: A Search for the Good after Auschwitz*, Evanston IL: Northwestern University Press.

Jones, James 2005: 'NATO Transformation and Challenges', *RUSI Journal* 150: 2, 114–18.

Kamarck, Andrew 2001: *Economics for the 21st Century: The Economics of the Economist*, Aldershot: Ashgate.

Kaplan, Robert 2002: *Warrior Politics: Why Leadership Demands a Pagan Ethos*, New York: Random House.

Kassimeris, George 2006: *The Barbarisation of Warfare*, London: Hurst.

Kay, Sean 2006: *Global Security in the 21st Century: The Quest for Power and the Search for Peace*, New York: Rowman & Littlefield.

Keegan, John 1997: *The Second World War*, London: Pimlico.

Kermode, Frank 2001: *Shakespeare's Language*, London: Penguin.

Kershaw, Ian 2007: *Fateful Choices: Ten Decisions that Changed the World, 1940–1*, London: Allen Lane.

King, Ian 2000: *Social Science in Complexity: The Scientific Foundations*, Huntingdon NY: Nova Science.

Klein, Gary 2003: *Intuition at Work: Why Developing your Instinct will Make You Better at What You Do*, New York: Currency.

Koselleck, Reinhart 1984: *Futures Past: On the Semantics of Historical Time*, New York: Columbia University Press.

Krugman, Paul 1998: *The Accidental Theorist and Other Despatches from the Dismal Science*, New York: W. W. Norton.

Laidi, Zaki 1998: *World without Meaning: The Crisis of Meaning in International Politics*, London: Routledge.

Leonard, Mark 2008: *What does China Think?* London: HarperCollins.

Leonhard, Robert, 1999: 'Centre of Velocity', in Robert Bateman (ed.) *Digital War: A View from the Front Line*, Novato CA: Presidio.

Lewens, Tim (ed.) 2007: *Risk: Philosophical Perspectives*, London: Routledge.

Lewis, Wyndham 1993: *Time and Western Man*, Santa Rosa CA: Black Sparrow Press.

Lieven, Anatol and Hulsman, John 2006: *Ethical Realism*, New York: Pantheon.

Lipton, Deborah 1999: *Risk*, London: Routledge.

Lloyd, G. E. 1990: *Demystifying Mentalities*, Cambridge: Cambridge University Press.

Looney, Robert 2005: 'The Success of Insurgency', *The National Interest* (fall).

Luhmann, Niklas 1998: *Observations on Modernity*, Palo Alto CA: Stanford University Press.

Lukacs, John 1976: *The Last European War*, London: Routledge & Kegan Paul.

Lukacs, John 2006: *Remembered Past: On History, Historians and Historical Knowledge: A Reader*, Wilmington DE: ISI Books.

Lyon, David 2007: *Surveillance Studies: An Overview*, Cambridge: Polity.

MacGillvray, Alex 2006: *A Brief History of Globalisation*, London: Robinson.

Mackinlay, John 2005: *Defeating Complex Insurgency Beyond Iraq and Afghanistan*, London: Royal United Services Institute, Whitehall Paper 64.

Maier, Christian 1993: *Athens: A Portrait of the City in the Golden Age*, London: Murray.

Mamdani, Mahmoud 2004: *Good Muslim, Bad Muslim: America, the Cold War and the Roots of Terror*, New York: Pantheon.

Manguel, Alberto 2005: *A Reading Diary: A Year of Favourite Books*, Edinburgh: Canongate.

Manguel, Alberto 2007: *The City of Words*, Toronto: Anansi.

Marcuse, Herbert 1991: *One-Dimensional Man*, Boston MA: Beacon.

Martin, James 2006: *The Meaning of the 20th Century*, New York: Riverhead.

Matthias, Peter 1967: *The First Industrial Nation: An Economic History of Britain*, London: Methuen.

Mayer, Michael 2007: *Forecasting Crisis: Climate Change and US Security*, Oslo Files on Defence and Security 6/07.

Mbembe, Achille 2003: 'Necropolis,' *Public Culture* 15:1 (winter), 11–41.

McNeill, Jay and McNeill, William 2003: *The Human Web: A Bird's Eye View of World History*, New York: Norton & Co.

Mills, Greg 2001: *The Security Intersection: The Paradox of Power in an Age of Terror*, Johannesburg: Witwatersrand University Press.

Mills, Greg 2007: *From Africa to Afghanistan: With Richards and NATO to Kabul*, Johannesburg: Witwatersrand University Press.

Mitchell, Ben 2007: *Bio Technology and the Human Body*, Washington DC: Georgetown University Press.

Morgan, Matthew 2004: 'The Garrison State Revisited: Civil-military implications of terrorism and security,' *Contemporary Politics* 10:1 (March), 5–9.

Musil, Robert 1979: *The Man without Qualities*, London: Picador.

Mythen, Gabe 2004: *A Critical Introduction to the Risk Society*, London: Pluto.

Mythen, Gabe and Beck, Ulrich (eds) 2006: *Beyond the Risk Society: Critical Reflections on Risk and Human Security*, New York: Open University Press.

Nagl, John 2002: *Counter-insurgency: Lessons from Malaya and Vietnam: Learning to Eat Soup with a Knife*, Westport CT: Praeger.

Nagl, John 2007: 'An American View of 21st Century Counter-Insurgency', *RUSI Journal* 152:4 (August).

Nancy, Jean-Luc 1993: *The Birth to Presence*, Stanford CA: Stanford University Press.

Naphy, William and Roberts, Penny 1997: *Fear in Early Modern Society*, Manchester: Manchester University Press.

National Security Strategy of the United Kingdom 2008: *Security in an Interdependent World*, London, Whitehall: Cabinet Office, CM 7291 (March).

NATO 2005: *NATO and the Fight against Terrorism*, Brussels: NATO Public Diplomacy, NATO Briefing (March).

Naylor, Sean 2005: *Not a Good Way to Die: The Untold Story of Operation Anaconda*, London: Penguin.

Norris, Clive 1999: *The Maximum Surveillance Society: The Rise of CCTV*, Oxford: Berg.

Norton, Richard 2003: 'Feral Cities', *Naval War College Review* (autumn), 129–36.

Nuttall, A. D. 2007: *Shakespeare: Thinker*, New Haven CT: Yale University Press.

Nye, Joseph and Smith, Roger 1992: *After the Storm: Lessons from the Gulf War*, Boston MA: Madison Books.

O'Hara, Kieron 2007: *Inequality.com: Power, Poverty and the Digital Divide*, London: One World.

O'Rourke, Patrick 2005: *Peace Kills: America's Fun New Imperialism*, London: Picador.

Osinga, Frans 2007: 'On Boyd, Bin Laden and Fourth Generation Warfare and String Theory', in John Andreas Olsen (ed.), *On New Wars*, Oslo Files on Defence and Security 04/07.

Outhwaite, William 2006: *The Future of Society*, Oxford: Blackwell.

Peters, Ralph 1999: *Fighting for the Future: Will America Triumph?* Mechanisburg PA: Stockpool.

Prins, Gwyn (ed.) 2000: *The Future of War*, The Hague: Kluwer.

Quadrennial Defense Review (QDR 2001) 2001: Washington DC: Defense Department.

Quadrennial Defense Review (QDR 2006) 2006: Washington DC: Defense Department.

Raphael, Frederic 2006: *Some Talk of Alexander: A Journey Through Space and Time in the Greek World*, London: Thames & Hudson.

Rasmussen, Mikkel 2007: *The Risk Society at War*, Cambridge: Cambridge University Press.

Rasmussen, Mikkel 2008: 'The Risk Society at War', talk at the London School of Economics, 21 February 2008.

Richards, David 2007: 'Interview with Major-General David Richards', *RUSI Journal* 152:9 (April).

Ricks, Thomas 2006: *Fiasco: The American Military Adventure in Iraq*, London: Allen Lane.

Robb, John 2007: *Brave New World: The Next Stage for Terrorism and the End of Globalisation*, New York: John Wiley & Sons.

Roberts, Nancy 2001: 'Coping with Wicked Problems: the case of Afghanistan', in L. Jones and J. Guthrie (eds), *International Public Management Reform: Lessons from Experience*, London: Elsevier.

Ruggie, John 1996: *Winning the Peace: American World Order in the New Era*, New York: Columbia University Press.

Rumsfeld, Donald 2004: 'Secretary Rumsfeld's Press Conference at NATO HQ', Washington DC: Department of Defense.

Rupert, Mark 2000: *Ideologies of Globalisation: Contending Visions of a New World Order*, London: Routledge.

Russell, Bertrand 1971: *A History of Western Philosophy*, London: George Allen and Unwin.

Sacks, Jonathan 2002: *The Dignity of Difference*, London: Continuum.

Saul, Richard 2006: 'Reactionary Blowback: The Uneven End of the Cold War and the Origins of Contemporary Conflict and World Politics', in Richard Saul and Alexandro Colas, *The War on Terror and the American Empire After the Cold War*, London: Routledge.

Schmidtchen, David 2006: *The Rise of the Strategic Private: Technology Control and Change in a Network Enabled Military*, Canberra: Land Warfare Centre.

Selbourne, David 1994: *The Principle of Duty*, London: Sinclair Stevenson.

Sennett, Richard 1998: *The Corrosion of Character: The Personal Consequences of Work in the New Capitalism*, New York: Norton.

Sennett, Richard 2003: *Respect: The Formation of Character in an Age of Inequality*, London: Penguin.

Shaikh, Fazara 2007: 'Luck running out', *The World Today* (December).

Shaw, Martin 2005: *The New Western Way of War: Risk Transfer and Crisis in Iraq*, Cambridge: Polity.

Singer, Max and Wildavsky, Aaron 1993: *The Real World Order: Zones of Peace/Zones of Turmoil*, Chatham, NJ: Chatham Publishers.

Smith, P. D. 2007: *Doomsday Men: The Real Dr Strangelove and the Dream of the Super Weapon*, London: Allen Lane.

Smith, Rupert 2005: *The Utility of Force: The Art of War in the Modern World*, London: Allen Lane.

Smith, Rupert 2007a 'Thinking About the Utility of Force' in John Andreas Olsen (ed.), *On New Wars*, Oslo Files on Defence and Security 4/07.

Smith, Rupert 2007b: 'Confrontations in War and Peace' http://www.dramatec.com.

Smith, Tony 1994: *America's Mission: The US and the Worldwide Struggle for Democracy in the 21st Century*, New York: 20th Century Fund.

Sontag, Susan 1979: *Illness as a Metaphor*, London: Penguin.

Sontag, Susan 2003: *Regarding the Pain of Others*, London: Hamish Hamilton.

Sooran, Chand, 'What is Hedging: Why do Companies Hedge?', http://www.finpipecom/hedge/htm.

Spiller, Roger 2005: *Instinct for War: Scenes from the Battlefields of History*, Cambridge MA: Harvard University Press.

Spufford, Francis (ed.) 1996: *Cultural Babbage: Technology, Time and Invention*, London: Faber & Faber.

Stearns, Peter 2006: *American Fear: The Causes and Consequences of High Anxiety*, London: Routledge.

Steinbrunner, John 2000: *Principles of Global Security*, Washington DC: Brookings Institution.

Stephens, Alan 2007: 'Effects Based Operations and the Fighting Power of a Defence Force', in John Andreas Olsen (ed.), *New Wars*, Oslo Files on Defence and Security 4/07.

Steward, Toby 2007: 'Unfulfilled Potential of the Military Police: Greater Exploitation of Police Skills in Operations', *RUSI Newsbrief* 27:1 (January), 9–11.

Stone, Norman 2007: *World War I: A Short History*, London: Allen Lane.

Strachan, Huw 2003: *The First World War*, London: Pocket Books.

Strachan, Huw 2007: *Clausewitz's On War*, London: Atlantic.

Strathern, Oona 2007: *A Brief History of the Future*, London: Constable and Robinson.

Sunstein, Cass 2005: *Rolls of Fear: Beyond the Precautionary Principle*, Cambridge: Cambridge University Press.

Surowiecki, James 2005: *The Wisdom of Crowds*, New York: Anchor.

Talentino, Andrea 2004: 'One step forward, one step back', *Journal of Conflict Studies* 24:2 (winter), 33–61.

Taylor, Charles 2007: *A Secular Age*, Cambridge MA: Harvard University Press.

Tertrias, Bruno 2004: *War Without End: The View From Abroad*, London: New Press.

Tilly, Charles 1985: 'Warmaking and Statemaking and Organised Crime', in Peter Evans, Dietrich Rueschmeyer and Theda Skocpol (eds.) *Bringing the State Back In*, Cambridge: Cambridge University Press.

Tilly, Charles 2005: *Trust and Rule*, Cambridge: Cambridge University Press.

Tilly, Charles 2007: *The Politics of Collective Violence*, Cambridge: Cambridge University Press.

Touraine, Alain, 2007: *A New Paradigm*, Cambridge: Polity.

Tripp, Charles 2007: 'Militias, Vigilantes, Death Squads', *London Review of Books*, 25 January, 18–31.

Trouillot, Michel-Ralph 2003: *Global Transformation: Anthropology and the Modern World*, London: Palgrave.

Truscott, Peter 2007: *The Ascendancy of Political Risk Management and its Implications for Global Security*, London: Royal United Services Institute, Whitehall Paper 67.

Tunsjo, Oystein 2007: *Constructing the Triangle*, London: Routledge.

Updike, John 2007: *Due Considerations: Essays and Criticism*, London: Hamish Hamilton.

Urry, John 2003: *Global Complexity*, Cambridge: Polity.

US-China Economic and Security Review Commission 2005: 'Report to Congress', Washington DC (November).

US Department of the Army 2006: *FM 3-24 Counter-insurgency* (December).

US Marine Corps 1996: *Command and Control Doctrine*, Quantico VA: USMC.

US Senate Foreign Relations Committee 2003: 'Iraq Reconstruction' S.Hrg 108–53 (11 March), Washington DC: US Government Printing Office.

Van Creveld, Martin 2006: *The Changing Face of War: Lessons of Combat from the Marne to Iraq*, New York: Ballantine.

Vatiokis, Michael 2006: 'Resolving Internal Conflicts in South East Asia', *Contemporary South Asia* 28:1 (April), 133–41.

Virilio, Paul (ed.) 1986: *Speed and Politics: An Essay in Dromology*, New York: Semiotext(e).

Virilio, Paul 1995: *The Art of the Motor*, Minneapolis: University of Minnesota Press.

Virilio, Paul 2000: *Strategy of Deception*, London: Verso.

Virilio, Paul 2005a: *Negative Horizon: An Essay in Dromoscopy*, London: Continuum.

Virilio, Paul 2005b: *The Original Accident*, Cambridge: Polity.

Vonnegut, Kurt 1965: *Cat's Cradle*, London: Penguin.

Waldrop, Mitchell 1997: *Complexity – The Emerging Science at the Edge of Order and Chaos*, London: Viking.

Weigley, Russell 1993: *The Age of Battles: The Quest for Decisive Warfare from Breitenfeld to Waterloo*, London: Pimlico.

Weisman, Alan 2007: *The World Without Us*, London: Virgin Books.

Weltman, John 1995: *World Politics and the Evolution of War*, Baltimore MD: Johns Hopkins University Press.

White House 2006: 'The National Security Strategy of the United States of America', Washington DC (March).

Williams, Andrew 1998: *Failed Imagination? New World Order of the 20th Century*, Manchester: Manchester University Press.

Williams, Michael 2006: 'Pre-emptive War and US Foreign Policy' *RUSI Newsbrief* 26:4 (April).

Williams, Michael 2008: *NATO, Risk and Security Management from Kosovo to Kandahar*, London: Routledge.

Wilshire, Bruce 1984: *The Essential William James*, Albany: State University of New York Press.

Windsor, Philip 1995: 'Cultural Dialogue in Human Rights', in Philip Windsor (ed.), *The End of the Century: The Future in the Past*, Tokyo: Kondansha International.

Winner, Laydon 1975: 'Complexity and the Limits of Human Understanding', in Todd La Porte (ed.), *Organised Social Complexity: Challenges to Politics and Policy*, Princeton NJ: Princeton University Press.

World Bank 2004: *World Development Report 2004* http://econ.org/wdr/wdr2004.

Wright, Robert 2001: *Non-Zero: The Logic of Human Destiny*, London: Vintage.

Wright, Ronald 2005: *A Short History of Progress*, Edinburgh: Canongate.

Zeman, Z. A. B. 1989: *Pursued by a Bear: The Making of Eastern Europe*, London: Chatto & Windus.

Zinni, Anthony and Koltz, Tony 2006: *The Battle for Peace: A Frontline Vision of America's Power and Purpose*, New York: Palgrave Macmillan.

Index

criticality 39; and subjective insecurity 67–71
Condorcet, Marquis de 63
conflict resolution 91
consequence management 102, 116–17; and aftermath 104; and cascading effects 106–9; and dangers of speed 109–14; and decision-making 104–6; and effects-based operations 114–18; ethics of 129–30; and a 'mess with a message' 122–9; and problem of choice 103; and risk 103; and war without victory 118–22
Cordesman, Anthony 112
counter-insurgency 23, 103, 114, 128, 155, 161, 163, 175
courage 64, 179, 180
crime, and children 137; committing of 135; domestic 134–7, 138, 139; and monitoring of prisoners 136, 138; prison populations 135; and rehabilitation programmes 134–5; and surveillance 136–8
Crime Net Management system 137
Croatia 90
Cuban Missile Crisis (1962) 73–4
Cultural Operations Research Human Terrain 163–4
cyber attacks 75

Darwinism 58, 124, 133, 154, 164, 179
Davis, Mike 83, 92
De Landa, Manuel 54
de-bounding, and anarchism on the margins 134; challenges 134; and disease 83–93; implications of 77; and responsibility 129; and risk-perception 76; security issues 77–84; and social risk 75, 88; and spatial dimension 74–5, 87; and temporal dimension 76
decentralization 168
decision-making, and acts without consequences 105; and anticipation of

negative effects 116; consequences of 103, 105–6; debates on 104–5; and decision dominance 105; and risk 103; and the state 123; and unpredictability 105–6
decisive battle, challenges to 50, 51–2; and outcome of war 51–2; theatrical appeal of 50–1
Defense Science Board 161
DeLillo, Don 182; *Cosmopolis* 8; *Falling Man* 132; *Great Jones Street* 62, 173
democracy 153–4, 161, 170
Democratic Republic of Congo 90
demonstrations 109
Dennett, Daniel 6
Department of Homeland Security 98
Desert Storm (1991) 3, 4, 6–11, 111, 127
Devji, Faisal 182
disease 102; anxiety concerning 83–4, 86–93; control of 85–6; effect in war-time 85; as existential threat 93; fearful of 84–6; and forgotten knowledge 91; frightened of 84; and funding on eradication/prevention of 92–3; and global death-rate 87; historical approach 84–5; and known unknowns 89–90; and knowns 89; and lack of perspective 84; and maximizing of profits 98; and medical authority 93–4; risk of 87–8; and security 84–5, 87–93; social dimension 88; spatial dimension 87–8; temporal dimension 88; and unknown unknowns 90–1; urban 85, 92
Doctor Strangelove (film) 42
Doctorow, E.M., *City of God* 46–7
Dorner, Dietrich 70; *The Logic of Failure* 69
Douglas, Mary 91–2
Dulles, John Foster 40
Durkheim, Emile 179
Dyer, Wayne 13

94; meanings of 63–4; as necessary gamble 165; and obsession with the present 25; as organizing principle for allied decision-making 24–5; and organizational practice 26–7; as product of a probability 165; proliferation of 126; reality of 100; and reflection 6–7; as social construction 100; and system failure 37; as unbounded 74–6; and the workforce 79–80

risk age 11, 26–7, 43–4, 60, 122; and anticipation of negative effects 116; and effects-base operations 115–18; emergence of 28; and force protection 112; importance of networks 112; and inter-state conflict 173–4; and the latent 173; as latest stage of modernity 177; and limits to knowledge 95–6; and *Möglichkeitsurteile* 97; and new security paradigm 132–4; and politics 172; and readjustment/readaptation 170; and search for security 126; and security analysis 102; and speed 111–14; uncertainties in 104, 106; and wicked problems 128–9

risk assessment 16, 141–2

risk aversion 6, 100, 164, 167–8, 175

risk avoidance 130

risk colonization 26

risk governance xi

risk management 10–11, 24, 60, 97, 118, 120, 124, 125, 130, 176; and anarchy on the margins 134, 148–50; and assessment of risk 169–71; and complex adaptive systems 150–4; concern with 26–7; geopolitics of 131–72; and intelligence/information 162–3; problems with 141–2; and rise of China 134, 142–7; and terrorism 134–42

risk society 6–7, 14, 19, 26, 63; and anxiety 64–7; and avoidance of ownership 123; and blow-back 70–1; and change of consciousness 68; and complexity

67–71; and consequences of different actions 69; and control of risk/uncertainty 76; and de-bounding of risk perception 74–6; dealing with probabilities not certainties 130; and the environment 71–2; and fear/anxiety 74; and the future 183–4; and interconnectedness 69–70; and poverty 72; and privatization of violence 72–3; and uncertainty 183; and war metaphors 73; and weapons of mass destruction 72

risk trap 126

risk-mapping 102

risk-taking 169–71

Rittel, H. W. J. (with M. M. Webber), *Dilemmas in the General Theory of Planning* 154

Ritter, Mark 79

Robb, John 165, 166

Rogers, General 76

Roosevelt, Franklin D. 10, 63, 86

Rorty, Richard 12

Rosanvallon, Pierre 34

Roth, Philip x

Royal Military Police 162

Rumsfeld, Donald ix, 67, 88, 90, 91, 95, 99, 100, 104, 120, 121, 127, 133–4, 171

Russell, Bertrand 44, 95

Russia 3–4, 38, 42, 58, 75, 83, 85, 89, 115, 131, 135, 146

SACEUR 160

safety state 11–19

Sainte-Beuve, Charles Augustin 65

Samuelson, Robert 63; 'Rediscovering Risk' 63

Santayana, George 178–9

Sante Fe Institute 152

SARS 74, 84, 86, 87, 91, 149

Saudi Arabia 11

Saving Private Ryan (film, 1998) 182

scenarios/game playing 2–3, 43

DATE DUE

APR 2 8 2011	
MAY 2 4 2012	